D1242159

Feeding Washington's Army

Feeding Washington's Army

Surviving the Valley Forge
Winter of 1778

Ricardo A. Herrera

The University of North Carolina Press CHAPEL HILL

Set in Merope Basic by Westchester Publishing Services
Manufactured in the United States of America

The University of North Carolina Press has been a member
of the Green Press Initiative since 2003.

Library of Congress Cataloging-in-Publication Data
Names: Herrera, Ricardo A. (Associate professor), author.
Title: Feeding Washington's army : surviving the Valley Forge winter of 1778 /
    Ricardo A. Herrera.
Description: Chapel Hill : University of North Carolina Press, [2022] |
    Includes bibliographical references and index.
Identifiers: LCCN 2021049433 | ISBN 9781469667317 (cloth ; alk. paper) |
    ISBN 9781469667324 (ebook)
Subjects: LCSH: Washington, George, 1732–1799—Headquarters—Pennsylvania—Valley
    Forge. | United States. Continental Army—Supplies and stores. | United States.
    Continental Army—History. | Valley Forge (Pa.)—History, Military—18th century. |
    United States—History—Revolution, 1775–1783—Destruction and pillage.
Classification: LCC E234 .H47 2022 | DDC 973.3/341—dc23/eng/20211025
LC record available at https://lccn.loc.gov/2021049433

Cover illustration: Harrington Fitzgerald, *Valley Forge Winter, the Return of the Foraging Party*
(ca. 1880–1900, oil on canvas). Museum of the American Revolution.

To Dolora

Contents

Illustrations and Tables

TABLES

Preface

This project began while I was a historian on the Staff Ride Team, U.S. Army Combat Studies Institute. I was building a staff ride on the Philadelphia Campaign of 1777–1778 and writing the stands, the locations where participants discuss a particular action, decision, or piece of terrain, for the Valley Forge portion. Staff rides use battlefields and larger areas of operations as classrooms and primary documents over which students, traditionally military, walk, talk, analyze, and discuss decision making, leadership, and their applicability to the modern military force. Among other things, staff rides are predicated upon the movements, maneuvers, and actions of military forces. The period between the army's marching into Valley Forge in December 1777 and marching out in June 1778, however, is largely static. The ride needed movement, if only for an hour in a longer day spent at the park. Activity, not immobility, is at the heart of the endeavor; thus, the challenge of examining Valley Forge, an encampment.

While pausing at Anthony Wayne's statue, I drew from Wayne Bodle's first-rate study of the encampment, *The Valley Forge Winter: Civilians and Soldiers in War*. Wayne gave attention to the army's patrolling and foraging activities, as soldiers and civilian interacted during the winter of 1777–78. The answer to my problem was to reframe Valley Forge as an eighteenth-century predecessor to the modern Forward Operating Base (FOB), a fixed, albeit temporary defensible position from which military forces operate. From FOB Valley Forge, the Continental Army maintained a security line to the east and south and sent patrols into the countryside to contest the space between the encampment and British-occupied Philadelphia. Soldiers from FOB Valley Forge marched out to forage in search of food and supplies for the army. All this was much more than passively and miserably sitting in freezing huts and starving. Here was action, here was the movement to sustain something of the staff ride's conceptual momentum. The focus of the stand at Anthony Wayne's statue would be the Continental Army's actions to feed itself, its sustainment operations in current parlance.

The story behind the army's efforts to sustain itself in February of 1778 is much larger and more important than the actual act. The bigger story is one of a maturing general, George Washington, and his officers and soldiers.

The Continental Army, if one argues for a line of continuity that traces to its birth on 14 June 1775, was but thirty-two months old in February 1778. In that period, the army had lost more fights than it had won. The main army under Washington had won signal victories at Trenton and Princeton, but its record of wins to losses was anything but respectable. Yet, Washington and the army had persevered, learned, and matured. By February 1778, Washington was able to give subordinate officers like Nathanael Greene, Anthony Wayne, Henry Lee, and others broad orders that gave them the latitude needed for the exercise of their initiative.

This book's genesis lies in my teaching at the U.S. Army's School of Advanced Military Studies (SAMS) and in my previous position on the Staff Ride Team. Scholarship informs my teaching, much as teaching informs my scholarship. The two are inseparable. Out of the need to introduce movement, one hour of teaching at Valley Forge, came an article. A second and third article, several conference papers, and a blog post later emerged. This book is the ultimate expression of that teaching moment. In small things, greater ones often inhere.[1]

Feeding Washington's Army

The Army Must Soon Dissolve

Following months of active campaigning, in December 1777, Gen. George Washington led the Continental Army into winter quarters at Valley Forge, a place whose name in American history is synonymous with privation, suffering, and endurance. From the late spring of 1777, through the onset of that year's winter, the army had marched and maneuvered well over 200 miles from its encampments at Morristown, New Jersey, to Cooch's Bridge, Delaware, to Chadds Ford, Pennsylvania, and beyond. Eventually, the army's journey led to Valley Forge. It had marched to fight and fight it did. Washington's Continentals and local militias had clashed with Gen. Sir William Howe's British regulars and Hessian auxiliaries at Cooch's Bridge, Brandywine, Paoli, Germantown, Whitemarsh, and other places over the course of the Philadelphia Campaign. The Continentals and militiamen had lost more battles than they had won, and yet the Continental Army had held together. As the end of the normal campaigning season (late spring though autumn) neared and then closed, General Washington convened several councils of war with the army's other generals to determine whether the army should wage a winter campaign or enter quarters until the spring. In the end, Washington determined that his soldiers would winter at Valley Forge. It was the least bad option within a limited range of possibilities.

Washington's decision to order the army into a winter cantonment at Valley Forge came about only after a lengthy series of considerations with the generals, congressional delegates, and local politicians. In the end, the approaching winter, the army's physical circumstances, and political and strategic necessity joined forces to limit Washington's courses of action. Ever the risk taker, Washington was also ever the realist. The army that wintered at Valley Forge was near enough to Philadelphia to challenge British occupiers for control of southeastern Pennsylvania; but doing so exacerbated the Continental commissariat's near inability to feed its soldiers. Washington's undertaking—buttressing Pennsylvania's government, exercising the writ of the Continental Congress, and denying the British exercise of political power—however, precluded his making any other decision. Faced with this complex and challenging strategic and political environment, Washington and the army made the best of a poor situation, constrained as they were by the strategic calculus of war. December 1777 was bad enough for the army, but worse was yet to come.

FACED WITH THE COLLAPSE of the commissariat and the all too real potential of scattering the army across eastern Pennsylvania so that it might feed itself, Washington was on the horns of a dilemma. Without food, the army would be compelled to abandon Valley Forge and surrender all hope of challenging the British for control of southeastern Pennsylvania. Choosing the more difficult path—maintaining the army's position at Valley Forge—Washington set in motion the Continental Army's riskiest and most complex operation it executed while there, the Grand Forage of February 1778. Washington had nothing but poor prospects before him. The army had to maintain its position in the Great Valley. Faced with by this, Washington acted decisively so that his soldiers might survive, so that the army might take the field in the spring and continue the war for American independence. The Grand Forage of 1778 was an act of desperation and a demonstration of Washington's willingness to accept risk while meeting a crisis. By February, the army was on the verge of dispersal or dissolution. Its logistical system had collapsed. Without food, soldiers faced starvation. Without food, Valley Forge could not be held. Confronted by a stark range of choices, Washington acted, and launched a grand forage to gather up as much livestock, forage, flour, and other needed goods to feed the army.

The expedition involved some fifteen hundred to two thousand soldiers of the Continental Army, a substantial portion of the roughly sixty-five hundred able-bodied, armed, and uniformed Continentals at Valley Forge. It included elements of the Pennsylvania, Delaware, Maryland, and New Jersey militias and contingents of the Continental and Pennsylvania navies. The forage spanned southeastern Pennsylvania, southern New Jersey, northern and central Delaware, and northeastern Maryland. It lasted nearly six weeks and engaged an estimated twenty-three hundred British soldiers (about one-sixth of the able-bodied British force in Philadelphia), as well as several vessels and crews of the Royal Navy.[1]

The Grand Forage of 1778 is largely unexamined. Historians and biographers of the major actors have treated it narrowly or failed to grasp the full picture. Generally, works that do treat the American encampment and the British occupation of Philadelphia have given the forage only the most casual attention. The uneven coverage of the forage is due to two central factors. First, compared to the campaigns and battles that bookended it, the Grand

John Trumbull, *General George Washington at Trenton*. Yale University Art Gallery.

Forage was small indeed. In terms of raw numbers, the thirty-eight hundred or so Continentals, Britons, Pennsylvanians, Delawareans, Marylanders, and New Jerseyans who took part quite simply paled in comparison to the several thousand soldiers who had fought at Brandywine and Germantown before the encampment, or would fight at Monmouth afterwards. Yet, while the forage was smaller than the Philadelphia Campaign or the Battle of Monmouth, a closer study reveals in fine detail some of the operational, logistical, and civil-military complexities, constraints, and opportunities commanders in the War for Independence faced. An examination of this foraging expedition reveals a side of warfare that that the larger battles of the War for Independence cannot, the vital efforts at sustaining the soldiers who fought. Hence, a closer study of the combatants' military and logistical operations reveals the great extent to which they devoted their time and energy at feeding themselves and how they accomplished those tasks. By considering operational and logistical efforts together, a better and more nuanced picture of the armies' capabilities emerges.[2]

Indeed, in the February foraging, the Continental Army demonstrated its tactical and operational maturity and acumen, as well as its improvisational skills. The Continental Army was an active force that challenged the British whenever and wherever possible, but only on Washington's terms—when he could help it. Washington planned carefully and accepted risk as he balanced it against opportunity. Moreover, the Virginian trusted his commanders to execute his broad concept of the operation. He gave them the latitude to interpret his orders expansively and to deviate from them when necessary, trusting, however, that they would hew to his broader intentions. The army's activity that winter is a startling contrast to popularly-held images of the army and the encampment.[3]

Herein lies the second reason for the Grand Forage's obscurity: the power of myth as popular history. For most Americans, including military officers, the Valley Forge cantonment is little more than a national morality play highlighting the virtuous self-sacrifice and patriotism of George Washington and his ragged band of Continentals. Sketched in broad outlines, they marched along frozen, snow-choked roads, leaving their bloody footprints to mark their route-of-march in the cruel Pennsylvania winter. While these patriots, ignored by Congress, their parent states, and local farmers, starved and froze, they endured in the service of the "glorious cause"— independence. By way of contrast, Gen. Sir William Howe and the British Army enjoyed the winter and the pleasures of Loyalist society, as they gambled, dined, drank, and whored, while snug and warm in occupied Philadelphia, the erstwhile American capital. Many recall the appearance of Baron Friedrich Wilhelm de Steuben, formerly a Prussian officer, who single-handedly, and with vulgar charm, transformed the Continental Army from a group of individualistic and undisciplined republican-warriors into citizen-soldiers, part of a well-drilled machine able to stand up to British bayonets.[4]

In the mythic telling, the Continental Army emerges as a static force, a "Greek chorus" trumpeting stoic martial values and patriotism. While there are kernels of truth to these legends, they reduce the Continental Army to passive witness and caricature. Instead, this book contends that the Continental Army at Valley Forge was a field army engaged in active operations. The myths ignore the Continentals' nearly constant combat and reconnaissance patrols, and the foraging the army undertook to supply itself and to deny those supplies to the British. In the scope, planning, and execution of the Grand Forage, Washington revealed his burgeoning acumen as a planner and commander, and his long-standing willingness to accept risk. Equally important, the Grand Forage revealed the maturity of the army's leadership and some of the logistical staff. The operation was too distant and too dispersed for Washington to exercise direct control; thus, he relied on the experience and judgment of his generals, dozens of field and company-grade officers, the army's logistical staff, the navies, and militias. Washington exercised centralized command, but placed his confidence in his subordinates. Meanwhile, his opponent, Gen. Sir William Howe, demonstrated a singular lack of interest in the largest and riskiest operation undertaken by the Continental Army in the winter of 1778. His belated response to the opportunity presented by the forage was halting and hesitant at best. Valley Forge lay exposed, yet he did not seize the moment. When Howe did act, his subordinate commanders entrusted with the mission showed little of the aggressive spirit that had been a hallmark in the previous campaign.[5]

As for the Continental Army, its distress was due to several factors, most of them beyond its control. Chief among them were the ever-tottering commissariat and quartermaster general. In its quest to protect liberty against power and avarice, Congress had purposely limited the authority of the commissary general and the quartermaster general and their purchasing and distributing agents. Constraints on power and greed may have protected liberty, but they also impeded the army staff's ability to feed, clothe, and supply the army. Without logisticians, the army could not fight. Moreover, worthless Continental currency, the weather, the roads, and, of course, the British Army also conspired to bring the Continental Army to its knees.

BY JANUARY 1778, the army's commissary and quartermaster departments had collapsed. Maj. Gen. Nathanael Greene noted bitterly, "the troops are worn out with fatigue, badly fed and almost naked." The soldiers, "some thousands of the Army," had been "without shoes for months past—It is difficult to get sufficient supplies to cloath the Army at large." The "naked" soldiers, wrote Greene, "have been upon the eve of starving and the Army of mutinying." Lack of food and poor hygiene resulting from "the want of acids and Soap" left soldiers "getting sickly in their Hutts." As for the army's horses, they were "dying from by dozens every day for want of Forage." Both and man and beast suffered.[6]

Writing from the army's "Camp on Schuylkill," Brig. Gen. George Weedon observed the region, and reckoned it a "plentiful but Distressed Country." The British Army had marched through the area in the closing days of 1777, and had subjected it to "ravagements" that were "shocking to behold." Nonetheless, Weedon continued, "Debilitated as our Troops are from the exceeding hard Service during this whole Campaign, Their Zeal for the Country does not abate, and tho they suffer greatly for want of Shoes and other Necessaries they seem determined to surmount all Difficulties and turn hardships into Diversion." But gilding the rhetorical lily and diversion did not fill bellies, clothe backs, or keep feet shod.[7]

Col. Timothy Pickering, a member of the Board of War and Washington's former adjutant general, was "very sensibly pained" over the army's distress. The lack of food and clothing, he feared, "may not be of short duration." Meat, whether fresh or salted, seemed unobtainable. Indeed, he doubted "where an ample and constant supply of flesh can be obtained." Perhaps, wondered Pickering, the army might reduce the meat rations and increase the bread allowance to compensate for the reduction. After thinking about this possibility, Pickering dismissed it, for he "suppose[d] it scarcely possible to diminish the ration of meat and increase that of bread," for the army had as little flour as it had flesh.[8]

Difficulty upon difficulty had plagued the commissariat for months, even before the cantonment. William Buchanan, Commissary General for Purchases for the Continental Army, complained about his inability to purchase beef, pork, or whiskey at the prices fixed by the Board of War. Even when local representatives fixed prices, they proved too low. Writing to President Thomas Wharton of Pennsylvania, Buchanan thought the rate established by Pennsylvania's Council of Safety for the purchase of wheat "sufficiently liberal," yet he found that it failed "to satisfy many avaricious People." The farmers, wrote Buchanan, "refuse to sell or thresh for sale any of that Article unless" purchasing agents met their "exhorbitant demands." If farmers refused to sell, then Buchanan's deputies and their assistants would be forced to impress wheat and flour, for, as Buchanan informed Wharton, the "Army must want inevitably want Bread very soon." This, however, did not hearten Buchanan. He found impressment "extreemly disagreeable," and asked Wharton and his councilors for their "advice and Assistance" in developing some other method than force. Try as Buchanan and his deputies might, their efforts were often in vain.[9]

As much as Buchanan deplored farmers' avariciousness, he did not want to forcibly seize foodstuffs or any other private property. Congress, on the other hand, its fear of power notwithstanding, had put aside ideological purity and fears of military tyranny in favor of practicality. It was willing to take a risk and trust that its own army would uphold its commitment to civilian control and respect for private property. It was not an easy decision. As early as 6 October 1777, Congress had authorized the commissaries general to "impress and seize waggons, shallops, and proper store-houses." It granted this authority until January 1778. The following month, delegates granted Buchanan the power to "purchase or impress wheat in the sheaf." It also directed Buchanan to "apply" to Pennsylvania's government for "assistance." Authorized or not, Americans considered the impressment of private property an abuse of power—little better than legalized theft. As was so often the case during the American Revolution, people looked back on history for repeated abuses of power by imperial authorities. Their own governments seemed to be following British practices. To most people, impressment was little more than the military usurpation of civil authority, liberty under attack by all-grasping power. Buchanan understood this as he tried to walk the fine line between military necessity on the one hand, and personal liberty and property rights on the other. It was to no avail. Even the soldiers themselves questioned the commissaries' motives.[10]

No matter how sincere their commitment to revolutionary ideals, their respect for liberties and rights, or their energy in doing their duty, soldiers and civilians alike damned the commissaries left and right. Samuel Tenny ("Tenney"), surgeon of the Second Rhode Island Continentals, was at his wits' end. He, along with the rest of the army, had been without food for several days. "I am still alive and not altogether unmindful of absent Friends," he wrote. However, "when you are inform'd that we have been five Days without Provision, the former will appear a little strange." Tenny poured his scorn upon the commissariat, particularly Thomas Jones, Deputy Commissary General for Issues. Jones was responsible for distributing the provisions that Buchanan's staff had purchased. Surgeon Tenny believed that there was a "set of men about the Army endeavouring to ruin it with D. Commy Genl of Issues at their Head." Jones, Tenny noted, is "detected in his villainies; & we all hope he will suffer, with Thieves, spies, & money-makers, in this world, & with Hypocrites & unbelievers in the next." Whether Tenny was wholly serious or merely venting his rage is difficult to tell. Nonetheless, his fury was sincere and shared by more than a few soldiers. Tenny's villain Jones was not the sole culprit. Instead, the commissariat was plagued by financial problems that were much more complex and invidious than Tenny could imagine.[11]

AMERICANS HAD FINANCED their war for independence through paper Continental dollars. As early as June 1775, Congress had authorized printing $2 million, which it increased to $6 million within another six months. Before the end of 1776, $25 million in Continental scrip circulated. Backed solely by faith and hope in the United States, both of which sank with British victories, the value of Continental money plummeted. By 1778, the exchange rate of paper to specie was 5:1, and it only got worse throughout the course of the war. It was not until 1777 that Congress made any effort to animate the states in levying taxes. Without the power to impose taxes, all Congress could do was importune the states to tax, take Continental dollars out of circulation, and raise their value through the resulting scarcity. However, faced with the need to arm and equip their militias, the states printed their own money, and virtually ignored Congress's requests. As for foreign loans, they were miniscule until about 1780, so Congress and the states printed ever more money. By 1777, the commissary and quartermasters' departments had expended $9,272,524.00; the following year, that rose to $37,202,421.00. At no time during the war did Congress or states ever establish any semblance of order over their finances. That would have to wait until sometime in the future. In the meantime, the value of American dollars fell in proportion to their numbers in circulation.[12]

Much as the value of American fiat currency fell, so too did the strength of the Continental Army. The main army's returns, a tabulation of bellies to fill, were as variable as the weather. The army's assigned strength fluctuated between a low of 14,892 soldiers (excluding militia) when it marched into the cantonment area in December 1777 and a high of 22,309 when its last units departed in June 1778. The number of soldiers actually fit for duty, however, tells a different story. That number never exceeded 13,751, which was registered in June 1778. Fully one-third of the main army was combat ineffective at the height of its strength while at Valley Forge. At the time of the Grand Forage, the number of soldiers fit for duty in February and March 1778 was 6,264 and 5,642 respectively. The number suitably clothed, armed, equipped, and ready for active campaigning was considerably less. The great disparity in numbers was due to a host of factors, including soldiers falling ill, dying, or deserting. In other cases, units performed duties away from camp, and recruiters failed to drum up recruits.[13]

Other complex factors affected the army's sustenance and the soldiers' condition. Bad weather and worse roads compounded the dismal logistical picture. An outbreak of atrocious weather in the first week of February continued throughout the month. On 5 February, the Schuylkill River, which divided the army's main encampment on the right bank from its local magazine on the left, was impassable because of flooding. On 6 February, Col. Israel Angell, commanding the Second Rhode Island Continentals, noted: "This morning was very raw and Cold . . . , and Rain'd as hard as Ever I Saw it." The next morning, the snow was "about ankel Deep." In nearby Lancaster, diarist Christopher Marshall noted that the "roads [are] near impassable." The "situation of the camp is such that in all human probability the Army must soon dissolve," wrote Brig. Gen. James Mitchell Varnum on 12 February. Historian Wayne Bodle has suggested that the army was fast approaching collapse, and probably would not have lasted through March 1778 unless it could obtain more food.[14]

THE PROBLEM WAS NOT that Pennsylvania was barren; it was not. There were supplies to be had in the counties of Bucks, Chester, Northampton, Philadelphia, Lancaster, and York, and in the states to north, south, and east, but transporting them to the army was difficult. The roads were poor, and even under clement conditions the journey was difficult for heavily laden wagons. Col. Ephraim Blaine, deputy commissary general for purchases for the Middle Department, noted the "neglect" within the quartermaster's department for "not keeping up a continual supply of Waggons from the Magazines with provisions." Blaine had "not received one Brigade of Waggons from Lancaster or the Back Counties this three Weeks" due, in part, because the quartermasters had "no power to press [wagons or drivers into service] and have great Difficulty in procuring a Single Team" of horses. Sadly, he noted, "the army will Suffer." Increased military traffic, to the extent that this was

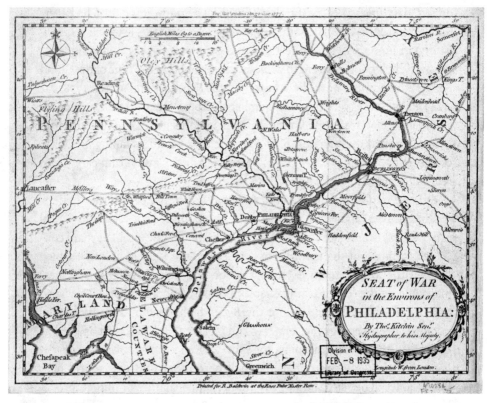

Thomas Kitchin, *Seat of War in the Environs of Philadelphia*. Geography and Map Division, Library of Congress.

possible, merely churned up the roadbeds, which in the freeze, thaw, and rain cycle made an already arduous journey hellish. Furthermore, wagoneers often siphoned off brine from barrels of salted fish or meat in order to lighten their loads, thus spoiling the food. Many simply jettisoned barrels along the roadside, while others cut short their daily mileage, began their journeys late, frequented taverns along the route, or failed to prepare forage and fodder for their animals, resulting in a late start the next morning. A tottering commissariat; reluctant farmers and manufacturers; dishonest, inept, and lazy contractors; near-worthless currency; inadequate transport; inclement weather; dreadful roads; and more made maintaining the cantonment a difficult proposition.[15]

Meanwhile, the British Army competed for food and forage, and conducted raids and patrols throughout the countryside, which compounded the Continental Army's problems. To the southeast of Valley Forge, the British

Army wintered in Philadelphia. If considerably more comfortable than were the Continentals wintering in their huts at Valley Forge, the British found that feeding themselves was no easy task. As redcoats patrolled the countryside around the city, British commissary agents escorted by large formations did their best to provision the army from local farms. Howe took care to safeguard his foragers and what they gleaned from the countryside. On 26 January 1778, Howe's Hessian aide-de-camp, Capt. Friedrich von Muenchausen, noted the dispatch of "three regiments . . . this morning to cover our foragers and wagons, all of which returned unmolested." They "brought almost 200 tons of hay" into Philadelphia. Often enough, however, lone farmers and millers brought their goods into British lines.[16]

Sir William's foragers particularly favored the lands east of the Schuylkill, where Loyalism was more pronounced, the enemy's presence was lightest, and there was less risk of being caught on the wrong side of a rising river. Col. Walter Stewart, whose Thirteenth Pennsylvania Continentals foraged through northeast Philadelphia County and Bucks County, estimated that enough flour and other provisions to feed from eight thousand to ten thousand men "goes daily to Philadelphia, Carried in by Single Persons, Waggons, Horses &ca." But while a large quantity of Bucks County's bounty entered British lines, something that astounded Washington, British agents discovered that providing for the army and navy was still difficult. In southeastern Pennsylvania, specie and escorts to city markets might encourage many farmers, but fresh provisions were still difficult to obtain. Every family farm had different subsistence needs, and their political loyalties were as varied as their numbers. The region was anything but pacified.[17]

British foragers had swept through Valley Forge and the surrounding area before the Continentals occupied it in December 1777. After the onset of winter, life between the lines became increasingly dangerous for soldiers and civilians alike as the two armies competed for popular affections, political power, and subsistence. The region easily contained one hundred thousand civilians, who also needed to eat. Marauding bands of furloughed Continentals; deserters from both sides; bandits; and Continental, militia, and British patrols looked for easy pickings of all sorts. Continental pickets summarily executed farmers bringing produce and livestock to Philadelphia. Maj. John Graves Simcoe, commanding the Loyalist Queen's American Rangers, wrote that to "prevent this intercourse, the enemy added, to the severe exertions of their civil powers, their militia" to enforce the Continental Congress's will, although the number were by "no means sufficient for . . . stoping the Intercourse between the Country and City."[18]

Richard Purcell, *The Honble. Sr. Wm. Howe, Knight of the Bath, & Commander of His Majesty's forces in America*. Anne S. K. Brown Military Collection, Brown University Library.

The contest for control over the lands between Valley Forge and Philadelphia led observers to bemoan the effects of the struggle. Brig. Gen. Jedidiah Huntington thought, "We are watching a Country that has Little to reward us." He hoped, however, "it is for the best that we are stationed here [at Valley Forge] though I must say I do not see it." He believed that the British were in such desperate straits that they had forsaken any hope of regaining the affections of the people, or of their cheerful submission to the crown's authority. Indeed, as Huntington observed, "their burning the Country as they have done is an Evidence they despair not only of Conquering but of holding it in subjugation, save by the Sword."[19]

Timothy Pickering's assessment was, if anything, even sharper than Huntington's. He pronounced Chester County "the most disaffected in Pennsylvania," and went on to damn the people as "barbarous wretches." He took bitter satisfaction seeing their distress, "now [that] their kind protector, the British, have plundered them without mercy or distinction." In this contest for the people's loyalty and support, Pickering aptly noted that "These barbarities will doubtful have their natural effect; to excite the resentment & alienate the affections of these people." Pickering's vengeful side was such, however, that he "was pleased to see how one old Dutchman & his sons . . . had been cruelly plundered." He took grim satisfaction when "One of the sons watched his opportunity & killed two [British soldiers], wounded two & took one of the plunderers, and the old man (who before had his rifle) said he would go home, put his rifle in order & get revenge." Physical destruction merely exacerbated political and armed conflict, which in turn contributed to further destruction. Armies that sought to gain allies among the people, instead alienated them, and created enemies. The war was as much a contest for people's affections and their support as it was a contest of arms. Destruction wrought for the sake of vengeance was satisfying, but its immediate consequences and the long-term effects militated against any sort of succor, settlement, or reconciliation. Emotion had the whip hand.[20]

The struggle over Pennsylvania's lands and peoples hindered both armies' ability to feed themselves. The inability of Sir William's agents to sustain the army locally forced British commissaries to transport large quantities of food from New Jersey, Delaware, England, and Ireland, but the "greatest reliance, especially for livestock, was placed on large detachments of soldiers who roamed both sides of the Delaware." Fuel could be had in the local area, but forage and fodder for horses and cattle had to be "supplemented by hay shipments from other areas, particularly Rhode Island." As for the Continental Army, its situation was so desperate that Washington ordered commanders responsible for the magazines that were to supply the army for the upcoming spring campaign emptied and brought to Valley Forge. The garrisons protecting the magazines were forced to fend for themselves.[21]

The Continental Army's dire circumstances might have reduced it to the passive, suffering host of legend. They did not. Indeed, the army's straitened condition impelled it into action, and it prepared to undertake its largest operation while at Valley Forge. Recent intelligence indicated that the British were preparing to mount a large foraging expedition sometime in mid to late February, at a location unknown to Washington. On 12 February, Washington ordered Greene to scour the countryside between the Delaware and Schuylkill rivers and Brandywine Creek for livestock and send all of it to the army. The task was of the "utmost Consequence," hence Washington's reliance on his ablest general. Greene would therefore "prevent the enemy from receiving any benefit" from the sheep, cattle, swine, and horses even as he eased "the present Emergencies of the American Army." Washington's concept of the operation was twofold: feed and supply the Continental Army and deny the very same foodstuffs and materials to British. This was not a combat mission; thus, it was imperative that Greene take measures for preserving his force.[22]

WHILE CONTEMPORARY ESTIMATES of the size of the force that Washington placed under Greene's command ranged from twelve hundred to two thousand soldiers, the roughly fourteen hundred stated in the order Colonel Angell recorded provides a likely total of the number that marched out of Valley Forge. Washington instructed Greene to give farmers certificates in lieu of cash. In addition to foraging, Greene and Wayne were to destroy "All the provender on the Islands between Philadelphia and Chester which may be difficult of Access or too hazardous to attempt carrying off." The expedition effectively collapsed the Continental Army's eastern screen and uncovered those approaches to Valley Forge as it sent forth so much of Washington's combat power to gather food and supplies. Already overstretched by its mission and low effective strength, the army was unable to support the militia or mount sizable patrols east of the Schuylkill while the Grand Forage took place. Washington's only forward security was now the under-strength Pennsylvania Militia, which, despite active service in the preceding year, was better suited for home defense than as a proper adjunct to the army. Washington pleaded with the president of Pennsylvania, Thomas Wharton, Jr., to call out and strengthen the militia in order to secure the countryside east of the Schuylkill. This was not a new matter. Washington had urged Pennsylvania's government to turn out the militia in strength during the invasion summer of 1777. He continued his repeated urgings until the army marched out of Valley Forge in June 1778. The state's government had done its best by issuing repeated appeals to the men, but as it and Washington well knew turning out the militia in these trying circumstances was only slightly less difficult than feeding his soldiers.[23]

Wharton and the county lieutenants faced the insurmountable task of mustering enough militiamen to do their duty. They had faced this problem from the outset of the British invasion, and it continued to dog them throughout the occupation. Indeed, Pennsylvania's struggle to muster its militia in adequate strength was representative of a larger problem faced by every state throughout the war, that of raising, equipping, and fielding adequate numbers of militiamen, not to mention raising recruits for the Continental Line. The problem was never solved. Just over a month before the Grand Forage commenced, Pennsylvania's government ordered out "Two classes of Militia from the county of York, two from the county of Cumberland, two from the county of Northampton, and one from the county of Northumberland." It directed the county lieutenants of Philadelphia and Bucks "to supply . . . twenty Light Horse[men], each without officers, as they must be necessarily divided into small parties, where officers will be useless." The militia was to screen between the Schuylkill and Delaware rivers, while mounted patrols "should be kept on the several roads for intelligence and other purposes." As an added inducement, the state promised to recompense the mounted troopers for losses or damages to their "horses, arms and accoutrements." Naturally, "The Gentlemen who turn out as Light Horsemen will be excused from serving when called in their classes."[24]

In spite of these incentives, county lieutenants reported grave difficulties in getting the militia to answer the call to duty. Col. Richard McAlester of York wrote that his county's militia "seems determined not to march." Pay was the issue; the call of duty and satisfaction derived from virtue and selfless service only compensated a man so far. Men who had been called out before made "Grate Complaints . . . respecting their pay, which they say they have not Recd." Were the state to settle the matter of pay or the counties able or willing to collect taxes for that purpose, McAlester believed "they wd Goo something freelyer." Under the circumstances, however, it was "allmost Impossible to Git a Cunstable to do his Duty in Respect of the Militia, or any other Person, to undertake the Colecting the Money—they will rather Goo to Prison." McAlester noted the "App[e]als" that were "held in Sundry Places for the 6th & 7th Classes" of militia, and that the "Next week there is several Companys . . . ordered to march." A conscientious man, Colonel

McAlester was "out in Diferant Parts to hurry them out, but the Coldness of the wether, & the Grumbling about the Pay is in Every mouth." The lack of pay affected all of the militia. Col. William Coats, Philadelphia County's lieutenant, was "Busily employ'd in holding appeals, and Collecting . . . substitute moneys" from those not inclined to serve, but well-off enough to pay for a substitute. The county paymaster reported to Coats that pay was in arrears to tune of £2,000, enough "to pay off several of the classes of Militia."[25]

Brig. Gen. John Lacey, Jr. of the Pennsylvania Militia also noted the poor turnout. Lacey commanded the state's forces covering the eastern approaches to Valley Forge and was responsible for denying forage and subsistence to the enemy. Lacey's numbers were so low that "we Cannot by no Means Act together, Either by pattroles or in Case of allarm; by which means some of the Roads Leading to my Camp are Left Unguarded and open to Surprise from the Enemy." He recommended removing his headquarters some three or four miles away from the enemy in order to prevent such an occurrence, despite Washington's remonstration that his "present position is at too great a distance from the city, and puts it in the power of the disaffected, very easily to elude your guards, and carry on their injurious commerce, at pleasure." Lacey did his best, and regularly shifted his bases and patrol routes, but the militia's poor turnout prevented Lacey from doing much.[26]

The militiamen who had earlier reported numbered around 300 and were due to return home by 1 February, and "As for the Light Horse Ordered from Philada and Bucks County, not one of them yet appear." Lacey learned from the counties' lieutenants that "they have not Rec'd any Orders to Raise or Send any." As January turned to February, Lacey was forced to consolidate his men "into One Body, as it is impossable to do any service in the Weak and scattered Condition." The militiamen spent "two thirds of their times . . . hunting [for] Provisions" because they were too far removed from the reach of the commissaries. By 11 February, Lacey's 300 were now "Redused to between Sixty and a hundred." "Redused" numbers were bad enough. They were compounded by "An axident" in which 6,000–7,000 "Cartriges" were "taken fire" and "blew up." The explosion burned five men and set fire to nearby tents, which destroyed "a number of Blankets and Cartriage Boxes in them, the numbers not Exactly known." The day following the orders to Greene and Wayne to mount the Grand Forage, Washington reassured Lacey that he had pressed President Wharton on the weak state of the militia, and had "let him know that unless the number of Men (one thousand) which Genl [John] Armstrong promised should be kept up, are regularly and constantly in the feild, it will be impossible to cover the Country on the other side of Schuylkill."

Wharton's, Lacey's, Washington's, and the counties lieutenants' efforts were almost all for naught: with only sixty men fit for duty, Lacey was compelled to report: "My force is at Last reduced to Almost a Cypher."[27]

THE PROBLEMATIC NATURE of the eastern approaches was not solely the province of Pennsylvania's militia. The inability of the Continental Army's cavalry to "secure a strong outpost at Trenton" compounded the militia's insufficient defense of the eastern approaches. For both political and logistical reasons, Washington had dispersed the bulk of the four regiments of Continental light dragoons throughout New Jersey in small detachments rarely larger than a troop. As conceived, the cavalry at Trenton was to have stiffened and supported the militia that was to have cut off Philadelphia to the north and northeast. Reality, however, confounded the plan. Brig. Gen. Casimir Pulaski, chief of the army's cavalry, arrived at Trenton with elements of the First Continental Light Dragoons on 8 January 1778. Expecting to find three days' forage for his horses, Pulaski discovered that there was none to be had nor had provisions been made for its delivery. On top of this, sailors of the Pennsylvania State Navy were quartered in the town. Having scuttled their galleys after Fort Mifflin's fall in November 1777, the "Gally men" claimed "prior possession, think they are intitled to hold it," and refused to budge. The lack of quarters and food for the light dragoons merely exacerbated the situation, which caused Pulaski to appeal to the "Civil majistrates" for assistance in establishing a magazine and Washington for ordering out the sailors. If nothing suitable could be done, Pulaski suggested shifting his forces northward about twenty-five miles to Flemington. In the meantime, Pulaski divided his troopers into squads and further dispersed them. While this eased the pressure on the limited quarters and food, it dissipated Pulaski's and thus Washington's mounted force and its combat power.[28]

Washington was not about to order out the sailors "if the only objection to Trenton be a little difficulty that may at first occur in procuring the most desirable Quarters for the Officers and men." He assured Pulaski that the barracks and town would provide "ample Quarters" for both. Room was found, but the issue of forage plagued Pulaski throughout the winter. Ironically, what forage Pulaski obtained was ferried over the river to Trenton from Bucks County. For the horses' sake, quartering in Pennsylvania would have made more sense, but Congress had resolved that "New Jersey demands, in a peculiar degree, the protection of the armies of the United States." Washington faced a dilemma: he had to both protect New Jersey and sustain his cavalry, and Congress had limited his options. Hence the demands of civil authority competed with and overrode military necessity, and forced Washington to attempt squaring the civil-military circle. Circumstances forced Washington to rely on Pennsylvania forage and fodder shipped to New Jersey. Extending protection to New Jersey meant that patrolling north of Philadelphia was out of the question. Ferrying horses and troopers across the river exposed New Jersey to the enemy and the light dragoons to the force of the Delaware River's current and ice floes in winter and to the Royal Navy. It was no wonder that Howe's foragers made their way undisturbed in the Northern Liberties and beyond.[29]

By relying on the Pennsylvania Militia, Washington was making the best of a poor bargain. The army buttressed Pennsylvania's weak government and denied the British free rein in southeastern Pennsylvania. Yet in doing so, Washington and his Continentals walked the fine line between the exercise of power and the practice and defense of liberty. Had the army intervened more forcefully in civil affairs, it might very well have upset the "delicate relation between the army and state government." Still, the chief problem was the lack of Continental soldiers. Shifting Continentals into the void east of the Schuylkill would certainly have stiffened the militia but would also have undercut the state's already weak image and hold on the region. More importantly, however, it would have expanded the army's area of operational responsibility, and the army simply could not afford to take on more. The Thirteenth Pennsylvania Continentals, the First Continental Light Dragoons, and others had foraged in the region and patrolled it before the foraging expeditions and with no perceptible effect against the enemy or in strengthening Pennsylvania's already uncertain authority.[30]

Washington realized that the militia's strength, presence, and ability were, at best, contemptible in British eyes and that General Lacey was unable to patrol his area adequately. The best Washington could do was to plead, cajole, and exhort the state's government and its militia. So weak was the Pennsylvania Militia that British patrols daily marched or rode out of Philadelphia four to five miles, all the while ignoring the militia. Under these trying circumstances, Washington's decision to launch a grand forage revealed the limited range of options available to him and the consequent risks of his decisions. Washington therefore set in motion his greatest gamble while at Valley Forge. Circumstances had dictated the general's options. Washington, his army, and even the hopes of the Revolution now confronted a "fatal crisis." The success or failure of Washington's command in Pennsylvania, on whether or not the crisis would prove fatal, depended on the success of the risky foraging expedition his men were about to undertake.[31]

CHAPTER ONE

Every Thing Wanted for the Use of the Army

No single institution, event, decision, or person was responsible for the suffering of Washington's soldiers. Their distress was due to cascading problems that emanated from a variety of sources, human and environmental, that fed into one another and compounded into a maelstrom of misery. Any one of the challenges confronting the Continental Army at Valley Forge was bad enough on its own, but when they combined, they very nearly brought the army to its knees. The specters of disease, dispersal, desertion, and mutiny cast a shadow over the army. Indeed, they posed as much or more of a threat than did the British Army.

Warfare has always been more than battles and campaigns. It has always been, as it was in the Valley Forge winter and always will be, a complex and frequently messy human endeavor bringing together politics, histories, theories of war and their practical applications, economics, human effort, personalities, and more. Warfare is both destructive and creative. It tests individual and institutional endurance, abilities, and beliefs. In the seemingly simple matter of feeding the Continental Army at Valley Forge, all these considerations, in greater or lesser degrees, came together. Nevertheless, the army held together during this fatal crisis, which is testament to Washington's leadership, his officers' and soldiers' trust and faith in him, and their trust and faith in one another. There were outliers to be sure; such is the case in all armies and organizations. Yet, Washington's army maintained its post and contended, and eventually overcame (if only momentarily) the myriad of problems besetting the efforts to feed its soldiers during the fatal crisis of 1778.

THE CRISIS THAT THREATENED the army's survival resulted from long-standing problems within the quartermaster general's department and the commissariat. Congress, ever fearful about corruption and the loss of republican virtue, had created a system and regulations designed to prevent the concentration of power and authority in a single person or institution. Having little history of working together harmoniously as colonies, the loose confederation of states only infrequently rowed together. These semiautonomous republics were so suspicious of centralized power that they contributed to the unintentionally cack-handed performance of the departments charged with supplying and feeding the army. Consumed by ideological purity, the preservation of republican virtue, and a deep-seated mistrust of military power, Congress had instead, by dispersing power and authority, unintentionally hobbled energy and threatened the life of the army.[1]

Neither the quartermaster general's nor the commissary general's departments had ever functioned well. Indeed, over the course of the war they almost always remained unable to properly sustain Continental soldiers for long. Although both departments lacked firm, capable leaders in the autumn and winter of 1777 and into 1778, they and most of the soldiers and civilians within them strove their hardest to clothe, equip, and feed the Continentals. Naturally, there were the outliers who attracted the lion's share of attention. Still, most struggled Sisyphus-like against forces more powerful than they. Immediate conditions like the weather, roads, greed and property owners' fear that they themselves might to hungry—and, of course, the enemy—compounded the greater institutional difficulties. Even before George Washington's command trudged into Valley Forge, these elements were combining in powerful and ominous ways that taxed the army's meager resources and capabilities. The Continentals' march into winter quarters spoke volumes about their situation and their circumstances. Once encamped, conditions worsened for the army and brought it to the precipice of collapse.

NOT LONG AFTER the Continental Army's birth on 14 June 1775, Congress established the offices of the Quartermaster General and the Commissary General of Stores and Provisions. It then delegated to the commander-in-chief of all Continental forces, Gen. George Washington, his choice of department heads. Washington selected Thomas Mifflin, a wealthy Philadelphia merchant for quartermaster general and Joseph Trumbull, a merchant and the eldest son of the governor of Connecticut to head the commissariat. Congress was not altogether sure of what the offices' specific duties should be or how they should be staffed, so it left the matter largely to Mifflin and Trumbull to work out the details of their organizations. Although not authorized, Mifflin and Trumbull exercised their initiative and hired merchants as purchasing agents, who often bought goods on their own accounts and then submitted the bills to Congress, which also paid them from 2–2 ½ percent commission, a well-established practice.[2]

At first glance, paying commissions to agents of the state sounds surprising, but in the case of Mifflin's and Trumbull's departments it was essential.

John Trumbull, *Thomas Mifflin, Major-General in the Continental Army*. Yale University Art Gallery.

The United States was not a unitary national state. It was a confederation of independent republics with the Continental Congress acting as the fig leaf of a general government. Its credit and trustworthiness were nonexistent. Faith and hope were all that the Congress possessed. Therefore, individuals had to do what the weak state could not. In performing their duties, the deputies ventured more than simply money; they put forth their names and integrity on behalf of the army and the so-called United States. Mifflin, Trumbull, and their purchasing agents relied on personal relationships,

John Trumbull, *Joseph Trumbull*. Connecticut Historical Society.

patronage, and reputations to perform their duties. As merchants, Mifflin and Trumbull were generalists who worked in shipping, banking, wholesaling, retailing, warehousing, insuring, and contracting, albeit not simultaneously. They had extensive commercial and personal networks within their colonies and beyond, and therefore seemed to have the requisite skills to run complex purchasing, contracting, and distribution systems. Their deputies, therefore, resembled them on a smaller scale.[3]

Over the winter of 1776–1777, Mifflin devoted time and energy toward reorganizing and reforming his department. Having experienced first-hand the difficulty of supplying the army, he was well-acquainted with his department's shortcomings. Mifflin submitted to Washington a plan for the restructuring of the of the army's quartermaster department. Washington approved of Mifflin's design and submitted it to the Congress, which adopted it on 14 May 1777. The new plan authorized separate subordinate departments for forage and wagons, confirmed what Mifflin had been doing previously by authorizing him to appoint subordinates as needed, and ordered that the quartermaster general submit monthly returns to the Board of War to keep an eye on supplies and expenditures. While Congress had acted to increase efficiency and accountability within the quartermaster's department, it acted in a wholly different manner with the commissariat.[4]

Similar to Mifflin, Trumbull had recommended a plan designed to streamline the flow of authority and increase efficiency in his department. Congress, however, beat Trumbull to the punch when, in the words of New York delegate James Duane, it "reformd and establishd [it] on a wise and salutary plan." Delegates divided authority in the commissariat by creating the Commissary General for Purchases and the Commissary General for Issues. Trumbull was to direct purchases, while Charles Stewart of New Jersey would oversee issues. Instead of a single head, the commissariat now had two, each of whom reported to Congress. As coequals, neither had seniority or authority over the other. As such, planning, coordination, and direction were beholden to personal goodwill throughout their departments, down to individual purchasers and issuers. Congress alone could compel Trumbull and Stewart to work in harmony should they be at loggerheads. Congress further emasculated the department heads by denying both men the authority to appoint their deputies, yet it held them responsible for their deputies' actions. Furthermore, Congress refused to pay Trumbull or his deputies commissions even as it demanded they deposit $5,000.00 surety bonds to guaranty their compliance with directives and their honesty. Commissary Trumbull had proposed a commission of .5 percent for him on all purchases and 2.5 percent for his deputies, but Congress disapproved it. Dissatisfied with the arrangement, Trumbull resigned in July, and in August Congress appointed William Buchanan, a merchant from Baltimore, as his replacement. Buchanan had been the deputy commissary general for purchases for the Middle Department, which covered Washington's command. Unfortunately for the army, Buchanan lacked drive and ability.[5]

Trumbull's resignation was bad enough, but Congress's reforms created cascading effects in the department of issues. From 18 June to 15 September, four of Stewart's deputies resigned in succession. When delegates approached potential candidates, they refused to accept positions unless paid commissions, while others refused to "give bond." And those who were willing to serve had no experience. Out of its sincere desire to prevent corruption and the concentration of power, and to preserve republican virtue, Congress had only succeeded in setting the stage for a severe trial. Both departments "fell apart" because they lacked senior leadership, and the deputies had little experience. Throughout, demoralization, confusion, and disorganization reigned. Worse, however, was yet to come.[6]

Despite Congress's acceptance of Mifflin's plan, he was deeply frustrated. Mifflin wanted a command. He had led a brigade in the 1776 campaign, had helped prepare Philadelphia's defenses that winter, had overseen the evacuation of supplies from the city, and had played a key role in raising Pennsylvania militiamen. Congress, which had earlier promoted Mifflin to brigadier general because of his performance, recognized his later accomplishments and promoted him to major general in February 1777, a sure mark of its esteem, despite his office entitling him only to the rank of colonel. While engaged in the preparation of Philadelphia's defenses, Mifflin had shifted responsibility for his staff duties to his deputies Joseph Thornbury, Clement Biddle, and Henry Emanuel Lutterloh, who did their best to run the department from July 1777 through March 1778. In March 1777, Mifflin subtly indicated to John Hancock that he wanted to surrender the quartermaster's office and assume a field command. Congress, however, failed to take his hint or ignored it. Mifflin was "far too valuable" as quartermaster general and in raising forces. In the wake of Philadelphia's fall to the British Army in September 1777 and Washington's conduct of the campaign, Mifflin was out of sorts. He tendered his resignation to Congress on 8 October 1777, and retired to Reading, "considerably malcontent," pleading his ill health and broken constitution.[7]

Crisis management and ad hoc remedies had marked the first two years of Congress's direction of the quartermaster and commissary generals' offices. It never anticipated or planned for events or contingencies, but instead reacted to developments, each one a potential calamity. Its oversight had been a peculiar one that ranged from laissez-faire—in the cases of allowing Mifflin and Trumbull to appoint their deputies and determine their departments' practices—to a jealous protection of prerogative in reforming the commissariat. Except for small variations, the pattern continued until the end of the war as Congress responded to tunes called by outside actors.[8]

Congress sat on Mifflin's resignation for a month before accepting it, and then promptly appointed him to the newly-constituted Board of War (its members were to come from outside of Congress). Unable to decide on Mifflin's replacement, Congress requested that he continue as quartermaster general until it arrived at a new appointment. Miffed, the general threw up his hands, and passed the buck to Col. Henry Emmanuel Lutterloh in January 1778. Lutterloh, Mifflin's deputy who had been serving at the army's headquarters throughout the 1777 campaign, could shoulder the burden from this point forward. Mifflin and the Congress continued their *pas de deux* through the winter, testing one another's resolve and patience in a complicated dance of power, pride, ideology, and duty. Finally, Congress agreed to Mifflin's demand that he carry but one responsibility. His former colleague, Joseph Trumbull, soon joined him on the board, but illness prevented Trumbull from serving. Maj. Gen. Horatio Gates; Col. Timothy Pickering, formerly adjutant general; Richard Peters, former secretary of the old standing committee, the Board of War; and Lt. Col. James Wilkinson joined Mifflin. As glaring as Mifflin's resignation was, truth be told, he had not supervised his department much since the summer of 1776. The absence of such a senior officer in so important a department was telling, but so too were the shortcomings in other departments, such as the clothier general, whose charge it was to uniform the army.[9]

JAMES MEASE, CLOTHIER GENERAL of the Continental Army, had fallen short in his charge to procure clothing for its soldiers. Much of the problem was due to Congress's inattention to the matter. It was not until 1779 that it even imposed some rudimentary organization over that department. As with the quartermaster's and commissary's departments, Congress's suspicions about centralized power knew few bounds, and it also constrained the clothier-general's authority. On a more practical note, the American states simply did not produce enough cloth or shoes to clothe and shoe the army. Further complicating the matter, individual colonels or states determined the color and facings of their regimental coats, broad uniformity be damned. Moreover, state authorities were in the habit of seizing clothing transported across their state lines, generals felt free to order the plunder of clothing and other shipments, and some drivers abandoned parcels where they pleased. Under these circumstances, Washington functioned as his own clothier general, frequently looking to the states to make up for the shortfall in what James Mease and his department could not accomplish. Without an effective central government, individual states clothed their regiments according to their sartorial tastes, but more often as best they could.

"The approaching Season, and the scanty suppl[ies] of Cloathing in public Store," wrote Washington to Gov. Thomas Johnson of Maryland, had prompted the general to send Lt. Col. Peter Adams of the Seventh Maryland Continentals home "to procure, if possible, a Quantity for the Troops which come from thence." Brigadier General Smallwood had also written to Johnson about the Marylanders. He cited the approach of winter and his fear of "the improbability of procuring supplies of Cloathing." Smallwood's concern for his soldiers "produced sensations that must affect any Person of Humanity," which led him to bring the matter to Washington's attention. Noting the "Distress which generally prevails in the Army for want of Blankets & Cloathing" and how the lack of such basic items hindered or precluded altogether the "Progress of our Military Operations." Washington reinforced Smallwood's appeal, and emphasized the "distress of the Army in this instance, I am sorry to inform you, is now considerable, and it will become greater & greater every day if some releif should not be had." The army's needs were myriad and spoke to the inability of the clothier general to supply soldiers their most basic wants of "every Species." Soldiers were short of blankets, shoes, and stockings. Properly uniformed, Washington believed, "we may be able to obtain some signal, if not decisive advantages over the Enemy by a Winters Campaign: If not, we shall not be in a situation to attempt anything on a large & general Scale." Lieutenant Colonel Adams went forth, armed with $2,000.00 to purchase for the Maryland Line what he could.[10]

Washington wrote similar appeals to the governors of New Jersey, Delaware, Maryland, and Virginia, and had "sent Officers" to carry home the point. He hoped Gov. Patrick Henry of Virginia would call upon the Virginia legislature to make a "very moderate Assessment upon the different Counties" to help clothe Virginia's Continental Line. Without an adequate manufacturing capacity or the energy and power that might be had from a stronger central government, the states would have to make up for the shortcomings of the clothier general.[11]

Even before Washington had begun importuning governors and contemplating the army's next moves, the Board of War had called for the Pennsylvania council's assistance in clothing Washington's soldiers. The board informed Washington as early as 18 October that it had proposed a "Plan" for impressing blankets, shoes, stockings, and other items "from the dissaffected in Chester County & other Parts of the State." Board secretary Richard Peters had no idea "With what Vigour & Dispatch" the council would act. He, like Washington, was "certain" that it had to do so with the "speediest Exertions," lest "Consequences of an alarming Nature must follow."[12]

The council acted swiftly. On 21 October, it "authorized and required" eight militia officers to impress "Blankets, Shoes & Stockings for the use of the army" from the people of Chester County who had given aid or assistance to the British or who had refused to take oaths of "allegiance & abjuration." It was not to be outright seizure, however forceful the act. The council ordered the officers to give certificates to the owners in recompense. Legal distinctions aside, impressing goods and compensating owners with nearly worthless Continental currency made this tantamount to seizure. The council's good intentions, no matter how swiftly acted upon, were for naught. Peters reported to Washington on 7 November, that the "Board have not the least Prospect of obtaining Blanketts at any Rate or Shoes in any reasonable Time" in the manner prescribed—so much for the efficacy of local control or responsibility. Instead, Pennsylvania's council requested that Washington "appoint," if he had not yet done so, "proper spirited Officers to collect Necessaries" in Pennsylvania for Washington's soldiers. Having shifted the onus upon Washington, the council urged him that his officers "should without Hesitation take from the dissaffected in Chester County particularly; every thing wanted for the Use of the Army."[13]

All of these efforts had some impact, but they were not enough. While encamped at Valley Forge, regimental commanders called upon their states for uniforms. Col. Henry Beekman Livingston of the Fourth New York Continentals nearly despaired over the condition of that state's Continental Line. Shortages of uniforms were such that New York's Continentals were "now the most Ragged Part of the Army," claimed Livingston. Their "Constant Duty" had worn the New Yorkers' uniforms down to tatters. Livingstone stressed to New York delegates Francis Lewis and William Duer that the "Want of Cloathing, Pay, and Provisions, Thins our Army." Playing on their sensibilities, Livingston feared "that if a Seasonable Supply is not obtained of each of those articles Particularly the Last that we shall soon be a very unequal match for Genl. How even in our own Trenches." He lectured the "Gentlemen" that good intentions and words were not enough, "in case you have taken it into your Heads to Feed, Pay & Cloath your Army with Resolutions." Without clothing, shoes, and of course food, "Discipline is almost Subverted among us."[14]

Try as it might, Pennsylvania's council had proven itself unable to exercise its writ of government and its authority. As if to compound its admitted inability to act, the council had ceded its police authority to the army and had even increased the reach of the army's geographic scope to the entirety of the state. The commonwealth's government expanded the army's sanction without regard to the seizure of personal property to include "every thing wanted for the Use of the Army." Even when armed with the council's approval, Washington dourly reported he was "extremely sorry to find we have no prospect of obtaining supplies of Cloathing, except by forcing them from the Inhabitants." Whatever the amount of clothing seized, Washington believed it would fall short of the army's needs. Furthermore, he believed that resorting to such extremes "would greatly distress the people & embitter their minds." More immediately, however, were the compounding effects of haphazard leadership, reform, and resignations as the 1777 campaign season came to an end and the army marched into its winter home. Continental and state authorities were difficult enough to influence or control. Mother Nature, however, was an altogether more difficult and challenging matter.[15]

IT WAS NOT MUCH of a consolation for the army, but the winter of 1777–1778 was not as severe as the previous one. In the preceding winter, Washington had struck back in a daring series of battles at Trenton and Princeton. Then, ice floes had closed the Delaware River to navigation. Indeed, they prevented two brigades of the Pennsylvania Militia, over three-thousand soldiers, from crossing the Delaware as the main army attacked Trenton. By comparison, however, the winter of 1777–1778 was "moderate," if uneven. There were two periods of severe cold, first toward the end of December (six degrees above zero, Fahrenheit) and into early January and again in early March (eight degrees above zero, Fahrenheit). These seasonal variations resembled in small scale the erratic temperature oscillations that marked the "Little Ice Age," a centuries-long phenomenon that spanned the years 1300–1850. Thus, the Valley Forge winter was merely one season within an age where the temperatures were, on average, 3.6 degrees Fahrenheit cooler than normal. Rather than an extended period of snowy, icy desolation, the Little Ice Age was "an irregular seesaw of rapid climatic shifts, driven by complex and still little understood interactions between the atmosphere and ocean." Supremely cold winters and easterly winds would abruptly shift to spring and summer deluges, followed by clement winters, or droughts, and heat waves. Indeed, the years following 1770 experienced evermore violent "climatic swings."[16]

Little more than week after the army had occupied Valley Forge, four or more inches of snow fell on it. A heavier snow fell on 8 February 1778, followed by heavy rainfall on 10 and 11 February. Yet another heavy snow fell from 2 to 3 March, when observers noted that that it was deep enough for sleighs in Philadelphia. Throughout the winter, frequent thaws and rains followed freezing temperatures, all of which made for muddy fields and appalling roads. Streams overflowed their banks, and roads became muddy wallows. Foot, hooved, and wheeled traffic only made matters worse. The "broken Roads" rendered movement "sometimes impracticable," which compounded the army's conditions all winter long. The natural environment determinedly had its say. After having mulled over in several councils of war the proposal that the army launch a winter campaign, Washington had finally decided to have the army winter at Valley Forge.[17]

On Thursday morning, 11 December 1777, the army set off from Whitemarsh for Valley Forge. Reveille had sounded early, and at 4:00 A.M., the "whole army ware Ordered to Strike Tents & Parade Redy to march when Ordered." It set off just over three hours later, with Brig. Gen. Anthony Wayne's Pennsylvanians in the van. Under ideal conditions, what ought to have been only a day's march took Washington's command some nine days. Early on, it encountered British forces, and throughout the march, it trudged along narrow, muddy, or frozen roads. At Swede's Ford on the Schuylkill River, soldiers had built a narrow footbridge upon thirty-six wagons resting in the streambed, which they "crossed in Indian [single] file," a manner guaranteed to impede progress even as it kept feet and legs dry. On days like 14 December, officers like Capt. Paul Brigham of the Eighth Connecticut Continentals had "Expectd to march Early But Did not." Rather, "Nothing more Extraordinary" happened that day, save "our receiving a Jill of Wiskey pr. Man, Which we have been deprived of for a Week or more!!" Besides the much-missed water of life, soldiers badly needed shelter, food, and new uniforms. The ranks were chock full of "invalids without number." Soldiers had been "marching by night & day," and living in the field, often without tents, for months. They were "thinly clothed, many without shoes or stockings, indifferently provided for, no vegetables." Lt. Col. John Laurens, an aide-de-camp to Washington and son of the president of the Continental Congress, confessed he "could weap tears of blood" when considering the "want of provisions." Without these basic necessities, the army would disintegrate, and with it all hope of challenging British forces in the field. Disaster beckoned.[18]

By Wednesday, 17 December, nearly a week after having set out from Whitemarsh, commissary agents like John Chaloner were "Direct[ing] the teams to cross [the] Shulkill at the flatland or Pawlings ford as we move this day for the Valley Forge." While the army approached Valley Forge from the east, the commissaries' trains approached from north, which meant another day without much to eat, and without much to commemorate a "day of thanksgiving" on Thursday. Congress had set aside 18 December as "Thanksgiving Day thro the whole Continent of America." Lt. Col. Henry Dearborn of the Third New Hampshire Continentals reflected on the day. He harbored some doubts about the army's ability to commemorate it properly, for "god knows We have very Little to keep it with this being our third Day we have been without flouer or bread." Like the rest of the army, Dearborn had been leading a hand-to-mouth existence, with shelter nearly as inadequate as food. That morning, he recorded, "we are Living on a high uncultivated hill, in huts & tents Laying on the Cold Ground." Dearborn's breakfast had been "Exceeding Poor beef," first boiled, then warmed and served in a "frying Pan." Compared to some soldiers, Dearborn was fortunate. In the evening, he "Dined & sup.d" with Maj. Gen. John Sullivan. Want and hunger aside, Dearborn was stoic about his situation. He was "thankful" for himself and his comrades to be "alive & not in the Grave [as was the case] with [so] many of our friends." Lieutenant Colonel Dearborn's quiet fortitude no doubt spoke for many soldiers.[19]

The following morrow was a "fine plesant morning for the Season." Junior officers like lieutenants Samuel Armstrong of the Eighth Massachusetts Continentals and James McMichael of the Thirteenth Pennsylvania Continentals knew the army was to "march to a place Call'd Valley Forge." Finally, the army's soldiers knew their destination. Although a mere five miles away, the march took all day, and they did not arrive until "after Sun Sit." Tedious the march may have been, but it was not without incident, and, in the words of Col. Israel Angell of the Second Rhode Island Continentals, "plaged So bad With our waggons" that the single track was hopelessly congested, rutted, and mud churned. The roads, he noted, "was Excessive Bad and our horses very poor and weak." As the column approached its winter home, a wagon "over[set] and killd one woman," a doleful event to be sure, and testimony to the appalling march and road conditions. At times, the weather had been "Verey Cold and Snowey." In a postwar recollection, Sgt. Lewis Hurd, then a private in Col. Charles Webb's Second Connecticut Continentals, found the situation as "distrsing as at any one time During the war." At times, Hurd and his comrades had been without "Shelter Clothing or Provision [for] Sum Days."[20]

Entering the "woods" near Valley Forge, Lieutenant McMichael discovered "our ground was laid out" in proper fashion, welcome to be sure. Soldiers built fires and cooked what food they had. Despite having had "nothing to Eat nor to drink" that day, McMichael and doubtless other officers and men scrounged and combined rations. In McMichael's case, "our Boy went to work to Bake Bread and of this we Eat like Insatiate Monsters." For others, however, it was "Suppers of raw Corn" scavenged from nearby fields. That evening, as well as on the previous days and for many to follow, soldiers made do "with one Gill of Rice other Days with 2 ounces of Meat Pr Day sum times 2 or 3 Days at a time without any thing Except hors feed oat meal Bran beef Hydes and old Bones that is gathered up." Fed or not, soldiers "Piched . . . tents," mounted guard, and bedded down for the night. All else would be sorted in the morning.[21]

The next morning, Maj. Gen. William Alexander, New Jersey's putative Scottish nobleman Lord Stirling, "accompanied by the Ingenieurs," rode ahead of the army, surveyed the cantonment, and selected the "proper spott for hutting" the Continentals. They designated division and brigade bivouacs, and within them, "Field Officers" from throughout the army adjusted and refined brigade and regimental cantonments. At the forefront of soldiers' minds, however, was food. Teams and wagons hauling provisions arrived, and raised soldiers' hopes, but in short order their hopes were dashed. Colonel Angell had thought the distribution "was very pleasing to the troops," but his seems to have been a minority view. Following the arrival of rations, inspectors quickly condemned the meat after having "Judged it not Wholesome for to Eat." The inspectors in Brig. Gen. Ebenezer Learned's brigade, captains Joseph Pettingill, John Wiley, and Seth Drew of the Ninth, Eighth, and Second Massachusetts Continentals, deemed it "not fit for the use of human beings." Moreover, the captains three reported the beef was so "unwholesome & destructive to nature" that nobody could "make use of Such fude."[22]

Learned had ordered the commissary to distribute salted, preserved meats, "as much as three Barrells to a Brigade, which" worked out to about eight ounces per soldier, half the mandated ration set by Congress in 1775. Fellow inspectors in Brig. Gen. John Patterson's brigade found much the same with their meat rations. As the commissaries distributed the salted provisions, Patterson in turn promised "some fine beef and flour in two days."

All their soldiers could do was trust. Lieutenant Armstrong thought "the men seem'd a little Contented" with the meager fare, and he expressed a quiet pride in the soldiers who had "bore up with such bad Usage." Indeed, that they had done so "with so little Mutiny" spoke well for them. Armstrong believed the soldiers' willingness to endure privation was due to the officers' example, their having "Endured the same" as their soldiers, although he wryly noted "there was more mutiny among the Officers than among the men." Leadership and followership by example clearly had their limits.[23]

THE ARMY'S FIRST FULL DAY at Valley Forge was but another in the slow-moving, staggering debacle that was its supply and transportation system. Food, uniforms, and much more had been in short supply in this land of plenty throughout much of the campaign, and it only worsened as the seasons turned from summer, to autumn, and then to winter. No matter the item, it was hard to obtain. Salt, a vital ingredient for food preservation, had become "so scarce" in places like Reading and Easton, Pennsylvania, "that there was the greatest probability of the Inhabitants suffering by want of it," recollected Col. Robert Lettis Hooper, Jr., deputy quartermaster general for Northampton, Bucks, Berks, and Philadelphia counties, Pennsylvania, and Sussex County, New Jersey. So hard to obtain was it, that it "was extreamly Difficult at Reading to procure from the Country People any provisions without a Barter in Salt."[24]

Soldiers were in "distress for the want of flour" as well, wrote John Chaloner, assistant commissary general for purchases. Chaloner and his fellow commissaries had been "feeding the troops from hand to mouth these several days past," he wrote on 16 December. As Chaloner penned these words, the army was "without one barrele of flour and have been so twenty hours." Without flour, the army would continue to "suffer." If that were not enough to spur action, Chaloner appealed to institutional and individual public character and pride—their honor. Should the commissariat fall short, "the reputation of all concerned in the victualing department will fall a sacrifice to the indolence and indulgence" of men uncommitted to their duties. Chaloner had fought long and hard to feed his charges, and despite his best efforts he had often fallen short. He confessed that he was "in the utmost distress for want of provision" to provide for the soldiers.[25]

Chaloner's voice was not a lone one. Other commissaries joined him in a discordant chorus of distress. Assistant Commissary for Purchases Azariah Dunham related a tale of woe over pork, salt, and corn to his superior, Col. Ephraim Blaine, deputy commissary general for purchases for the

Middle Department. Based out of Monmouth, New Jersey, Dunham did his best to supply the forces to his southwest, but he was unable to obtain salt "for [the] takeing in of Pork." Autumn was the time to slaughter swine and put them up for the coming months, but without salt that was impossible. The locale, Dunham reported, was "almost Destitute of it." East Jersey's proximity to British-occupied New York was a key element in its lack of provisions. Over the previous spring and winter, both armies had maneuvered, camped, and fought in the broader environs, which meant that "no Corn could be rais'd." Moreover, while in the area, they had emptied farmers' stores and laid-in supplies, including salt pork. It was a vicious cycle of want, denial, exploitation, and deprivation. Yet, all was not lost. Dunham persevered in his quest for food and salt for the army.[26]

Dunham reported that he had sent a "brigade of Waggons for Salt to Tarry Town," north of New York City. Shortly after dispatching the wagons, however, he heard a rumor "that that place is burnt," although he "wish[ed] it may prove otherwise." Limited provisions and rumors of a burned town aside, Dunham had good news to report. He was going to forward a herd of 278 head of cattle on 18 December. Once delivered, Dunham hoped "my people may be Discharged as soon as possible" so that they might drive to the army another herd he was expecting from New England. Promising news aside, Dunham added that he was deeply in debt, "more than £22000," for his purchases, and desperately in need of reimbursement. Dunham was "Dayly Involveing myself further in Debt," and he implored Blaine "to send the Needfull [funds] to extricate me." His credit could only go so far, his funds even less. Having purchased all the cattle possible from "within the Circle of my Acquaintance," Dunham could not "purchase where I am not known on Credit."[27]

SLOWLY, THE DAYS GROUND ON to Christmas. The army received the day with hope but little else, particularly joy or full bellies. Soldiers felt these shortages acutely. Lieutenant Armstrong had noted their growing discontent over their "not having their last Allowance of Provisions Regularly." He recorded on 21 December that soldiers had drawn their rations of "flour one day," but no meat for over a day and a half. Sadly, it had not been that day. What flour the troops had drawn had failed to sate their hunger. It was not long before Continentals "began to Grumble again for want of Bread." When the soldiers finally drew meat rations, they amounted to little better than "Carri[o]n Beef," scarcely suited "to make Broth of, and indeed there was Scarcely anything more than bones" to it. On the following morning, after having been "without Provision, all the day before," the army "drawed two days Allowance of flour but could get no meat." Young Armstrong's regiment, the Eighth Massachusetts Continentals, "baked" their flour into "Cakes," and then marched out of camp, toward the "Enemy." While away, "we kill'd Some Sheep & went to broiling in on the Coals &c Eating it without any Salt." Time and distance away from the "flagpole," as soldiers for time immemorial have noted, had its benefits. Nevertheless, Christmas was but another day of scant rations for most of the army, and "We was without provisions therefore." Armstrong's superiors sent him and a foraging party out to search for food. Later that afternoon, around "three or four," Armstrong's party "got [49 wt.] of Salt Beef & 110 wt. of fresh Beef and two hundred & a half of flower." Whatever satisfaction Armstrong had was short-lived, for shortly after returning to camp he was sent out on a patrol and did not return until around 10:00 P.M. "This," he noted, "was my Christmas frolick."[28]

Armstrong's Christmas frolic was part of a larger effort begun on that day's eve. "So great is the want of Beef and Bread in Camp," reported Col. Thomas Jones and John Chaloner to Thomas Wharton and Pennsylvania's council, that Washington ordered every brigade to dispatch an officer and twenty-two soldiers "to collect and send into Camp a temporary supply." Jones and Chaloner had little hope of success, for "this Country is drained and affords a very trifle" in the way of provisions. Nonetheless, the soldiers went about their duty, some parties having greater luck than others. On Christmas, "Another party will march to morrow morning a greater distance, and it is to be hoped be more Successful." Purchasing commissaries had strained themselves to feed the army. Their efforts had paid off the day previous, when drovers herded in "about seven hundred Cattle." With an army numbering 10,000 or more souls, this amounted to about "a Weeks allowance" of beef. As for flour, it was "quite Exhausted."[29]

Jones and Chaloner believed magazines at Lancaster, York, and Wright's Ferry (today's Columbia, Pennsylvania) held "a considerable quantity," but "a trifling has come in for many days." The problem was a want of "Waggons" and teams, which, they reported, the "Quarter Master do not furnish." They implored Wharton and Pennsylvania's council to give whatever assistance they could to "enable" the quartermaster to provide the commissary with "Teams sufficient to bring on daily One Hundred Barrels." Like their fellow commissaries, Jones and Chaloner were "distressed beyond description." They hoped that Wharton and the council could exercise their power "to order Waggons sufficient to bring on the above supply daily."[30]

Disorganization and confusion characterized commissary and quartermaster operations. Political decentralization, suspicion, and confused lines of authority and direction emanating from Congress, the new Board of War, and the states and on through the army often prevented or retarded staff officers' efforts. Rather than benefitting from thoughtful, centralized, and coordinated direction, instead commissaries and quartermasters dissipated their energy and efforts by often working at cross purposes, as Continental and state commissaries and quartermasters competed against one another for the same resources. The Board of War compounded the confusion, competition, and inefficiency when it persuaded Congress to introduce a parallel commissary system in January 1778, and forbade the existing commissariat from interfering with the new department. Whatever energy or efficiency they achieved through unified effort was more often honored in the breach than not.[31]

HAD THE COMMISSARIES been able to purchase all of the provisions required by the army, their ability to transport those goods would still have been severely limited. As the army approached Valley Forge, Colonel Jones, Deputy Commissary General for Issues, wrote to President Wharton of the "approaching Calamity that threatens our Army for the want of Provisions," which was "occasion'd by the Scarcity of Waggons." Even if there had been wagons, there were few teams of horses available to haul them. Jones complained that "there is not half teams employ'd in halling flour," and because of that he had not a "single Barrell" to distribute. Although Jones had sent two express riders to Lancaster and Reading with directions to urge "forward all Provision Waggons," the effort was for naught. "Some Gentlemen" who had come from Lancaster informed Jones that they had "not seen any Provision teams coming from thence." Col. George Ross, deputy quartermaster general at Lancaster, and the issuing commissaries there and at York and Reading confirmed as much. Without an immediate delivery of "at least 200 to 250 BBs. [barrels of] flour to Camp," Jones feared the army would dissolve within a week.[32]

Nearly a fortnight before Jones had written to Ross, the quartermaster had shared news with him about wagons and drivers. "Notwithstanding every exertion to procure Teams," Ross was unable to secure any around Lancaster because they were involved in moving "all the Flour from York to this side Sasquehannah" River. Some teams, wagons, and drivers, however, were not involved in shifting the magazine. Instead, they remained untouched because of the "vast number" of men on duty with the militia, which Ross deemed a "great hindrance." Continental and state exertions were so much at cross purposes that militiamen risked fines for venturing out with their teams and wagons. Militiamen had approached Ross, offering to "furnish their Teams & to make their Tour of Duty for two months, if that will excuse them from the Militia." Could this be effected, Ross thought, "Business would go on Cleverly," but Pennsylvania's council and the Continental Congress were at sixes and sevens. Ross had a dozen teams, some twenty-four to forty-eight horses "straying about, not a driver to be had."[33]

Reliance upon civilian teamsters not subject to military discipline was another element that compounded the army's supply problems. Moreover, there was little accountability for property and little in the way of enforcing what little there was. Thus, contracted civilians disposed of public property that made their work more onerous. A congressional committee sent to camp in February 1778 found "the Property of the Continent dispersed over the whole Country." It discovered "Waggons left to the Mercy of the Weather, & the Will of the Inhabitants." Wagoneers had entrusted picks, spades, and shovels to the safekeeping of people without obtaining receipts. Delegates claimed that a general's orders resulted in the recovery of 3,000 or more "Spades, & Shovels, & the like Number of Tomahawks" that were in the possession of people near the camp. Much the same held true for "Tents, & Tent Cloth" that had lain in a barn throughout the summer, and had only recently been recovered. Improperly maintained, the wagons fell into disrepair. What transportation the committee saw at camp was "now performed by the Men, who without a Murmur patiently yoke themselves to little Carriages of their own making, or load their Wood & Provisions on their Backs."[34]

Want of wagons and teams had dogged the army from the time of its creation in 1775, but that want was not always because there were none to be had. In some cases, local laws frustrated Continental authorities, but in others owners were reluctant to part with their wagons and teams because quartermasters or other officers had not obtained proper authorizations to call upon or impress wagons. Moreover, local officials were hesitant to act or assist the army without legal authorizations. Without the force and surety of law, owners were liable to bear uncompensated all expenses without the ability to apply for redress or recompense for whatever losses they might incur. In other cases, the reimbursement offered simply did not compare with the wages offered by private individuals. Congress had decreed that it would pay 30s per day per wagon, driver, and team of four horses. Teamsters refused the trifling pay when they were able to earn £3–4 daily on the market. The cause may have been glorious, but the wages were not. The lack of firm or committed leadership in the departments compounded the situation. Judging by the performance of some quartermasters, commissaries, and teamsters willing to work for the mandated pittances, Congress got what it refused to pay for, and the soldiers suffered for it.[35]

Pennsylvania's council addressed the matter of compensation in a letter to its congressional delegates. It stressed that wagon owners, "for a considerable time past," had been steadily "loosing money" because of the "wages which the honourbale Congress has fixt." Teamsters had to provide for themselves and their families, while horses needed food, and wagons needed maintenance. Without adequate pay, "the loss must fall on the owners, when Justice and equity says it should be bourne by the publick." For equity's sake, therefore, the council recommended that Congress raise the rate from thirty shillings for a wagon, team of four horses, and driver to forty-five or even fifty shillings; "otherwise when the wagons . . . are worn out they will not be replaced." Horses, iron, and labor were simply too high to replace or repair wagons for the amount allowed by Congress. Col. John Bull, adjutant general of Pennsylvania, confirmed as much in a letter to President Wharton, when he noted that the wages of "Common" farm labor had trebled, "at Least," and other "articles which the Farmer cannot Dispence with" had risen to prices "Proportionately Dear." Bull thought it "more then Probeble" that farmers would only raise enough crops for their own needs. Congress held fast to its stingy compensation. Depressed currency, low reimbursement, inflationary prices, and owners' reluctance to part with goods and labor—all of these problems forced army and state agents to impress wagons and teams, and impel drivers to manage them.[36]

Impressment had been an integral element in the army's survival mechanism during its frequent moments of crisis. Indeed, as early as 1776, Continentals had been impressing supplies for periods authorized by the states or by Congress. Periodically, Congress and the states renewed impressment authorizations. During the Philadelphia Campaign, the army had been authorized no fewer than three times, and generally with the admonition that those who had failed to swear or affirm to oaths of loyalty should bear the brunt of the sacrifice. Desperate as the army was, its foraging parties often paid little heed to peoples' loyalty oaths. Upon the approach of foraging parties, the Rev. Henry Melchior Muhlenberg, pastor of the Lutheran church in Trappe, Pennsylvania, and father of Brig. Gen. John Peter Gabriel Muhlenberg, commented that "There is a great distress again today because wagons, horses, provisions, and victuals are to be impressed, or rather grapes are to be picked from thorns and figs from thistles." For wagon owners, Pennsylvania tried to ameliorate some of the sting by appointing its own wagon masters down to the town level. Local wagon masters may have helped lessen the pain for some, but impressment involved far more than wagons, teams, and drivers. It included food and clothing. No matter what the item, however, property owners lost in the end when agents and others gave them receipts or paid in Continental dollars. Continental and state authorities, in turn, also lost something.[37]

Sanctioned or not, impressment alienated property owners. Even though officers and agents gave certificates, the steadily sinking value of Continental dollars meant that property owners lost money when the army seized their goods, even if only temporarily. More fundamentally, impressing property was the heavy-handed intrusion of the state into private lives and a violation of individual rights—legal sanction or not. It risked alienating people and turning them against the army and the cause of independence. Thus, when Continentals or states' agents pressed property they ran the risk of creating enemies in a war for which peoples' affections and loyalties were key. Washington had taken this to heart early in the war. He understood the nature of the struggle, but was also sensitive to property rights. Throughout the war, he was reluctant to impress property.[38]

Congress, "firmly persuaded of General Washington's zeal and attachment to the interest of these states" recognized as much when it complimented him about his "forbearance in exercising the powers vested in him by Congress." While such restraint was "laudable," Congress reminded the general more forcefully that his "delicacy in exerting military authority . . . may, on critical exigencies, prove destructive to the army and prejudicial to the general liberties of America." Getting to the point with yet more force, Congress "directed" Washington to "subsist" off of farmers and others nearby, and to seize whatever the army needed or might be of use to the "enemy." In ordering Washington to take off the gloves, Congress enjoined him to take "from all persons without distinction, leaving such quantities only as he shall judge necessary for the maintenance of their families."[39]

Impelled by necessity and urged on by Congress, agents and foragers set about in their quests for food, clothing, and the wagons to bring those supplies into camp. Impressment supplemented the ongoing purchasing, so when farmers and others refused to accept mandated prices, commissaries and quartermasters could fall back on legally sanctioned coercion. William Buchanan, who had replaced Joseph Trumbull as commissary general for purchases, reported to Thomas Wharton about his deputies' difficulties in obtaining beef, pork, and whiskey at the prices fixed by the Board of War. Although Buchanan found the "price fixed for Wheat . . . sufficiently liberal," it was not at all enough to "satisfy many avaricious People." Buchanan was reluctant to exercise the power; he found it "extreemly disagreeable"; and before resorting to it asked for Wharton's and the Pennsylvania Council's "advice and Assistance in devising some mode that may prevent the necessity of using force."[40]

Farmers' avarice was not confined to locales in which army operated. It extended far beyond, even into New England, which supplied many of the army's needs for beef, flour, salt, and other goods, however haltingly. Within Connecticut, Elisha Clark, a deputy commissary general for issues reported to Jeremiah Wadsworth, a deputy commissary general for purchases, that he was unable to acquire any grain. He had traveled "above Livingstone Manner and made all possible Inquiry about Wheat" and other grains, but met without success. Farmers refused the mandated price of $3.00/bushel. The wheat they had "not thrash'd nor will they as yet." Instead, they gambled on prices rising, "as they think it will be higher." Frustrated by the ordeal, Clark seemingly threw up his hands, and declared "their can be no encouragement to Bartor with that sort of people."[41]

However reluctant authorities were of exercising coercion, they resorted to it. Col. Charles Stewart, commissary general for issues, had discovered "not a Barrel of Flour or one fatt Ox or Cow on hand" the day the army had marched into Valley Forge. "His Excellency," General Washington, was "amazed and highly offended at this failure" to properly feed the army. It was more than a matter of humanity; it was a matter of military effectiveness and readiness. Starving soldiers or those foraging for their own sustenance could not fight. Washington, according to Stewart, "collected the General officers who declared their Difficulty to prevent a Mutiny among the Troops for two Days past." This state of affairs had prompted the commander-in-chief to dispatch from each brigade a captain, a commissary of issues, and twenty-two soldiers to "seize and bring in flour, Beef Pork & Wheat." The foraging parties combed the countryside as far as ten miles from camp. Colonel Stewart feared the measure would prove ineffective. He was certain that Washington found the foraging "oppressive & highly disagreeable," as did the farmers. The following day, Richard Barnard, a Quaker farmer, noted in his diary and ledger that "Joshua Lawrance Came here with some armed men . . . & took from me too wagon load of hay & 25 bushels of Corn." Impressment was not merely intrusive; it could be personal, but also entrepreneurial.[42]

COL. CHARLES STEWART.
Member of the Continental Congress.

Col. Charles Stewart, Member of the Continental Congress. The Miriam and Ira D. Wallach Division of Art, Prints and Photographs: Print Collection, New York Public Library Digital Collections, The New York Public Library.

Capt. Stephen Olney of the Second Rhode Island Continentals fondly reminisced about "one good supper" several of his messmates "obtained." They left camp to purchase food and startled a homeowner "while knocking at the door" and offering payment for whatever food he was able to spare. The man's chickens raised a ruckus and "began to squall." One of the young officers called out, "'what are those D___d Hessians about[?]'!" Rather than answering the door, the man "chose to keep his bead." Olney conjectured that the "Dred of Hessians or the thought of selling property for our bills of credit [had] so stupefied" him, that he refused to answer the door. Captain Olney judged that "the chickens made a most excellent stew, and verified the old adage — Stolen meat tastes Sweet." In retrospect Olney may have been gilding the lily, but not by much.[43]

The First Rhode Island Continentals' Sgt. John Smith took it upon himself to lead a private foraging party on 21 December. The day had been "warm," always a "Pleasant" occasion in December. Fine weather aside, Smith and his messmates had had "Nothing to Eat but a Little flower made with Coarse Indian meal." This was not enough, so the sergeant led some soldiers out of camp that "Night." While they were out, "the fortune of war" graced them and "Put into our hands a Poor Sheep which we Roasted & boild which Gave the Company a Good Super which we Eat & turnd in." As a good sergeant, Smith had looked out for his company but in doing so he and his foragers had stolen a sheep from a local farmer. They and others like them had not only ventured out of camp, but by violating military discipline, had crossed into a moral and ethical gray zone by stealing in order to survive. It was a situation that pleased nobody.[44]

Washington recognized the crucial relationship between the army, the people, and the success of the War for Independence. He railed against the "cruel outrages and roberries lately committed by soldiers," and deemed them "unwarrantable." Joining virtue to practicality, Washington drove home the painfully obvious, "Were we in an enemy's country such practices would be unwarrantable; but committed against our friends are in the highest degree base, cruel and injurious to the cause in which we are engaged." If he could not gain popular adherence to the cause of independence and support for the war, the least he hoped to do was to avoid embittering the neutral or swelling any further the ranks of the Loyalists. There was no little irony that a revolution waged, in part, against the fear of encroachment by central authority was now resorting to intrusive central authority, including the seizure of private property, to save itself. What success they met with was not enough to sustain the army.[45]

When foragers or purchasing agents approached, they spared few property owners; rank, prominence, or service to the revolution did not shield many from their reach. John Lesher's case is emblematic. Lesher, a Berks County, Pennsylvania Militia captain, farmer, and owner of the Oley Forge, remonstrated at length to President Wharton and the commonwealth's Supreme Executive Council about his repeated losses from Continental troops in 1777 and 1778. Captain Lesher had represented his county in Pennsylvania's 1776 constitutional convention and was a member of the General Assembly from 1776 through 1782. Ironically, he was also a commissioner active in purchasing supplies for the army.[46]

Writing in January 1778, Lesher "conceive[d] I am no more master of any individual thing I possess." His property had suffered "damages" by soldiers and "Continental Waggons, in taking from me 8 Ton of Hay, destroy'd. Apples sufficient for 10 hhds [hogsheads] Cyder, Eating up my Pasture, Burning my Fences, &c., and 2 Beeves I was oblig'd to buy at 1s. per lb., to answer their immediate want of Provisions, and at Several other times Since I have Supply'd Detachments from the Army with Provisions." In late December or early January, the army had impressed "14 Head of Cattle & 4 Swine, the Cattle at a very low Estimate, to my infinite Damage, as they were all the Beef I had for my workmen for carrying on my Ironworks." Lesher was unable to force a compromise with the foragers in order to retain the hides and tallow: "I had rather deliver'd the Beef and reserv'd the Hides, Tallow, &c., but no Arguments will prevail, all must be deliver'd to a Number of Armed men at the point of the Bayonet." As a forge master, Lesher was responsible not only for his family but for "Colliers, Wood Cutters and other day Labourers," altogether numbering "near 30 Persons." Support for American independence was one thing, but impoverishment at the hands of the Continental Army was another.[47]

Turning to lecture the president and council, Lesher reminded them of the connection between soldiers' conduct, the success and nature of the Revolution, and the government's responsibility to protect the people. It struck him "with Horror to see a number of our own Officers & Soldiers, wantonly waste & destroy the good Peoples Properties; [for] by such conduct they Destroy the Cause they seek to maintain." While few were spared, there were, in Lesher's judgment, a privileged few who escaped the reach of foragers. "Instead of Judicious men appointed in every Township," he continued, "or as the Case may require, to Proportion the Demands equal according to the Circumstances of every Farmer & the general benefit of the whole, these men, under the Shadow of the Bayonet & the appellation Tory, act as they

Please, our Wheat, Rye, Oats & Hay taken away at discretion and Shamefully wasted, and our Cattle destroyed." Some farmers, Lesher continued, "have not a Bushel of Oats left for Seed, nor Beef sufficient for their own Consumption, while some others lose nothing, as a man who has 100 head of Cattle lost not one; such Proceedings I think to be very Partial" and injurious to the cause of independence. "[U]nless some Speedy & Effectual method be taken to put a stop to such irregular Proceedings," he wrote, "I Shudder at the Consequence."[48]

SHUDDER INDEED. The army must have appeared to Lesher and others an all-consuming creature with a voracious, unyielding, and never-sated hunger. It was an engine of the most conspicuous sort of consumption. Between December 1777 and June 1778, the army consumed 4.5 million pounds of bread, flour, and biscuit, and nearly 4 million pounds of meat and fish; something over 2,272 tons of breadstuffs and 1,985 tons of meat and fish (see Table 1.1: Ration Consumption). The numbers, painstakingly compiled by Valley Forge historian Jacqueline Thibaut, are estimates extracted from incomplete records; the consumption figures for March and April 1778 are missing, as are those for certain other categories in other months. Nonetheless, the record opens a door to the logistical challenges faced by the Continental commissariat.[49]

The average monthly consumption of breadstuffs—for the five months for which records exist—works out to nearly 454 tons per month, and for meat and fish nearly 397 tons per month. The prescribed daily ration, met more often in the breach than not, allotted each soldier one pound of bread, another pound of meat, a pint of milk, and a quart of beer, one ounce of rice, six ounces of peas or beans, and just under an ounce of butter, or their equivalents. Officers, depending on their rank, were authorized additional rations as a component of their allowances. Inexact and incomplete as the ration figures are, supplying the Army with an average of nearly 1.7 million pounds of food per month was a herculean task. In the last week of February, the army required 15,903 rations daily, which had to be transported from magazines, mills, and other sites.[50]

In order to fulfill that requirement, over 113 wagons per day were needed for transport. A two-horse cart could transport 800 pounds of provisions and other supplies, whereas a four-horse wagon could haul a ton. The army had only eight wagons in camp. Even with those wagons, it was doubtful that teams could be had. So many Continental, state, and private "Waggon horses . . . have been found unfit . . . that the Army will . . . suffer for

TABLE 1.1 Ration consumption

Month	Bread	Flour	Biscuit	Total pounds breadstuffs	Meat and fish in pounds	Daily number of rations	Total pounds per month
December 1777, including militia	unknown	unknown	unknown	1,041,979.8	1,071,282.5	23,061	2,113,262.3
January 1778	185,505	715,859	unknown	901,364	1,053,222	unknown	1,954,586
February 1778	235,686.5	506,234.5	unknown	741,921	616,634.25	19,749	1,358,555.25
March 1778	unknown	unknown	unknown	unknown	unknown	unknown	unknown
April 1778	unknown	unknown	unknown	unknown	unknown	unknown	unknown
May 1778	189,908.5	694,021.5	unknown	883,930	546,154	unknown	1,430,084
June 1778	283,703.75	694,021.5	1,357	979,082.25	683,639	21,697	1,662,721.25
Total per category	894,803.75	2,610,136.5	1,357	4,548,277.05	3,970,931.75	64,507	8,519,208.8

Tonnage estimates reflect an adjustment to breadstuff weights resulting from a reduction in the May 1778 total by 81,466.5 pounds in order to correct a table error and the addition of 42,534 pounds of tongue not originally considered in Thibaut, "This Fatal Crisis," table between 126–127.

want of an immediate Supply of Provision, & forage." Col. Clement Biddle, commissary general for forage, predicted that the shortage of wagons and teams, and therefore food, would hamper the spring campaign. Perversely, the only bright side to this picture was the Malthusian decrease in hungry bellies as the winter progressed.[51]

Purchasing was preferable to impressing, but Continental dollars were nearly worthless. Accepting them in exchange for goods was tantamount to theft, so farmers and manufacturers were reluctant to sell their goods to purchasing agents. There was more to it, however. Indeed, their reasons were as varied as they were. Some speculated, betting on rising prices to offset the risk of seizure by the armies. They avoided the public market established by Washington, and husbandmen hid their horses and wagons upon the approach of foragers or purchasing agents. Some inhabitants were loyal to the crown and refused to assist the Continentals. In all likelihood, most were concerned with their families' welfare. Empty promises in the form of near-worthless Continentals dollars or promissory notes would not provide for families or their needs. It was a matter of survival.

On 29 December, Congress reacted to the army's plight and formed the ad hoc Committee on Emergency Provisions. It consisted of the ad hoc Board of War, and three delegates: Cornelius Harnett of North Carolina, Elbridge Gerry of Massachusetts, and Abraham Clark of New Jersey. By the following day, 30 November, Francis Lightfoot Lee of Virginia had joined it. Congress charged the committee to "fall upon immediate Methods for Supplying" the army. Writing to President Wharton, the committee acknowledged its discomfort with impressment, the "Umbrage to the Inhabitants," and "deplore[d] the Necessity" of sending out foraging parties, but the army's "wants" had to be fulfilled. George Washington's soldiers were not alone in seizing food and other supplies.[52]

AT THE OUTSET OF THE WAR, British officials had assumed that they would be able to sustain all of King George's men with local purchases of food and other nonmilitary goods. Instead, that became the exception rather than the rule. The British Army had captured and held New York, but had failed to secure an area extensive enough to sustain its victualling needs. Instead, the army relied heavily upon British butchers, bakers, candlestick makers, and others to supply them. It was to little avail. Throughout the war, the focus on capturing and holding ports was understandable and necessary, but without a large enough force to seize and defend rich agricultural areas, soldiers could do little more than secure these logistical hubs from which they mounted expeditions in search of the enemy, but more often in search of food and other supplies to supplement dwindling stocks. Foraging was a constant element in British operations, and "demanded an inordinate effort" from the soldiers. Gen. Sir William Howe launched six large foraging expeditions in January 1778, another six in February, and ten in March. Continentals and militia patrolling and foraging around Philadelphia forced the British to intensify their efforts and expend even more energy in the search for supplies. From the outset of the Philadelphia Campaign, the British Army had been in search of food, forage, fodder, and other supplies even as it sought battle with the Continental Army.[53]

Philadelphia, economically and politically important to the American cause, was but another port the British had to defend. Although historian R. Arthur Bowler deemed 1777 "the best year of the war . . . in terms of provisions' reserves," they still fell short of the six-month rule-of-thumb preferred by commanders. From August through late October, the British Army subsisted off the land and ate well, but not long afterward the easy availability of foodstuffs declined to the point that Howe's commissary general, Daniel Wier, informed the Treasury Office that the bulk of the army's supplies would have to be shipped from Britain.[54]

Historians have estimated that it took one-third of a ton of food per year to feed a soldier in America, and that an army of 20,000 soldiers required thirty-three tons of food daily. From 1777 through the close of 1778, Britain dispatched 124 victualers and transports, averaging "220 tons burthen," to supply soldiers in North America. It was not enough. Besides soldiers, there were the hundreds, if not thousands of horses used by the army in Philadelphia. On average, each one required twenty pounds of fodder and nine of oats or corn daily. Much of the fodder came from Rhode Island, brought to the army by contracted merchant shipping. The American threat to Howe's supply line was such that he deployed around 3,000 soldiers to escort wagon trains traveling to and from Chester, fifteen miles southwest of Philadelphia. Still, it was not enough. In response, Howe sent out large foraging expeditions, sometimes lasting for as long as a week, sometimes employing upwards of half the army. Moreover, twice and thrice-weekly woodcutting parties required covering forces of 500 and more soldiers to protect them. As Maj. Charles Stuart of the Forty-Third Regiment of Foot had observed from New York in the summer of 1777, the threat of attack by militia and Continentals "absolutely prevented us this whole war from going fifteen miles from a navigable river." Previously, Stuart had railed against "the neglect of those in high office, who omitted making magazines of every species of forage when we were in possession of the greater part of the province of New York." Their neglect, Stuart charged, had forced the army to "enter into a kind of 'petite guerre,' which has kept the army the whole winter in perpetual harassment, and upon a modest computation has lost us more men than last campaign." Small as it was, the British Army could ill afford to wage a wasting war of attrition. Yet, it had no other options.[55]

Foraging parties continued their searches as the army settled into occupation duties. Robert Morton of Philadelphia singled out troopers of the "Light Horse," likely the Sixteenth or Seventeenth Light Dragoons, for having taken hay, and over fifty bushels of potatoes from his family. He "rec'd a Rec't for the load of hay." On the British Army's return from Whitemarsh, northwest of Philadelphia, Morton pointed to Hessian soldiers who "Bro't off about 700 head of cattle." Not long after that, another column ventured west as "Lord [Charles] Cornwallis with a detachment of about 5000 men cross'd the Schuylkill towards Derby [Darby] to cover a Foraging Party of Waggons." Cornwallis then led his force northward, where it briefly tangled with the advance guard of Washington's army as it marched west to Valley Forge. Colonel Pickering damned the "great devastations" wrought by the "barbarous wretches." But, when Cornwallis returned to British lines, Capt.-Lt. John Peebles of the Forty-Second Regiment of Foot, better known as the Royal Highland Regiment or the Black Watch, observed less judgmentally that the column had made "a good hawl of forage, some cattle, & plunder."[56]

Peebles's remark about plunder reveals something of the extent to which soldiers took license while foraging and their officers looked away or were unaware of the despoliation. British and "Hessians" had "ransacked" a house belonging to the Morton family and had visited "destruction similar" at Israel Pemberton's country home. Cornwallis's command, which Peebles had remarked on, had, according to Morton, "plundered a number of the inhabitants of everything they had upon their farms, and abused many old, inoffensive men." Morton was convinced that this was "permitted, under the command of their officers, to ravage and destroy property." It was as if the army was inciting "the inhabitants to rebellion" by its indiscipline. Howe took notice.[57]

On 18 December 1777, Howe's orderly book recorded that he had given "repeated orders . . . against Plundering & Depredations." Throughout the tenure of his command, which dated to 1776, Howe had received a constant stream of complaints about the lawlessness of his soldiers, and was "Very Much Mortified" by their behavior and by having to enjoin subordinate commanders "for their Exertion to Surpress such Unsoldier Like Behaviour so absolutely Repugnant" to military discipline and the larger mission of suppressing the rebellion and gaining adherents to the king's cause. Even before this latest injunction, courts-martial had convicted and sentenced soldiers to floggings and executions. Lawlessness notwithstanding, foraging continued, and alienation grew apace. The army and its horses had to be fed.[58]

On 21 December, Howe ordered well over half of the army, "24 battalions" according to one observer, and over eighteen field guns and howitzers of varying calibers, to prepare for a forage. Soldiers were ordered to bring three days of provisions and "Waggons of Each Corps three Days Rum." The next morning, Howe, seconded by major generals James Grant and Charles Grey and Brig. Gen. Alexander Leslie, "cross'd the Schuylkill at Grey's Ferry," occupied "Derby," and sent covering parties to protect the "Waggons Foraging, also the small craft that loaded at Tinicum Island." The "grand foraging Party" lasted until 28 December. Continentals had harassed the foragers and killed or captured over a dozen, and the weather had been "Very Cold and disagreeable, I assure you," but it did not affect the progress of foraging.[59]

Captain-Lieutenant Peebles reckoned that Howe's foragers had brought in "between 3 & 400 tons of hay every day," over 2,000 tons in total, which he believed would satisfy the army's needs for four months (by Howe's estimate, it was only half that). Maj. Carl Leopold Baurmeister, adjutant-general of Hesse-Cassel forces observed critically, that the forage had been brought about by the "neglect" of British forage masters and commissaries who had allowed the stocks to fall to a "scanty supply." Nonetheless, Baurmeister deemed the expedition "very successful." Foragers had seized "450 sheep and 180 head of cattle," along with the hay, most of which had been loaded "on ships," which then sailed up the Schuylkill, "above Gray's Ferry Bridge," where it was offloaded. Thirty transports had taken part in the operation. The freezing weather, however, caused "two Briggs and a Schooner" to become icebound. The crews were unable to free the vessels, and the Delaware River's current drove them aground on the New Jersey shore near Gloucester. As unfortunate as the loss of the three transports was, it was soldiers' and civilians' crimes that enraged Howe.[60]

On the first day of December's grand forage, Howe's orderly book noted that "two Men are Orderd for Immediate Execution for the Crime of Plundering." Howe was "Determined to Punish with the utmost rigour Every Man Detecte'd In Depredation of any Kin'd." He more than realized the consequences of criminality. Besides alienating Americans, it ate at the very fabric of the army, its orderliness and discipline, and threatened to turn the force into an armed mob. Most soldiers obeyed Howe's injunctions, but for some they went unheard or ignored. Near the end of the forage, courts-martial had tried and convicted "Isaac Green a Negro," and "James Hammuel Inhabitant of the City of Philadelphia." The court sentenced both men to "One Thousand Lashes," little better than a slow, painful death sentence. Green and Hammuel were not alone. Other defaulters' names entered the orderly book for plundering, along with their findings of guilt, or rare acquittals. With so much of the army engaged in feeding itself and its animals, it had little time to fight. The British Army's logistical shortfalls, therefore, gave the Continental Army much-needed breathing space. Time spent foraging was time given over to Washington's soldiers for their own foraging. With need and opportunity calling, Washington launched his largest and most ambitious operation while encamped at Valley Forge, the Grand Forage.[61]

CHAPTER TWO

Like Pharaoh I Harden My Heart

Try as they might, the Commissary General, the Quartermaster General, the army's foraging parties, the Board of War, and Congress were unable to feed the army or rectify the larger systemic problems that had created and sustained the crisis. As January ended and February began, George Washington faced a momentous decision. Unable to wait for cattle drovers and herds from New England or to readily obtain flour from nearby Lancaster, Washington's choices were stark. Let the army continue starving and risk mutiny and dissolution, disperse it to locations closer to food sources and surrender southeast Pennsylvania to the British, or send out a large foraging expedition to glean from the countryside and the people all that could be had. A grand forage was but a temporary expedient to longstanding structural problems. Moreover, it risked the encampment's security by dispatching a large portion of the army's few combat-ready soldiers and created an opportunity for Sir William Howe to attack the cantonment or even the Continental foragers. Confronted by these choices, Washington opted to risk the army's security so that it might maintain its position at Valley Forge. On 12 February, Washington issued orders to Maj. Gen. Nathanael Greene "to take, carry off and secure all such Horses as are suitable for Cavalry or for Draft and all Cattle and Sheep fit for Slaughter together with every kind of Forage that may be found in possession of any of the Inhabitants." Greene was to march the next morning.[1]

Washington had received "recent intelligence" about Howe's intention to make yet "another grand Forage into this Country." This suggested that Sir William was going to dispatch a large contingent of his army, perhaps half or more of it, in search of food, forage, and fodder. He had done so twice in December 1777, and Washington had been unable to challenge the British columns. Were Howe to launch a grand forage while Greene's column was beyond the fortifications of Valley Forge, Washington hazarded their making contact, and coming to blows. Were that to happen, Howe's tactical acumen and superior numbers meant that British arms would likely prevail. It was a fight Washington could ill afford. Yet, there was hope. British operational patterns did not suggest that Howe would seek battle. His only attempt had been at Whitemarsh in early December, but nothing had come of that venture. Washington likely took this into consideration as he balanced the

Charles Willson Peale, *Nathanael Greene*. Courtesy of Independence National Historical Park.

risk against the army's needs and the opportunities offered by a foraging expedition. He had taken Howe's measure as commander over the course the 1776 and 1777 campaigns, and had come to understand his opponent. Skilled he was, but Sir William's need to feed and preserve Britain's precious few soldiers overrode whatever inclinations that he might have had toward combat.[2]

Greene's foragers were to concentrate their efforts in the area "between the Schuylkill and the Brandywine," west of Philadelphia. The Schuylkill was a barrier to British movement. Unfordable near Philadelphia, its few bridges limited the speed and size of whatever British forces might cross, which gave added security to Greene's foragers. While foraging, officers under Greene were to make valuations and counts of all the "horses Cattle Sheep and Provender so taken" from people, and issue them certificates redeemable in Continental dollars. Washington ordered Greene to destroy "All the Provender on the Islands between Philadelphia and Chester" that his soldiers were unable to impress. Naturally, they were to "take an account of" property and property owners' names "as far as the nature of the Service will admit." Greene directed Col. Clement Biddle, commissary general for forage, to "to issue the necessary warrants & Instruction, for the execution of this Service & to superintend the commissaries & Quarter masters."[3]

WHEN WASHINGTON HAD CONCEIVED his idea for the Grand Forage, it seems that he had initially selected Brig. Gen. Anthony Wayne to command the operation. It made sense. Wayne hailed from nearby West Chester, was intimately familiar with the area and its people, and as a local man he might lessen tensions or anxieties among the farmers. Wayne was a capable, tough-minded, aggressive, and competent—if vain and headstrong—officer who could be relied upon. His frequent exhortations to Pennsylvania authorities about the condition of his soldiers spoke to his concern for soldiers' welfare and smart turn out. Notwithstanding Wayne's humiliation in the battle of Paoli (20–21 September 1777), his tactical judgment was sound. Not long after drafting orders to Wayne, however, Washington changed his mind and instead chose Greene to command, with Wayne as the Rhode Islander's deputy. Greene was Washington's most capable lieutenant. The two had formed a close bond during the New York Campaign of 1776. Although Greene had committed his fair share of errors, he learned from them, and matured and developed into a solid and reliable soldier. He had gained Washington's trust and confidence. His rearguard action at the Battle of Brandywine on 11 September 1777 had bought time for the army to retire from the battlefield, and was one of the more impressive feats of soldiering performed that day. Greene was humble, clearsighted, and a capable organizer who did his best to accomplish whatever mission fell to him. Despite his upbringing as a Quaker, Greene was anything but a pacifist. During the foraging he more than once demonstrated a hardnosed and unforgiving side. He was precisely the soldier Washington needed in command.[4]

Greene recognized the army's difficult situation, but was doubtful about the forage's ability to accomplish much. Shortly after receiving his orders,

Greene wrote to Wayne to coordinate the details of their pending expedition. He "Inclosed" a message from Capt. Henry Lee of the First Continental Light Dragoons that touched upon the pending forage. Lee commanded an outpost south of Valley Forge, and was an especially active and observant young cavalryman, well known to the army's senior officers. Although a copy of Lee's communication does not exist, Greene's tone strongly suggests that Lee had doubts about the potential for success, doubts that Greene shared. Greene questioned whether the foraging would gather much for the army, but "His Excellency thinks we had better make the experiment nevertheless." Greene then ordered Wayne to "consult and fix upon the plan for execution" with Colonel Biddle, who was to oversee the expedition's issue of warrants to farmers and others for their seized or destroyed property as well as to direct the subordinate commissaries and quartermasters accompanying the forage. Greene, who was busy meeting with a congressional committee charged with enacting needed reforms for the army, trusted Wayne and Biddle to develop "the plan for execution," a sign not just of Greene's other commitments and his standing with Washington and Congress, but also of his trust in the two officers. His doubts and commitments notwithstanding, Greene dove into the task with all his customary drive and energy.[5]

The farms, pastures, fields, woods, and rolling countryside of Philadelphia, Bucks, and Chester counties were a complex geographic and human terrain. Bounded by the Delaware and Schuylkill rivers, and intersected by numerous streams, some of them navigable by small craft, family farms of about 130 acres predominated. Most of the people raised wheat, corn, various other crops, horses, swine, sheep, and cattle in this "long and fertile floodplain." Horses averaged around 14.3 hands high, while swine averaged about 175 pounds apiece, and provided about 125 pounds of dressed pork. Sheep, in contrast, weighed in at around fifty pounds and gave somewhere between ten to fifteen pounds of mutton. Typically, local cattle weighed around 770 pounds, and yielded around 450 pounds of dressed beef. Some specimens of the livestock, however, were much smaller. In December 1780, Washington wrote with dismay about the "immensely poor" examples he encountered in Connecticut. He reckoned "they were so small that I am convinced they would not average 175 lbs. the 4 nett quarters. some could not exceed One hundd. weight." Washington sourly observed that "next Summer a starving man wd. scarce eat the Beef they were about to put up after the Salt had extracted the little fat and juice that were in it." If this was the case in Connecticut, a center of cattle raising and a land little touched by war, what was to be expected in forager-ravaged Pennsylvania in 1778?[6]

Reflecting on the physical environment, Capt. Johann Ewald, a Hessian *jäger*, remarked on its "mountainous" terrain and "thick forests." He found the region "well cultivated and very fertile," just the sort of environment to sustain an army. Geography and economic interests had long tied southeastern Pennsylvania's farmers into a regional and transatlantic commercial network. Ports along the Delaware River were entrepôts for crops, livestock, and timber harvested by freehold farmers, husbandmen, and woodcutters. No port, however, was larger or more important than British-occupied Philadelphia, capital of one of the most ethnically, religiously, and politically diverse regions in British North America. In some ways, Pennsylvania was the United States writ small.[7]

Maj. John Graves Simcoe, a young British regular and commander of the Loyalist Queen's American Rangers, described the people of southeast Pennsylvania, their ethnicities, religious backgrounds, and degrees of loyalty or disaffection. "Disaffected" was something of a catchall term used by Britons, Loyalists, and Americans struggling for independence that described those who did not want to openly choose sides in the war. It ranged from people ill-disposed toward the combatants, but unable to act upon their opposition, to the indifferent, and those with sincere pacifist convictions. Simcoe described Philadelphia County as "mixed with People of all Complexions and Denominations," an unstated acknowledgement of the region's place within the empire. As a major port and the largest city within this contested portion of the British empire, Philadelphia's population was a tacit assertion of its role and significance. Some 55,000 people had lived in the county, with upwards of 30,000 in Philadelphia proper. Simcoe judged "the Majority is loyal" to the British cause, although "many [were] violently Rebellious and consist of Germans, English, Irish, Scotch, etc." Beyond the city limits, numerous hills marked the northern reaches of the county.[8]

North and northeast of Philadelphia sat Bucks County, a place generally well disposed to the king's arms and favored by British foragers. Around 18,000 to 20,000 people called it home. According to Simcoe "Germans of various Denominations" lived there, although later examinations suggest a largely English and Quaker population. Nevertheless, Simcoe deemed the Germans, the Quakers, and the Presbyterians "loyal," and indeed thought that "on the whole there is a great Majority of Friends to Government in this County." Friends of the government meant food for the army, intelligence about the enemy, and even recruits for Loyalist battalions. This boded well for the future, although there were suspect populations in Bucks, such as the "English Baptists, Low dutch & Calvinists," whom Simcoe distrusted and deemed among the "disaffected."[9]

Chester County was the focus of Greene's foraging. Situated on the right bank of the Schuylkill River, which provided a small measure of security, 30,000 or more people called it home. Simcoe through them "very Loyal." Most of the people were Quakers of Welsh descent, with pockets of German Reformed, Lutherans, and Pietists in the northern portions of the county. Simcoe noted that there were "at least 20 Quaker Meeting Houses, only 4 Presbyterian Meeting Houses and 7 English Churches." Simcoe put some faith in the "many . . . young Quakers in this or young Menonists" in other counties. He believed they "will assist greatly in suppressing the Rebellion." Simcoe had served in America long enough to recognize that Quakers and Mennonites, if not willing to abjure their pacifism and fight, were still essential to the re-establishment of British rule in Pennsylvania and beyond. They must have demonstrated a cheerful or willing acquiescence to British arms, else Simcoe would have consigned them to the ranks of the disaffected.[10]

Across the Delaware River, broadly similar geographic and settlement patterns existed. Although Greene's orders sent him to Chester County, he was mindful of southern New Jersey, having briefly occupied Mount Holly with his division in November. While there he had become familiar with the countryside's richness, and took this into account when he later developed a plan that branched off from Washington's original intentions. West Jersey, as some still thought of it, shared some of Pennsylvania's characteristics. Farmers who tilled its "rich loamy soils" and raised livestock, sold their surplus wheat, corn, and animal flesh in Philadelphia, an easy journey across the Delaware. The topography was largely gently rolling countryside intersected by numerous watercourses, and dotted with forests. Burlington County, up-river from Philadelphia, was mainly Quaker, with a mixed English, Swedish, and Dutch population. To the south were Gloucester and Salem counties with similar mixes. All told the three counties' combined population was less than 30,000, most of whom lived close by the Delaware River.[11]

Because of Chester County's proximity to Valley Forge and the frequency of British foraging, there was little chance of finding enough wagons and teams to haul away whatever might be garnered from Pennsylvania's farmers. Hence, one of Greene's first actions was to dispatch soldiers to Lancaster, some 46 miles west of Valley Forge, in order to impress, organize, and bring forward wagons and teams. If the recent past was any indicator, they had their work cut out for them. When the orders went out to Greene, the army had had not "a single wagon in Camp." As for supplies or wagons from Lancaster or Bucks County, the army had not "Received one Brigade of Waggons . . . this three Weeks." Quartermasters "complain[ed]" they had not the authority to press wagons or teams.[12]

IN THE MEANTIME, Greene organized his command. He had but one day to do so, and his planning, like Washington's, was emblematic of the rushed and "improvised" nature of the operation. The hurried design points to the army's desperate situation. "After Orders" following the initial set that directed Greene on the expedition designated one major general, one brigadier general, three colonels, four lieutenant colonels, four majors, sixteen captains, thirty-two subalterns, thirty-two "Serjeants," thirty-two corporals, sixteen drummers and fifers, and "1200 privates to parade Tomorrow [13 February] at Ten oClock with 3 peices of Artillery furnished with six days allowance of hard bread, 2 days meat." Although not specified, the gun crews and horses for the three pieces of artillery added to the composition of Greene's column. The caliber of the guns determined the number of artillerymen and horses. Given the nature of Greene's mission and the need for mobility, it stands to reason that the guns were lighter weight three, four, or perhaps six-pounders (pounder referring to weight of solid shot fired). Gun crews might range from four or five soldiers on a three-pounder, eight on a four-pounder, and upwards of twelve for a six-pounder. The number of horses required to draw each gun and its ammunition ranged from two, to four, to six per team. Therefore, if not included in the original count of 1,200 privates, the artillery added an additional twelve to thirty-six soldiers and from six to eighteen horses. Without a muster, however, this is conjectural.[13]

Before marching, the column drew 640 "Pounds Salted Provision;" officers, noncommissioned officers, and privates would assume both foraging and covering party duties, likely combining their roles. Washington expected Greene's command to subsist from the countryside for upwards of a "fortnight." The "After Orders" also specified six days of rum at the rate of one gill per soldier daily. They drew 224 "Gallons of Rum or Whiskey," just over five and one-half days' worth — clearly, Chester County was expected to supply the shortfall from the total of 1,280 rations of rum (or an acceptable substitute), or forty gallons daily for eight days. Considering the poor material condition of the army, only "those who [were] best clothed" were to march.

Moreover, each of the colonels was bring along his regimental surgeon "supplied with bandages &c." The orders did not designate wagons, for there were few in camp, nor did they include any reference to cavalry, most of it being away in New Jersey or on outpost duty.[14]

Estimates of provisions in the locale provided by Col. Ephraim Blaine, deputy commissary general of purchases, were a mixed picture. Blaine thought there were some 5,000 "Barrells Flour" in Chester County, and another 7,000 across the Delaware River in New Jersey. He estimated that in nearby Philadelphia and Bucks counties there were 1,500 and 4,000 barrels respectively. Other reports indicated that Delaware alone had some 17,000 bushels of wheat, 5,000 barrels of flour, 12,000 kegs of salt fish, and unnumbered quantities of corn, beans, and salted pork—all rich pickings for the army should it venture forth. New Jersey, Washington's sources told him, had many thousands of head of cattle. These supplies were equally tempting to Sir William Howe's foragers, but even were the Continentals not competing with the British for those supplies there was still a problem: transportation. The army did not have enough wagons to bring on the ample supplies estimated by Blaine. In an explanatory note below his table of estimates, Blaine made clear the awful arithmetic: "Suppose thirty five thousand Rations pr day issued in Camp and it's Neighbourhood, that will be Three hundred & fifty Barrells pr Day—Suppose Two hundred and fifty Waggons each to Carry Eight barrells, and upon an Average make a trip each Week, the Amot. will be Two Thousand Barrells, Suppose fifty more employed at a greater Distance in bringing forward Stores—This Number of Waggons will scarcely be Sufficient to Support the Army." Without wagons, horses, harnesses, and drivers to haul barrels of flour and other supplies, no matter how bountiful Chester County might be, or for that matter any other county, the army would want for food.[15]

The "After Orders" subtly suggested the physical condition of the army as well as Washington's need to accept ever more risk through an ad hoc organization with little unit integrity or cohesion beyond brigade membership. Soldiers serving alongside messmates and under their own officers, as much as officers commanded by their own superiors, benefitted from the camaraderie and familiarity developed through training and combat. They knew and trusted the soldiers to their left and right. Greene's foragers, however, were another matter. The named officers represented six divisions, seven brigades, and ten regiments, a motley crew if ever there was one. If the officers' regiments are any indication, the enlisted men hailed from Massachusetts, Rhode Island, Connecticut, Pennsylvania, New Jersey, and Virginia. In a

Richard Butler (1743–1791) Colonel in the 9th Pennsylvania Regiment. Painted 1790–1832–78

John Trumbull, *Richard Butler, Colonel in the 9th Pennsylvania Regiment*. Yale University Art Gallery.

practice adapted from the British Army, the Continentals had earlier created a specialized light infantry brigade whose soldiers were drafted from the army's various brigades. This, however, was an altogether different matter. Unit integrity, prized by the Continental Army as much as the modern U.S. Army, had to be thrown out the door because of the army's woeful state. The day that Washington had issued orders for the forage, Col. Richard Butler reported the wretched condition of his soldiers. There was "not a blanket to seven men" in the Ninth Pennsylvania Continentals. Butler had "been obliged to retain the Tents as substitutes for blankets." Those soldiers likely did not number among the foragers.[16]

Unfortunately, many of the names of the soldiers who marched out of Valley Forge that February morning have been lost to history, and like most soldiers in most conflicts, they are anonymous, and they are faceless. Their names, and, surely, they were recorded somewhere, have gone the way of so many orderly books, journals, letters, diaries, and other documents speaking to their existence and thus their identities and humanity. They have largely disappeared. Nonetheless, it is possible to construct a partial roster of soldiers and restore a small handful of those lost or forgotten who marched out that February morning (see table 2.1 below).[17]

TO THE LOW RATTLE AND THUMP of drums and the shrill sound of fifes, officers and noncommissioned officers roused their troops. Reveille had likely sounded sometime between 4:00 A.M. and 6:00 A.M. Soldiers formed in ranks; sergeants called the rolls; officers read aloud any last-minute orders for the day and then dismissed the men to attend to their personal needs and to prepare what meager fare they may have had. It was to be a day of marching. The morning of Friday, 13 February was "pleasant but Soon Clowded up and grew raw cold and unpleasant." By 10:00 A.M., in obedience to Washington's orders from the previous day, officers, soldiers, and musicians formed up into ranks. Greene and Wayne rode at the head of the column, while the field officers, the colonels, lieutenant colonels, and majors rode at the heads of their makeshift battalions. Senior officers had to see their soldiers, and their soldiers had to see them. Captains, subalterns, and noncommissioned officers marched with their companies, and fifers and drummers beat and played a cadence. Thus, wrote Capt.-Lt. George Fleming to his brother officer, Capt. Sebastian Bauman of the Second Continental Artillery, a "Detachment of fifteen hundred Men & four Field Pieces, under the Command of Genl. Green . . . marched towards Darby: what their destination is we know not."[18]

Trudging southeastward out of Valley Forge, the column tramped along miserable muddy paths, generously described as roads. The past few days had been a wet, stormy mix of rain and snow. To the north of Valley Forge, in nearby Trappe, the Rev. Henry Melchior Muhlenberg kept a journal, in which he noted the weather and what had transpired around him. Deep snow had lain on the ground when, on 11 February, a "heavy rain fell." It continued through the day, and brought "high waters and impassable roads." At

TABLE 2.1 Organization and participants

Number and rank indicated	Name	Parent unit
1 Major General	Greene, Nathanael	
1 Brigadier General	Wayne, Anthony	Wayne's Brigade
3 Colonels	Butler, Richard	Ninth Pennsylvania, Conway's Brigade
	Shepard, William	Fourth Massachusetts, Glover's Brigade
	Spencer, Oliver	Spencer's (Fifth New Jersey) Additional Continental, Conway's Brigade
Staff	Biddle, Clement	Commissary General for Forage
	Forsyth, Robert	Captain and aide-de-camp (adjutant) to Greene; adjutant, Fourth Virginia, Scott's Brigade
4 Lieutenant Colonels	Ballard, Robert	First Virginia, Muhlenberg's Brigade
	Harmar, Josiah	Sixth Pennsylvania, Conway's Brigade
	Sherman, Isaac	Second Connecticut, Huntington's Brigade
	Unknown	
4 Majors	Bradford, William	Sherburne's Additional Varnum's Brigade
	Bradish, David	Fifteenth Massachusetts, Glover's Brigade
	Cabell, Samuel Jordan	Fourteenth Virginia, Weedon's Brigade
	Hait, Joseph	Eighth Connecticut, Varnum's Brigade
	Mentges, Francis	Eleventh Pennsylvania, Wayne's Brigade
16 Captains	Doyle, John	Eleventh Pennsylvania, Wayne's Brigade
	Woodbridge, Theodore	Seventh Connecticut, Huntington's Brigade
	Others unknown	
Subalterns	Capt.-Lt. Simonds, Jonas	Second Continental Artillery
	1st Lt. Ransdell, Thomas	Eleventh Virginia, Woodford's Brigade
	2nd Lt. Horne, Benjamin	Fourth New Jersey, Maxwell's Brigade

(continued)

TABLE 2.1 Organization and participants (*continued*)

Number and rank indicated	Name	Parent unit
	2nd Lt. Jennings, Simeon	Second Rhode Island, Varnum's Brigade
	Morton, 1st Lt. Hezikiah or 2nd Lt. James	Twelfth or Fourth Virginia, Scott's Brigade
	Bvt. Lt. de Montfort, Julius	Hartley's (Pennsylvania and Maryland) Additional, Wayne's Brigade
	Others unknown	
32 Sergeants	Unknown	
32 Corporals	Unknown	
16 Fifes and Drums	Unknown	
1200 Soldiers	Unknown	Twelve are known, but not individually identified, to have come from Maxwell's Brigade (First Connecticut, Fourth Connecticut, Fifth Connecticut, Eighth Connecticut, and Second Rhode Island)
3 Pieces of Artillery	3-, 4-, or 6-pounders	Artillery Brigade
Gun Crews	12–36	Artillery Brigade

After Orders, 12 February 1778, RG 93, M853, NARA; 22, Anthony Wayne to Theodore Woodbridge, 23 February 1778, Woodbridge Papers, CTHS; Wayne to George Washington, 5 March 1778, 14 March 1778, *PGW*, 14:73, 74, 181; Washington to Jonas Simonds, 28 February 1778, *PGW*, 13:698–69. Simonds was a late addition, sent to New Jersey in February. Trussell, *Pennsylvania Line*, 88; Poor Orderly Book, HSP; First New Jersey Continental Regiment Orderly Book, NJHS; Wayne to Simeon Jennings, 23 February 1778, *NDAR*, 11:412–13. Julius de Montfort to Wayne, 10 March 1778, Wayne Papers, HSP; *OCA*, 137, 493, 511, 102, 233, 84, 274, 494, 116, 138–39, 266, 389, 203, 604, 497–98, 458, 301, 319, 193, 404; page-number order reflects the corresponding entries in the table. Col. Richard Butler was not listed in the after orders, but he did participate in the forage. Bvt. Lt. Julius de Montfort escaped captivity and joined Wayne in New Jersey. It cannot be determined if he was one of the original officers on the forage. The guns were likely 3-, 4-, or 6-pounders, which were lighter pieces and thus more mobile.

least it kept the armies "fairly inactive in their winter quarters," a small blessing for Muhlenberg, whose son was Brig. Gen. John Peter Muhlenberg. Both men were Lutheran divines, but while father Henry tended to his flock in Trappe, his son commanded a brigade of Virginia Continentals. The elder Muhlenberg reflected on the weather-induced respite for the armies, no doubt with his son in mind: "They are forging arrows and gathering strength to shoot them where divine providence shall ordain." Miserable as the weather was, Greene's column marched southward, with a "stormy, penetrating northwest wind" at its back.[19]

Greene led his ad hoc command to Springfield Meeting House, just under twelve miles southeast of Valley Forge and around nine miles west of Middle Ferry, which accorded quite well with an earlier, but never acted-upon recommendation from Wayne to Washington, advocating that the army station there from 1,000 to 1,200 soldiers as an "Advanced post" at Derby, with an additional mounted screening force covering all the roads into the city. The column's movement had been anything but a secret to either the Continental or British armies. Colonel Angell had noted it in his journal, the adjutants of Brig. Gen. Enoch Poor's brigade and of the First New Jersey Continentals, had recorded that Lt. Benjamin Horne, Fourth New Jersey Continentals, and "as many men from [Brig.] Genl. [William] Maxwells Brigade (not Exceeding 12) as he shall select" would prepare for the expedition. Sgt. Ebenezer Wild of the First Massachusetts Continentals noted "a large party detached from the whole army went off on some expedition. They carried a week's provision with them."[20]

As surprisingly widespread as knowledge about the Grand Forage was within the Americans' camp, it was also known by their enemies, and in some detail. Capt. Friedrich von Muenchausen, General Howe's Hessian aide-de-camp, wrote with extraordinary accuracy that Washington "today detached General Wayne with 1,500 men and four cannon down the river about three miles beyond Darby to gather available cattle, provisions, etc." Security at Valley Forge was so lax that John Charles Philip von Krafft, a former Prussian officer looking for an appointment in the Hessian service—but just as happy to seek one in the Continental Army—freely wandered about the encampment at Valley Forge for over two weeks. Krafft, who later received a commission as a lieutenant in the Hessian Regiment von Bose, wrote not only about "General *Green*," but also about "General *Ween* [Wayne]," and that they had departed Valley Forge at 10:00 A.M. Krafft's level of detail was astonishingly close to the numbers Washington had specified: "3 Colonels, 6 Lieut. Colonels, 16 Captains, 32 Subalterns, 32 Sergeants, 32 Corporals, 16 Drummers and Fifers, and 1200 men crossed the *Schwlkill* [Schuylkill River], but it was not known, in camp, where they were going." Security this lax and intelligence with this sort of specificity boded ill for the expedition.[21]

Shortly after establishing his headquarters at Springfield Meeting House, Greene set his men to collecting all the cattle, horses, wagons, and other necessary items in the area. He intended to fall back six miles to his "rear" on the fifteenth "to take post at one Edwards," a tavern which was to serve as a collection point for the foraging parties. Chester County's roll of tavern petitions lists Nathan Edwards as the sole Edwards operating a licensed tavern in the county (1764–1782). Located in Middletown, just over four miles west southwest of Springfield Meeting House, Edwards's Black Horse Tavern was on a major north-south thoroughfare, the Edgemont Road (roughly what is now Route 352), which ran from Chester to the Great Valley, just west of Valley Forge. At first consideration, Greene's usage of "rear" seems rather broad and his choice of location questionable—Valley Forge was to the north-northeast. Yet, upon reflection, the Edgemont Road, also known as the Great Road, made perfect sense. It was distant from Philadelphia, which put it out of easy striking range of British forces, and it led toward camp while still maintaining a safe distance from the enemy. With some of his forces interposed between the foragers and Philadelphia, Greene held the central position from which he could delay an enemy attack against his foragers.[22]

Concerned about being exposed to enemy attack and about the army's poor condition, Greene urged Biddle to "exert yourself in collecting forage otherwise the business will go on slow." Underscoring his seriousness, he enjoined Biddle to supervise the officers and men closely, and promised that he would "punish the least neglect with the greatest severity." Greene's injunctions reflected his interpretation of Washington's orders and his own views of the people in Chester County. In conclusion, Greene enjoined Biddle to "forage the country naked," and, not without some black humor. He wrote to Biddle, that "to prevent their complaints of the want of Forage we must take all their Cattle, Sheep and Horses fit for the use of the Army." It made perfect, hardhearted sense. Without livestock to feed, there could be no shortage of forage, thus there was nothing for farmers to complain about. It was a cruel solution to a cruel problem.[23]

HAD HOWE BEEN inclined or able to attack, Greene's foragers presented a tempting target. They were exposed, they were a small formation, and they were too far distant for support from the main army. But two factors conspired against the British. First, the weather that had turned the roads into a hellish mudscape for the Americans also limited British mobility, and now helped protect Greene's column from a possible British attack across the Schuylkill River. Captain von Muenchausen said as much when he wrote of a "very heavy rain" on 11 February, which forced the British to "dismantle the upper bridge across the Schuylkill." The bridge linked the Philadelphia garrison to a "redoubt on the other side" of the river. A pontoon or floating bridge crossed the Schuylkill at the Middle Ferry, spanned today by the Market Street Bridge. British redoubts protected the right bank at Middle Ferry, while there were left bank redoubts for it and the Upper Ferry. Susceptible to the rise and fall of the tides, high water, and ice, British engineers regularly removed the bridge or replaced it when it washed away. Cut off by the removal of the bridge, the only way to relieve the guard on the west bank was "by some large boats."[24]

Upstream from Middle Ferry was the Upper Ferry, today crossed by the Spring Garden Street Bridge. The Haverford Road led to the west. With boats, infantry could cross and provide support to the Middle Ferry post on the west bank. A redoubt protected this crossing and anchored the left of the British line of fortifications. To the east, nine more redoubts, with abatis (interlaced tree trunks laid on the ground with stripped and sharpened branches pointed toward an enemy approach) between them, stretched across the neck of land north of Callowhill Street and tied into the rightmost redoubt anchoring the line on the Delaware River. Gray's or the Lower Ferry, downstream from Middle Ferry, at today's Grays Ferry Avenue Bridge, was an unfortified site leading to the Derby Road. A westward bend on the Schuylkill River above Gray's Ferry isolated the crossing site and kept it beyond a convenient supporting distance for reinforcements. Supporting redoubts would have only stretched British forces thin. In all likelihood, patrols provided security and early warning from that direction.

Positioned as they were, the British bridge and defenses at Middle Ferry were also a suitable location from which to launch attacks or expeditions into Chester County. Without the bridge, however, that was not possible. Hence, the "sudden heavy rain" on the eleventh gave the Americans a measure of security. Forced to rely on boats, there was no way a large British force could cross the river and interfere with the American foraging. As it was, the streets in Philadelphia were "all in a flood." The second factor in Greene's favor was the British Army's nearly constant need to replenish food and fuel stocks (the garrison consumed 800 cords of wood weekly), which meant that foraging constituted the majority of the army's activities. The army's clocklike pattern of dispatching foraging and woodcutting

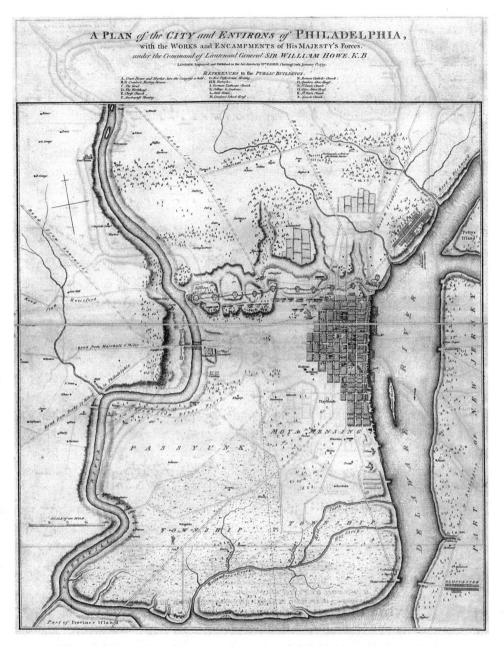

William Fadden, *A Plan of the City and Environs of Philadelphia: With the Works and Encampments of His Majesty's Forces under the Command of Lieutenant General Sir William Howe, K.B.* Geography and Map Division, Library of Congress.

parties spoke to its operational tempo. The size of the parties spoke to their importance and the perceived threat from Continental and militia forces. Greene, however, was not on Howe's mind. The day following the downpour, British forces marched northeast, "four miles beyond Frankford," covered by three regiments. The British were out until the fourteenth, when they returned with a "good deal of forage." While British forces had seen to gathering their quotidian needs, Capt. Richard Hovenden's Loyalist troop of Philadelphia Light Dragoons and Capt. William Thomas's company of Bucks County Volunteers "pushed ahead" and captured twenty-five prisoners. Nothing in the documents suggests that Howe was concerned about the presence of over 1,200 Continentals across the Schuylkill, all within striking range.[25]

Sir William had resisted temptation, but that was not to be for Greene's Continentals. Under the circumstances, the redoubt at Middle Ferry could not be denied. Cut off from supporting units on the east bank of the Schuylkill, it was altogether too inviting. Located on the western high ground opposite the crossing site, the central redoubt was on the northern edge of the road from Marshall with two "guardhouses." Two supporting redoubts "about 100 paces" to the south and north covered its left and right flanks. A "guard" of one noncommissioned officer and six privates typically manned each of the supporting earthworks. A curtain wall and covered way linked the central and southern positions, while abatis protected the front of the central post and continued on to the rear of the northern redoubt. The northern post oriented to the north, toward Suetts Mill and the Upper Ferry. Its southern-facing rear was open, but minimally protected by the abatis, while the central redoubt was open to the east, and the southern one open to the northeast. Across the river on the southern edge of Market Street, a "Fascine Red[oub]t" defended the eastern crossing site, while the two-battalion strong Seventy-First Regiment of Foot (Fraser's Highlanders) provided a quick reaction force from its neighboring encampment. Around a quarter of a mile west of the position, high ground rose above it, well out of musket shot, but well within artillery range. The roads to Lancaster, to the northwest, and to Derby, to the southwest, joined the Marshall Road in a trident-shaped intersection. Gardens occupied the southeast corner of the intersection at the eastern edge of the facing high ground. Today, the much-widened Market Street, the 30th Street Train Station, and the Internal Revenue Service regional headquarters, formerly the Main Post Office, cover the fortifications.[26]

On the night of 14–15 February, Capt. Christian Philipp von Ellrodt and Lt. Friedrich von Keller of the Regiment von Eyb (First Ansbach), Lt. Wilhelm Friedrich Ernst von Reitzenstein of the von Voit Regiment (Second Ansbach), and "sixty men" of the regiments Eyb and Voit held the Middle Ferry guardhouse. The position's isolation prompted Lt. Col. Robert Ballard of the First Virginia Continentals to propose an attack against it. Ballard and his command had been "out on the foraging business yesterday [14 February] down about Darby," around seven miles southwest of Middle Ferry, when he learned of the bridge's removal. Sensing an opportunity to temporarily smash a British toehold across the Schuylkill, he selected about 200 men "to attempt the Guard, [and] upon his earnest entreaty" Greene acceded. As Ballard's party advanced upon the redoubt around 3:00 A.M., a "Light horseman" spied it about 500 yards distant and galloped off to raise the alarm. Ballard "push'd on as hard as possible," but discovered the garrison secure in a stone house. Before Ballard's attack got to within one hundred yards, the guard opened "a very heavy fire . . . which was very warmly returnd on our part till we got within 50 yds," as the Continentals advanced, fired, reloaded, and continued driving forward.[27]

With the element of surprise vanished, Ballard had chosen to attack rather than retire. If he had hoped to seize the Ansbachers' position in a *coup de main*, he was sadly disappointed. The Virginian and his men "push'd on as hard as possible." By opening fire at 100 yards, the Ansbachers had thrown away their fire. Their chances of hitting an enemy soldier at that distance ranged somewhere between slim and none. At 3:00 A.M., even with a "waxing gibbous moon" shining brightly, the ability to present or aim muskets with any degree of accuracy was limited. Smoothbore muskets were notoriously imprecise at 100 yards. Many commanders withheld their fire until seventy-five yards, while experienced officers reserved theirs until the last fifty yards, when their soldiers' fire from unrifled muskets might strike with telling effect. The Ansbachers had given Ballard the opportunity to advance upon them.[28]

Facing inaccurate fire, Ballard pressed on until he and his soldiers were within fifty yards, killing distance. Most of Captain von Ellrodt's command was "secur'd in the Stone house," discharging a ragged, individual fire through open windows. There was no opportunity for neat, orderly volleys directed by officers. Try as they might, Ballard's Continentals found "it impracticable to force them out of the house" as soldiers from both sides fired at muzzle flashes, shadows, and imagined enemies. Unable to close with the

Ansbachers, Ballard ordered his soldiers to withdraw. He commended them for having "behav'd exceeding brave and would, I believe, have attempted Staving the Doors," such was their spirit. Acting in conjunction with Ballard was his fellow Virginian, Maj. Samuel Jordan Cabell of the Fourteenth Virginia Continentals. Cabell and his "party," reported Ballard, approached the river from downstream, and "fell in with a small party" of enemy soldiers. Reporting back to Ballard, Cabell thought his soldiers had "killd Several of them."[29]

As with all combat actions, large or small, confusion reigned during and after the event in its telling. Soldiers involved in the fight could do little more than guess at what effect their fighting had had upon their enemies. As word about the brief engagement (it lasted but fifteen to forty-five minutes) spread among Howe's German troops, the size of the American force was magnified and the Ansbachers were even more steadfast than before. Captain Ewald reported that Ballard lost ten killed and left behind seven wounded, including a "French officer." Ballard, however, notified Greene that "there was not a man of his men kild, [although] five were slightly wounded." Ballard also added that his men "kild one Hessian . . . , mortally wounded another . . . [and] two of his men on their march deserted." The Ansbachers reported suffering one killed and three wounded.[30]

Pvt. Johann Conrad Döhla of the Voit Regiment and Cpl. Johann Christoph Doehlemann also of the Second Ansbach Regiment doubled the size of Ballard's picked men to 400, and then Döhla accorded a promotion to Capt. Henry Lee by naming him a lieutenant colonel in command of the attack. In Döhla's telling, the Americans had opened the firefight with a "heavy rain of musket balls," but Ellrodt's "unfriendly answer" sufficed to drive off the attackers, who "retreated so quickly that they left few dead, but all the more shoes, hats, and bread sacks along the way." Justly proud of his regiment and countrymen, Lt. Johann Ernst Prechtel of the Ansbacher Voit Regiment emphasized the "watch, which consisted primarily of Ansbachers, held the positions so bravely, that the enemy had to retreat."[31]

Retreat Ballard's command did. Following the action, he wrote to Greene from Valley Forge. Lieutenant Colonel Ballard reported that his "party met with but little loss." He believed, albeit incorrectly, that the Ansbachers had wounded four or five soldiers "Slightly," and had killed one or two. In truth, five had had been wounded, none killed, but two had deserted "on their march." Ballard and his Continentals had marched around twenty or so miles in two days, had fought in a confusing early-morning firefight, and now "The poor fellows are exceeding fatigued," he wrote. Looking out for his soldiers, he thought that they "woud be glad of Some Whiskey" as a restorative. Suggesting the mixed nature of his party and not willing to host an open bar, Ballard "directed the Officer of each respective corps to make out a return for Whiskey." Had the command been solely of the First Virginia, Ballard would not have written "the Officer of each respective corps." As welcome as the water of life was, food was more important. Their two days of meat had not been enough. Indeed "Many of them say they haven't had a mouth full of meat this 4 days," which suggests the severity of the food shortage at camp, and the poor offerings around Derby, or that the soldiers had eaten their rations far sooner than they should have. Empty haversacks and Ballard's setback notwithstanding, the forage continued.[32]

DESPITE THE INTERRUPTION of the firefight at the Schuylkill redoubts, the business of the forage went on. Greene maintained a steady correspondence with Washington, and constantly updated him with the progress of the foraging. Two days after departing from camp, the scarcity of supplies and the skill of Pennsylvanians at hiding their goods prompted Greene to request from Washington assistance from an additional deputy quartermaster general "to conduct the business of that department." The foraging parties were not meeting with much success. Greene noted that their "collection was inconsiderable, [as] the Country is very much draind." Nonetheless, they did manage to find some cattle, sheep, and horses, all of which Greene had sent on to the encampment. He promised to continue sending "forage and all further collections" as rapidly as possible. If, however, meat continued to remain "scarce," Greene suggested that the commissaries "purchase a quantity of Sugar," which soldiers could mix with cracked, boiled wheat, and make frumenty. Greene recommended it as "palatable and nourishing," and thought it would make for a "very good substitute for meat." Clearly, Greene was a far better soldier than he was a nutritionist.[33]

In his letter, Greene reported that Colonel Biddle had encountered much the same state of affairs in his rounds. He "complains bitterly of the disaffection of the people," and had "got but few Waggons." Nonetheless, Greene was not dissuaded. He steeled himself against the people's distress: "The Inhabitants cry out and beset me from all quarters, but like Pharoh I harden my heart." In pharaonic fashion, when Greene's Continentals seized two men transporting provisions to the British, he ordered "an hundred [lashes] each by way of Example." Greene was "determin[ed] to forage the Country very bare," and assured Washington that "nothing shall be left unattempted."[34]

Greene did not anchor himself to his headquarters. Sometime in the afternoon or evening of the fifteenth, he rode southwest to Providence Meeting House, and there met with Colonel Biddle who reported the results of his actions. Biddle reminded Greene that there was "but a poor prospect of getting Waggons," and Greene pleaded with Washington to send forward all of the wagons that could be "spard." Cattle and sheep could be driven forward, but hay, flour, grain, and goods required transportation. Temptingly, what the land had in abundance was "Hay . . . , the plentifulest article that there is in the Country." He estimated that "Sixty or Seventy tons may be had in this neighbourhood," all of which would go far toward feeding the few winter-thin cattle, sheep, and horses pressed for the army. Greene then proposed expanding the geographic scope of the forage into Bucks County "as soon as the Bridge [over the Schuylkill] is passable," and in the meantime forage around Reading. After conferring with Biddle, Greene determined that some of foragers would "mount a press party on Horses" to secure wagons somewhere near "the back of Brandywine" Creek on 16 February. Biddle had heard through one of Washington's aides-de-camp, Lt. Col. Tench Tilghman, that the general wanted Biddle to "extend your Views beyond your present Circle of foraging." Wagons were the order of the day. While the ones brought forward with the foragers were transporting food, fodder, and forage back to the army, Washington wanted Biddle to "send some persons further back," deeper into Chester County, and have them impress, load with forage, and send back to camp "every Carriaje that can be found." He specified "the upper parts of the Brandywine and between that and the Camp," and urged Biddle to act quickly. If provisions did not arrive soon, "I fear," wrote Tilghman, "we shall not have a Horse left alive to eat it." Biddle and Greene knew well the army's "distress."[35]

In addition to acting on Washington's suggestion to extend the geographic scope of the forage, Greene also proposed expanding on Washington's original instructions to destroy "All the Provinder on the Islands between Philadelphia and Chester" that could not be transported. Instead, he suggested following Wayne's advice to "destroy all the forage upon the Jersey shore." For this, Greene selected Col. Richard Butler of the Ninth Pennsylvania Continentals to command the detachment. Butler and his command were to "Cross the River from Chester" and proceed to New Jersey. Greene's openness to considering Wayne's thoughts and his comfort in expanding on Washington's original directive speaks to his self-confidence and to his trust in Wayne's judgement and in Washington's trust in him. This decision highlighted Greene's willingness to accept risks when opportunity beck-oned and his confidence in Washington's acquiescence. The mutual trust and confidence shared by these three generals were the bedrock of their re-lationships, and enabled them to act boldly and take risks.[36]

Washington had received Greene's letter late on the evening of 15 February, and lost no time responding. He approved of Greene's "demand of Wag-gons," and directed Deputy Quartermaster General Col. Henry Emanuel Lutterloh to send "forward" every wagon that could "be spared from the Camp," but also those wagons "pressed in the neighborhood" of the camp. Greene was not, however, to relax his own efforts at procuring wagons, no matter his "Success in this quarter." As to having Colonel Butler incinerate New Jersey hay, Washington approved of it. If the Continental Army could not have it, it was far better to "destroy it that the Enemy may derive no ben-efit from it." Making war on food was making war on the enemy. Washington also approved of Greene's hard hand when he had made an example of the two men whom he had ordered punished with one hundred lashes for try-ing to move supplies into British lines. Despite his previous regard for pri-vate property and distaste for impressment, Washington now believed that the army's wants justified "any measures you can take." Were any of the "In-habitants" to hide or refuse turning over their "Carriages," Greene was to "make severe examples of a few to deter others." Greene anticipated Wash-ington's injunction. Before receiving it, he had already ordered "all the press parties" to seize as "prisoners" all farmers who "conceald their Cattle or Car-riages." He assured Washington that "examples shall not be wanting to fa-cilitate the business I [am] out upon."[37]

FIXED IN PURPOSE, but flexible in method, Greene reconsidered his pro-posal for the Bucks County incursion. Mindful of keeping the army's objec-tives secret, he believed that an attempt to press wagons in Bucks County would "explain our intentions too early" and would endanger the detach-ment, an interesting observation given how widely known his own foraging had been to friend and foe alike. Instead, Greene proposed issuing a press warrant to Col. Johnston Smith, a former gunsmith and now purchasing agent in Northampton County. Smith would hold the warrant in abeyance while he applied to Pennsylvania's "Executive Council "for an hundred wag-gons, to be got ready in three Days." Should the commonwealth's govern-ment prove unable or unwilling to exert itself, or should Washington deem that the circumstances justified bypassing the council, only then was Smith to "collect the Waggons with his press Warrant." The escorts for the newly-acquired wagons were to load them with forage from "some of the best Hay Towns between Camp and Lancaster," deposit the hay at the encampment, and proceed to Bucks County "with so much secrecy and dispatch, that it will be difficult for the Enemy to defeat it." Even as Greene wrote, "Nine or Ten Files of Men" in Lancaster were impressing "Waggons" to the tune of "150 Teams" to transport provisions.[38]

Try as he might, though, Greene had met with little success in Chester County. His foraging parties had taken all the livestock "fit for our use — but the Country has been so gleand that there is but little left in it." This was no surprise, given that Chester County was a favorite location for British foragers. They had scoured the region so thoroughly that Greene found the "face of the Country . . . strongly markt with poverty and distress." Howe's foragers had made off with the best horses and cattle. The "few Whigs" Greene encountered told him that "great numbers" of livestock had been driven into Philadelphia by Howe's soldiers and local farmers. Despite Greene's presence, those motivated by political loyalties or economic circumstances continued bringing their goods into British lines. John Chaloner, deputy assistant commissary of purchases, received from an Alexander Steel, 140 pounds of beef "taken from persons Carrying it towards the Enemy." Chaloner had it "apply'd to the Use" of Greene's foragers.[39]

Still at Providence Meeting House, Greene decided to modify his plans for burning hay on the Jersey river shore. Instead, he intended extending his foraging efforts across the river. Rather than Colonel Butler in command, "General Wayne will cross over into the Jerseys from Willmington." Wayne was to not only destroy hay, he was also to drive "in all the Stock from the Shores," and send it to camp. Greene recognized that whatever success Wayne had would not provide "immediate relief" to the army. In order to alleviate some of the soldiers' suffering, Greene decided to drive in all the cattle his parties had collected. Doing so, however, decreased the strength of his force. It made the smaller detachments, and even the main body under Greene, more vulnerable to the enemy, should they decide to venture forth. Moreover, this reduction in strength also decreased Greene's ability to forage. As it was, Greene had sent back "Great [but unspecified] numbers" of soldiers who had "fallen sick and got foot sore amarching." Because of his diminishing host, Greene also sent back two "field pieces to Camp — they being altogether useless to me." The cattle forwarded by Greene on the sixteenth, "near fifty Head," were no doubt welcome but not enough. Greene wished that he could have sent more, but the local people had become quite adept at "conceal[ing] their stock," as well as "their Waggons and Harness[es]." That same day, the camp had also received ninety barrels of "Pork and fish and thirty head of Cattle," which Col. Ephraim Blaine believed would "afford two days provisions." Similar to Greene, Washington had also decided to widen the geographic scope of the forage. On 16 February, he sent Capt. Henry Lee, Jr. and his troop of light dragoons into Delaware and Maryland.[40]

Just before Lee set out on his leg of the forage, he wrote to Greene about the "increasing distress of the Army for want of provisions." One of Washington's aides, Lt. Col. John Laurens, shared similar news with his father Henry, president of the Continental Congress. Over the past several days the army had not had "Above half allowance" of its meat ration and the "soldiers are scarcely restrained from mutiny by the eloquence and management of our officers." Camp, Laurens wrote, was littered with the "carcasses of horses." Those that "crawl[ed] in existence" exhibited a "deplorable leanness [for] . . . the want of forage." If not unexpected, the state of affairs was no doubt disturbing. "God grant we may never be brought into such a wretched condition again," prayed Greene. Yet, the foraging business had to go on. Soldiers searched "Woods and swamps" for cattle, wagons, horses, harnesses, and anything else that might aid the army. Clearly frustrated by farmers and others concealing their property, Greene tightened the screws as best he could. Continental scrip was sorely inflated, but it was better than nothing, and nothing was what Greene gave those who concealed their property. As a reward for their skill at secreting animals and goods, Greene gave "orders to give no receipts" to those who had "conceald" their property. Furthermore, the owners were to be notified of the uncompensated seizures — it was only right that they should know of their involuntary support of the army.[41]

Anger aside, Greene found "The business I am upon . . . very disagreeable." He did not elaborate on what he found unpleasant, but his letters suggest that it was the great effort expended by so many soldiers for so little gain, people concealing their goods and livestock, and the seizure of property. Nonetheless, he wrote, "I should be happy in executeing of it if our success was equal to our wants." Any hope that that local "Whigs" would give information "respecting Tories" and their cached goods was lost "for fear when we are gone they will be carried prisoners in Philadelphia." Without an active militia to protect those who supported the Continental effort or to enforce the political will of the Congress and the government of Pennsylvania, sensible Whigs kept to themselves. Still, detachments fanned out in an ever-widening circuit, searching for that which would be useful. Lt. Col. Josiah Harmar of the Sixth Pennsylvania Continentals followed through on the plan to forage west of the Brandywine's forks "a little above the rout of the enemy," while Col. Oliver Spencer of the Fifth New Jersey Continentals (Spencer's Additional Continental Regiment) made a large circuit north and west toward Goshen Meeting House, about ten miles southwest of Valley Forge, to gather cattle.[42]

Even with a much smaller force directly under him (there are no numbers available), Greene was still determined to continue foraging until all of the wagons were loaded with hay. As for "Grain there is but little to be got." Elements of his force had already burned a "considerable" quantity of forage on the Delaware River islands and "We got a number of very good Horses from off" of them in the bargain. Those good horses notwithstanding, Greene's "Officers in spight of every thing I can say to them," had also brought in quite a bit of poor horseflesh, wholly unfit for service. Rather than bother with weakened or aged horses, Greene intended to "notify" the owners of their horses' locations so that they might retrieve them and relieve the army of them their care and feeding. From those few Whigs who were willing to share information, Greene learned that the British were readying for a "grand forage some where." His sources believed that it would take place "on this side [of the Schuylkill], but I immagin they will alter their plan now if they designd it before" Continental foragers had scoured Chester County. Greene had "no doubt of Bucks County being their object."[43]

THE DAY OF 15 FEBRUARY was eventful. First, there had been Lieutenant Colonel Ballard's failed, early-morning attack against the Middle Ferry outposts. More followed. Later that morning, Col. William Shepard ("Sheppard"), Fourth Massachusetts Continentals, sent out a party from his "division" to "collect Cattle" around Springfield Meeting House, Greene's initial headquarters. Lt. Thomas Ransdell ("Ramsdel"), Eleventh Virginia Continentals, commanded the detachment of about "twenty odd men." Ransdell's detachment, however, "never returnd." Not for the life of him could Greene "immagin" what had happened. Adding to his frustration, Greene had "never heard of their being out" in the first place. Putting aside his ire, Greene conjectured that Ransdell, whom Shepard thought "an exceeding good Officer," might have "got lost."[44]

If lost, Greene feared that Ransdell had been captured after having "fallen in with the Enemies Piquet" at Middle Ferry. Imagining the worst, Greene conjectured that Ransdell's men had "made him a prisoner and carried him into the enemy." Desertion, the bane of all eighteenth-century armies, was bad enough, but to turn coat, make prisoner their officer, and then hand him over to the enemy was reprehensible. Yet, Greene thought it not "improbable, for most of his party were Virgina Convicts." Without evidence, all Greene could do was conjure possibilities, each one worse than the other, ranging all the way to the chance that the "Soldiers might kill the Offcer and go in themselves" to British lines. After allowing his darkest fears to surface, Greene took a moment and drew from "an account" he had received "from the City." Instead of imagining the worst, he was "well convinced" that a British patrol had taken Ransdell and his Virginians prisoner and then "marched [them] through" Philadelphia that "evening." But because Greene's "Intelligencer sais there was no Officer with the men," he gave into his fear, which made him "apprehend foul play—but its all conjecture."[45]

As it turned out, Greene's worst fears were not realized. Not long after he had dispatched his letter to Washington, Ransdell and his party returned. Where they had been and what they done remains a mystery. Whether they had succeeded in gathering cattle remains to be discovered. As for Ransdell, he continued in service as an officer of the Virginia Line, finally retiring from the Continental Army as a captain on 1 January 1783 after nearly seven years of soldiering.[46]

THROUGHOUT GREENE'S PORTION of the foraging, the dearth of transportation had dogged his soldiers' efforts; he was ready to return to camp. "The time for which I came out expires tonight," he wrote on the eighteenth, "but as the forageing business has been greatly obstructed for want of Waggons it will be necessary for me to continue a few days longer." Before acting upon any decision Greene first wished "to know your Excellencies pleasure respecting the matter." Coincidentally, the unintended delay met with Washington's desire that Greene continue foraging, but only if the "prospect of making it [were] worth the while." The army's straitened circumstances, "this several days past," had continued unabated. Rations had not been "Above half allowance" for several days, reported Ephraim Blaine, and "god only Knows when we shall have it in our power to Afford them a plentiful supply."[47]

By the evening of 19 February, Greene was prepared to present to Washington forty loaded wagons, but nothing more. It was not that the countryside was devoid of hay, rather that the army did not have the number of wagons it needed to support its operations. With more of them, Greene believed that he would have had an even greater impact, but instead his efforts "rendered us but little assistance from the lines." As for cattle, that was another matter. Colonel Spencer reported from Goshen that "there was but few Cattle to be got there." Lieutenant Colonel Harmar, operating around the "forks of the Brandywine" had not yet reported, but Greene, having "heard of Cattle going to camp from that quarter" attributed that success to him. Greene's foragers had "pretty well gleaned" Chester County. His "next move" was to order the return of his troops to camp, save a small rearguard. Harmar's party may have been that rearguard. Orders issued by Harmar suggest that he and his foragers may have returned to camp by 2 March at the latest. As for Greene and the soldiers under his immediate command, they returned to camp between 21 and 24 February, no doubt frustrated by the army's lack of transportation, the poor pickings in Chester County, and the unwillingness of so many to aid so few. His disappointment not-withstanding, Greene believed that the "little collections" made by his command and "some others" had "prevented the Army from disbanding."[48]

As Greene prepared to retire, Washington issued a "Proclamation on Cattle." He exhorted "Friends, Countrymen and Fellow Citizens" of New Jersey, Pennsylvania, Delaware, Maryland, and Virginia to rise up and support the army in its most recent hour of need. Washington called upon them to "prepare Cattle, for the use of the Army" in its spring campaign. The success of the army depended upon the "virtuous yeomanry" of those states to "put up and feed, immediately, as many of their Stock Cattle, as they can spare" for the use of the army. Promising a "bountiful price," Washington linked the self-interest and needs of "Proprietors" with the "illustrious cause of their Country," and assured them that their work on the army's behalf would "contribute in a great degree to shorten this bloody contest." But patriotic self-interest, self-sacrifice, and republican virtue went only so far. Revealing his determination, Washington brandished a stick in support of the monetary and patriotic carrot proffered by reminding those "so insensible to the common interest, as not to exert themselves, upon these generous principles" that their provisions would prove tempting to enemy foragers and others. By supplying the Continental Army, they might very well "save their property from plunder, their families from insult, and their persons from abuse, hopeless confinement—or perhaps a violent death." It is impossible to determine how effective the proclamation was. Nevertheless, it was calculated to widen the foraging and remind people of the continued existence of the army, its resistance against the British, and the potentially harsh measures that might result from failing to support the Continentals.[49]

Greene had been "out ten or Eleven days." Not without some justifiable pride, he wrote that he had executed his orders "with great fidelity" and had given the army some "relief . . . from the little collections I had made." Despite the exertions of the soldiers under his command, "We are still in danger of starveing," as had happened to "Hundreds and Hundreds of our Horses." Washington had dispatched Greene without the wagons so necessary for transporting forage, flour, and other provisions because he had none to send. He had left Greene to his own devices when it came to impressing wagons. Under the circumstances, there were no other options. Faced with the dearth of wagons, Greene did not shy away from impressment or outright seizure. His lack of cavalry prevented him from ranging farther afield in search of transportation and provisions. Limited to the speed and range of the infantry, he made the best of a poor situation.[50]

There are no tallies recording what Greene's foragers had gathered. His aide-de-camp, Capt. Robert Forsyth, was sure that "we swept off all the Horses, Cattle, Sheep & Hoggs the Waggons gears, Hay, Oats & grain some Leather and every Thing our Army wanted." Colonel Blaine, however, thought that Greene had "rendered us but little assistance from the lines." The expedition was an act of desperation. It underscored the army's want. Whatever the count of livestock, flour, forage, or wagons, the foraging expanded, as first Anthony Wayne separated from Greene to cross over the Delaware into New Jersey, and then Henry Lee rode into Delaware.[51]

CHAPTER THREE

General Wayne Will Cross over into the Jerseys

When Maj. Gen. Nathanael Greene ordered Brig. Gen. Anthony Wayne and his column "into the Jerseys from Willmington," Wayne and his command departed a barren countryside. Continental foragers had gleaned what they could from Chester County. Foragers had left behind only enough to sustain the farmers whose wagons, teams, hay, crops, and livestock they had impressed for the army's needs. By expanding the foraging area, Greene decreased the pressure on a limited base of forage and provision, and enabled farmers to begin the process of rebuilding, replanting, and hoping for the best. Should the seat of war remain in Pennsylvania, farmers could expect the worst.[1]

By dispatching Wayne, Greene and Washington took a calculated risk. Focused on its own foraging in Bucks County, the British Army had left alone the Continentals in Chester County. Wayne's column, however, even if augmented by the New Jersey Militia, would make for a tempting target. The Delaware River was as much an obstacle as it was a highway. Cut off by the river from the main army and the fortifications at Valley Forge, Wayne had nowhere to fall back in case of attack. Despite Gen. Sir William Howe's focus on feeding his army and his diffident behavior, there was a possibility that Wayne's detachment might prove too tempting a target for the British commander to ignore. Indeed, as historian Troyer Steele Anderson pointed out, "only a very serious mistake by Washington" could inspire Howe to risk an attack against Washington's army. In December 1777, Howe had declined attacking the fortified Continentals at Whitemarsh, just north of Germantown, and he refused to do so while they were at Valley Forge. Explaining his decisions during his 1779 Parliamentary defense, Howe pled the "entrenched situation of the enemy," his paucity of forces, and the Loyalists' questionable strength and commitment to the British cause as limitations on his scope of action. These considerations notwithstanding, Wayne's detachment, if not as grand a prize as the main army, presented an opportunity to strike while husbanding Britain's limited and increasingly precious manpower.[2]

Upon further consideration, however, another possible reason for British inaction emerges. For much of the Philadelphia Campaign, the British Army had focused its attention on logistics: feeding, clothing, and keeping

James Sharples Sr., *Anthony Wayne*. Courtesy of Independence National Historical Park.

warm and dry. Howe had consistently outmaneuvered Washington and bested him in combat. Yet, as he tried to bring the American to decisive battle, he had fallen far short. After Howe took Philadelphia, Philadelphia took Howe. The inconclusive skirmishing at Whitemarsh, 5–8 December 1777, had been Howe's last offensive action. Put off by the prospects of storming American fortifications, Sir William meekly returned to Philadelphia. Instead of a resounding triumph, Whitemarsh had all the thunder and fury of a damp squib. Thereafter, Howe concentrated his energies on sustaining his soldiers, and let pursuing battle with the Continentals recede into the background. Putting aside Philadelphia's political, economic, and symbolic importance, the campaign had now become a "fight for the control of even more crucial environmental resources." Yet, the British Army could not eat the Continental Army into submission. Howe's officers and soldiers could not help but take note of their commander and his halfhearted pursuit of British victory through battle. Whatever the case, Howe's attitude, personal example, his leadership, the need to feed and maintain the army, and the command climate he fostered clearly affected the army's discipline and subordinate officers' attentiveness to duty. Nonetheless, Howe's continued inaction was not a forgone conclusion. Perhaps this was the mistake for which he had been waiting: an isolated, understrength, slow-moving brigade encumbered by livestock.[3]

With Wayne in New Jersey, separated from the main army and the safety of Valley Forge's fortifications, he had but two choices if challenged by the British. Wayne could fight or flee. Combat promised British victory, whereas flight would be yet another encore performance for the Continentals, well-practiced as they were in keeping one step ahead of their enemies. A British battlefield victory might induce enough shock to the Continental Army's morale so as to weaken it, and prime it for an even greater fall. It might bring Loyal-leaning Americans to the king's colors and bolster the ranks of the Loyalist battalions. Immediate decision through battle was unlikely, but a resounding British victory might become the first step toward a successful resolution in this war of attrition. Wayne's survival, on the other hand, promised yet more of the same; another season of Britons seeking battle, another season of Americans avoiding battle, and another season of inconclusive war. Now was the time to strike.

SHOULD HOWE ACT AGAINST WAYNE, the Royal Navy's command of the Delaware River gave his forces unmatched mobility and reach along the river's course. The Delaware River Squadron, under Capt. Andrew Snape Hamond, boasted over ten vessels, including three frigates, a captured frigate designated as an armed ship, and other vessels. Over one thousand sailors, many of whom however had suffered from "Fever and Flux" in January, crewed Hamond's squadron, which mounted over one hundred and sixty guns, which far exceeded the combined firepower of the Continental and British armies.[4]

CAPT. SIR ANDREW SNAPE HAMOND. BART. R.N.
1738 - 1828.

Capt. Sir Andrew Snape Hammond, Bart., *R. N.* The Miriam and Ira D. Wallach
Division of Art, Prints and Photographs: Print Collection, New York Public
Library Digital Collections, The New York Public Library.

TABLE 3.1 Delaware River Squadron, Royal Navy

Rate	Ship's name	Guns	Crew	Commanders
5	*Roebuck*	44	280	Capt. Hamond, Andrew Snape
5	*Pearl*	32	220	Capt. Linzee, John
6	*Camilla*	20	160	Capt. Phipps, Hon. Charles
Armed Ship	*Vigilant*	20	150	Cdr. Christian, Brabazon
Armed Ship	*Delaware*	24	160	Cdr. Watt, James
Sloop	*Zebra*	14	125	Cdr. Orde, John
Galley	*Cornwallis*		40	Lt. Spry, Thomas
Galley	*Philadelphia*		30	Mid. Aitchison, Robert
Armed Vessel (Schooner)	*Viper*	10	50	Lt. Pakenham, Edward
Store Ship	*Adventure*		40	Lt. Tonken, Hugh
4	*Experiment*	50	320	Capt. Wallace, Sir James (station at mouth of Delaware River)
"Several Tenders, Pilot Boats, Gun Boats, &c."				

"Disposition of His Majesty's Ships and Vessels employed in North America under the Command of the Vice Admiral the Viscount Howe," 5 January 1778, "Disposition of Captain Andrew Snape Hamond's Squadron," 23 January 1778, Hamond to James Watt, 11 February 1778, "Disposition of His Majesty's Ships and Vessels Employed in North America under the Command of the Vice Admiral the Viscount Howe," 9 March 1778, *NDAR*, 11:39, 196, 321, 556; "Journal of H.M. Armed Schooner *Viper*," 9 May 1778, *NDAR*, 12:304; Gardiner, *Navies and the American Revolution*, 74.

As impressive as Hammond's command was, environmental factors limited his ability to bring its full power to bear. Hammond testified before Parliament in 1779, that "I don't know any river so difficult of navigation; large ships can only pass at certain times of the tide." The Delaware was an estuarial river, which fed into Delaware Bay and the sea. As such, the Delaware was subject to tidal movements just below Trenton, the fall line. Above Philadelphia, the river narrowed, which increased the velocity of the water flow, and limited the speed at which vessels could proceed upriver. Downriver from Trenton, the constricted shipping channel limited ships'

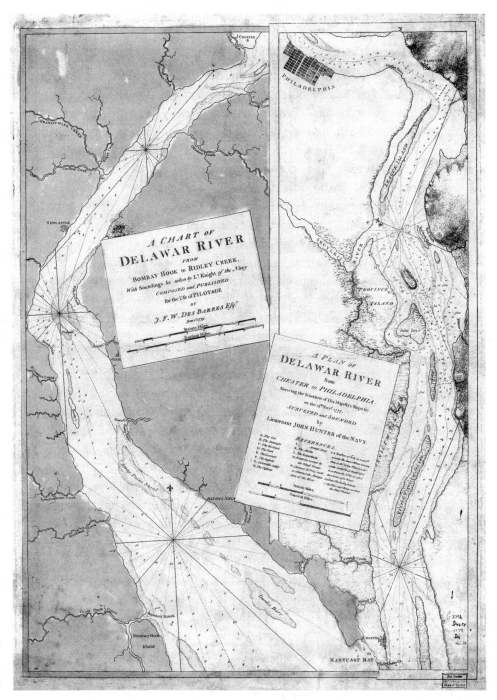

Joseph F. W. Des Barres, John Knight, and John Hunter, *A chart of Delaware River from Bombay Hook to Ridley Creek, with soundings & taken by Lt. Knight of the Navy*. Geography and Map Division, Library of Congress.

maneuverability, which, when combined with slower speeds, meant that enemy guns could easily range and command British riverine approaches to Bordentown. Even below Philadelphia, where the river was wider, any ship at anchor lay "within cannon shot of the shore in all places, within musket shot in some." Alongside and within the navigable portions of the river, the mud-flats, sandbars, and islands threatened deeper-draft ships and narrowed the shipping channels. As for the tides in this more navigable stretch, they ran "between 3 and 4 miles an hour." While three to four miles per hour may seem inconsiderable, it was not. The speed, combined with the volume of water moving downstream was powerful. When the tide flowed, it was "too rapid for ships of war to ride with springs on their cables." Springs allowed sailors to shift a ship's position while at anchor to bring its guns to bear on a target. All along the river, confessed Hamond, "the ships run great risk of being aground." Captain Hamond was not about to repeat the performances of H.M.S. *Augusta*, a third-rate ship-of-the-line mounting sixty-four guns on two decks, and the much smaller H.M. Sloop *Merlin*, a single-decked vessel carrying eighteen guns. Both ran around in October 1777, while supporting operations to open the river to British shipping, and had to be destroyed.[5]

Navigating the Delaware in good weather was challenging enough, but in winter the river held yet more surprises for mariners. Snow and freezing rain rendered sails into unmanageable frozen blocks, made sheets and running gear inoperable, and transformed upper decks into skating rinks. Hard freezes restricted river traffic, and when the river thawed, as it did periodically in the winter, ice floes moving downriver could severely damage ships' hulls. In early January, ice forced the entire squadron to tie up alongside wharves at Philadelphia, "to take Shelter from the Ice in the River." These constraints forced Hamond to rely on his more maneuverable, lighter weight (and thus more fragile), but shallower-draft vessels, such as the galleys *Cornwallis* and *Philadelphia*, and various gunboats. While the river did not choose sides, its nature acted as an American ally, and negated many of Hamond's advantages, albeit not completely. The Continental and Pennsylvania navies picked up that slack.[6]

DESPITE THE ROYAL NAVY'S overwhelming strength, what remained of the Continental and Pennsylvania navies' leadership was determined to dispute Hamond's command of the river. Unable to contest Hamond directly, Continental and Pennsylvania naval commanders chose to put the Briton off balance by striking at weak targets and forcing Hamond to disperse and dissipate his strength. This proved most fortunate for Wayne.

On 29 January 1778, the Marine Committee of the Continental Congress had ordered Capt. John Barry of the Continental Navy to "employ the Pinnace and Barges" of the frigates *Effingham* and *Washington*, and another barge, to harass enemy shipping. The orders authorized Barry to gather as many sailors as were "necessary to officer and man" the boats as he saw fit. Orders in hand, Barry ventured to Bordentown, New Jersey, to take charge of his new command. Arriving on 1 February, he found two serviceable barges, a third in need of repair, and a pinnace in similar condition. Barry recruited Lt. Luke Matthewman, previously his first officer on the brig *Lexington*, as second in command, and Mid. Matthew Clarkson, probably to command one of the boats. It is likely that Lt. James Coakley, a Continental marine from Barry's scuttled *Effingham*, also joined. As for the crews, Barry was only able to recruit twenty-five sailors; however, it took twenty tars to man each barge. Fortunately, Comdre. John Hazelwood of the Pennsylvania Navy granted his request for an additional fifteen sailors.[7]

After recruiting crews and fitting out the boats, Barry set off downriver, and "in two barges, passed Philadelphia through the ice" at some time in early February. A week or more before Barry's two barges slipped past Hamond's moored squadron, a most unfortunate event took place. Capt. Nathan Boys, former commander of the Pennsylvania galley *Franklin*, had borrowed two state navy guard boats. He intended to take them overland to Cooper's Creek, which emptied into the Delaware from Cooper's Ferry, across the river from Philadelphia. From there, Boys proposed rowing or sailing downriver and establishing a base of operations around Cohansey Creek, down river from Salem, New Jersey, from where he intended to "take some Vessels from the Enemy." Once Boys and his men arrived at Cooper's Creek, which empties into the Delaware River from present-day Camden, New Jersey, several miles upriver from Salem and Cohansey Creek, the crews absconded with the boats as their officers slept. A third, unrelated boat under Capt. Robert Collings, formerly first lieutenant of Pennsylvania's ship *Montgomery*, went overland from Burlington, New Jersey. Whatever prize money Collings and his crew made from capturing British vessels was to be divided to pay Hazelwood and the rest of the Pennsylvania "Fleet." Luckily for Collings's purse, Pennsylvania's navy was short of sailors.[8]

While Barry prepared his boats, Commodore Hazelwood reported that he sent "Six Armed Boats down by Land." He reassured Washington that, unlike the previous overland boating venture, the crews could be "depended on." As before, he was "in hopes" that the boats would "annoy the enemy below" Philadelphia. He requested Washington to send him sailors "trained to

Colin Campbell Cooper (after Gilbert Stuart), *John Barry*. Courtesy of Independence National Historical Park.

the Galleys" to man the boats and help cut off the British garrison's riverine supply line and prevent British raiding along the shore.[9]

Barry may have been making his way past Philadelphia as the contingent of Pennsylvania boats went overland. Unfortunately, reports at this stage are few and often vague. Nonetheless, with the river free of heavy ice Barry's boats could take advantage of the many inlets, marshes, and hidden spots along its banks to conceal themselves from prying eyes. As for the Pennsylvanians, once afloat some of them they may have joined forces with Barry in the Christina River, near Wilmington. Whatever transpired, Barry's presence was felt on the river or at least at Valley Forge. Brig. Gen. Jedidiah Huntington reported news of Barry, some Continental soldiers, and his "armed Boats" having "taken an armed Vessel . . . and two Transports from Rhode Island loaded chiefly with Hay." Huntington wrote that Barry's crews set fire to the hay transports, while they dismounted the guns of the armed vessel, presumably for their own use, and removed other "Articles" before abandoning the armed vessel as "several Frigates and other Vessels of force" closed in on the Americans. Rousing as the tale was, and the stuff of legend, there is no evidence to support Huntington's story of naval daring in early 1778. Still, Barry made himself a presence to be reckoned with on the Delaware. His next chapter opened in the state of Delaware.[10]

ON 17 FEBRUARY, Wayne and his detachment departed for Wilmington, from which he hoped to cross into New Jersey. When Wayne arrived, Capt. Henry Lee and his troop of light dragoons were also in town. Brig. Gen. William Smallwood, who commanded the two Maryland brigades holding Wilmington, had "not only this Party but General Wayne here with five hundred men to aid & dispatch on another Expedition." Wayne learned that Barry was anchored nearby with his boats, and the two met. After they had conferred, Barry agreed to ferry Wayne's Continentals across the river on 19 February. Luckily, there were no British cruisers in the vicinity. The crossing, however, did not go undetected. According to local historian Joseph S. Sickler, Hugh Cowperthwaite, a Loyalist, and "chief guide into Salem" County, New Jersey, made his way across the river to Philadelphia and reported to General Howe that "Wayne was loose in Salem County." His purpose, in the words of Capt. Friedrich von Muenchausen, was to "rob the country of cattle, forage, clothing, and leather goods."[11]

As was the case for southeastern Pennsylvania, southwestern New Jersey had suffered from the effects of the war. Regulars and militiamen frequented the countryside in search of livestock and other goods, while Whigs and Loyalists vandalized one another's property. This part of the state, particularly Gloucester County, boasted large concentrations of Loyal Americans and Quakers who, following the British occupation of Philadelphia, "lost no time in opening a brisk trade with the city." "Everywhere," wrote Pastor Nicholas Collin of Swedesboro, "distrust, fear hatred and abominable selfishness" reigned. Worse, however, followed in the wake of Wayne's foraging.[12]

The weather on the day of Wayne's crossing "remained good," while back at Valley Forge, Col. Israel Angell noted that "Nothing Remarkable happened in our Camps, Except the Soldiers being eternally Drunk, as their Money was not all gone." As for Wayne, however, upon landing he "proceeded to salem the same Evening." The next day, Wayne to wrote to Brig. Gen. Joseph Ellis of the New Jersey Militia and requested his "Assistance in this Essential business" of foraging. Wayne asked that he collect all the cattle and horses at Gloucester, Cooper's Ferry (present-day Camden), and Haddonfield. Wayne suggested that Ellis collect "the Whole at some secure place for the Immediate passing them aCross the Delaware — which I believe can't be well Effected short of Trent Town." Crossing the Delaware upstream from Trenton made good tactical sense. The narrow channel below and the falls at Trenton prevented the Royal Navy from intercepting whatever crossed. Wayne added that should Ellis detect an enemy crossing, he should "send on Intellegence thereof with all possible Dispatch — together with the rout[e] they are likely to take." Because of the possibility that Ellis's couriers might be intercepted, Wayne told Ellis to send his intelligence by "Different roads leading to this place." As for Wayne, he intended to march northward, keeping away from the shoreline, advancing "along the Roads that head the Creeks."[13]

Writing back, Ellis was "happy in just receiving your Orders" and promised to be "particularly carefull in attending to" them. Mustering no more than three hundred men, Ellis set his militiamen to work with a purpose. They quickly collected around Gloucester, Cooper's Ferry, and Haddonfield, all the cattle suitable for slaughter and "several Horses for the more immediate service of the Cavalry." Upon gathering the livestock, they were "taken & drove to some secure place as soon as the small Detachment . . . can possibly collect them." Wayne had also tasked the New Jersey brigadier with keeping a watchful eye on the "Motions of the Enemy." Ellis promised that he would pass on as quickly as he received it whatever intelligence his scouts reported. Wayne did not wait long. A few hours after Ellis wrote Wayne, he passed on "certain Intelligence" from a trusted "person" who had information that the British had planned to land a force at Burlington. From there, the intention was "throwing a Strong foraging Party down the Country." The weather, Ellis surmised, had delayed the British landing. Diarists had recorded rain, sleet, snow, and "very dirty" roads the previous day, 20 February. If the intelligence was correct, then Wayne, Ellis, and their commands were fortunate, for the "Boats intended for the Expedition were all in readiness."[14]

OVER THE NEXT SEVERAL DAYS, New Jersey militiamen and Continentals did their best to collect horses, cattle, forage, and foodstuffs. In Salem County, Wayne's forces collected cattle from Elsinboro up to Mannington, north of Alloway Creek. Like many of the farmers in southeastern Pennsylvania, a goodly number of south Jersey farmers hid their cattle in the woods, or in the tall swamp grass. Despite the presence of Wayne's force, many Whigs were wary of openly supporting Wayne for fear of what would happen once the Continentals departed, and British regulars and Loyalists returned. Although some saw it as their "Duty & Inclination . . . to give every possible assistance to the Common Cause of America," they demurred out of concern that it "would involve . . . [them] in so many unhappy consequences were" they to take part.[15]

Thomas Sayre, a farmer and justice of the peace from Lower Alloway Creek, just south of Salem, numbered among the "personally active" Whigs. He urged Wayne to have any of his officers "on the Route" to call upon him for assistance. Sayre promised to "aid them with my best information and as farr as my Example or advice will influence others you shall have it for your purpose." Thanks to Sayre, Andrew Yorke, quartermaster of the Second (Eastern) Battalion, Salem County Militia Regiment, and others like them, Wayne developed a good idea about who had horses and cattle and how many in Lower Alloway. While in Salem, he ordered Capt. Theodore Woodbridge, Seventh Connecticut Continentals, "to proceed to Lower Alleways Creek and enquire for the following persons who have Cattle or Horses":

> Wm Bradway Jur. has 6 head of Cattle
> Edward Handcock has 4 — Major Sparks has 4
> Ricd Moore has 8 — Peter Clever has 4
> John Stretch has 10
> John Wise has a good Horse or Mare
> Richd Smith a Mare
> David Adams a Mare
> David Ware has a good Mare but rode her off with a view of Secreting
> her — you will bring either him or his Mare to this place

Once Woodbridge had completed his mission, he was to "Call on" Sayre and "York," each of whom had cattle, and Sayre a "good Horse." Both men, Wayne closed, "will Assist you with their advice," which they apparently did. On the reverse side of the orders, Captain Woodbridge noted whom he visited and what he had impressed for the army's use. It far exceeded Wayne's expectations.[16]

The few days spent foraging in Salem County had been fruitful, farmers' efforts at concealing their property notwithstanding. While Captain Woodbridge and his Continentals were scouring Lower Alloway, enough cattle had been collected since 19 or 20 February to send forward on 22 February. Wayne ordered Lt. Col. Isaac Sherman, Second Connecticut Continentals, to "March with the Company under your Command Immediately." He directed Sherman to drive the "Cattle now Collected here," and head to "Wrangle Town," presumably a twenty to twenty-five-mile march, where Sherman's drovers would halt for the night. The next day, they were to proceed "by the Road heading the Creeks to Mount Holly where you will Quarter the Next Night," another twenty or so miles. Following a night at Mount Holly, Sherman was to set off for "Trent Town," where his detachment would await "further Orders." All told, Wayne expected Sherman's soldiers and their bovine host to march about seventy-five miles in three days, a wearying but not impossible task. Mindful of security and always enterprising, Wayne further ordered Sherman to send ahead of the main body an advance guard under a "trusty Officer," who was give warning about the enemy and allow Sherman's soldiers time to drive their herd rearward or "into the Country" at any sign of alarm. As they marched toward Trenton, Sherman's foragers were to fan out in "small active parties" and gather up the cattle along their route of march and "Capital Horses for Cavelry." Throughout the march, Sherman was to issue certificates to farmers and keep accounts, "so that there may be no Mistake[s]" when farmers redeemed their "Certeficates."[17]

The following day, cattle and horses in hand, Captain Woodbridge set off along the "same Rout that the Other part of the Troops have gone." Wayne wanted Woodbridge to do his best to "overtake" Sherman's command, which Wayne had designated the "Main Detachment." Woodbridge was to gather up any cattle or horses missed by Sherman's soldiers and to keep an eye out for any stragglers from the Main Detachment and "bring them on with you." Wayne's expectations for Sherman's and Woodbridge's parties' marching were overly optimistic. An experienced, mounted soldier on a good horse could easily ride thirty-five miles per day. Veteran infantry might march twenty to twenty-five miles a day for a few days, while quartermasters expected wagon masters to drive their teams at a rate of twenty miles daily (an infrequent occurrence due to frequent tavern halts, late starts, and poor preparation). Cattle could be driven twenty to twenty-five miles daily, but their daily caloric consumption, particularly in the winter when pasturage was thinner, made this a troubling proposition. If they were to be slaughtered to feed the army, emaciated cattle would not do. At some point, Wayne had to balance the needs of the army against the needs of its meat source. That matter aside, Sherman's and possibly Woodbridge's detachments made it to "Whippin Town or Rangle Town," where Col. Israel Angell, Second Rhode Island Continentals, and Maj. Richard Platt, aide-de-camp to Maj. Gen. Alexander McDougall, "mett with General Waines Division."[18]

EARLY ON, WAYNE had anticipated a British reaction to his presence in New Jersey. His distance from the main army, the size of his command, its physical isolation because of the river, the slow rate of march imposed by the cattle and forage, and Howe's need to respond in order to reinforce British authority and preserve New Jersey's provender for British forces made him too tempting a target for even Howe to ignore. Unable to match a sizable British force in combat, Wayne had decided on an alternate scheme. On 23 February, he ordered Captain Barry to "pass up the River, with your Boats, and Burn all of the Hay along the shore from Billings Port" to Salem. He was to take "an Acct. of the Persons Names to whom it belongs together with the Quantity" destroyed. This suggests that Wayne intended that the property owners be compensated for their losses. As a start, Wayne had it on good intelligence that at "one John Kellys place at the mouth of Rackoon Creek, there is near One Hundred *Tons*—and up Mantua Creek, there is [also] a Considerable Quantity." Supplementing Barry's crews, Wayne ordered Lt. Simeon Jennings of the Second Rhode Island Continentals to "proceed with the Detachment under your Command being nineteen in number . . . on board Captn. Barreys Boats." Jennings's detachment was drawn from his regiment and the First, Fourth, Fifth, and Eighth Connecticut regiments from brigadier generals James Mitchell Varnum's and Jedidiah Huntington's brigades. Barry's raids were to serve a dual purpose: to divert British attention from the expedition while denying the enemy forage. Once Barry had "Effected the Business on Which he is Ordered," he was to land Jennings and company in Pennsylvania.[19]

Barry began his work of destruction at Raccoon Creek on the morning of 24 February. Wayne believed that this "drew the Attention of the Enemy that way," and he reported to Washington the next day that "twenty flatt bottomed Boats with a Number of other craft full of Troops, rowed down the River by Glochester Point" at 1:00 A.M., 25 February, "but where they have landed I am not yet Informed." He sent out scouts along the river and "expect[ed] every moment to here" about the British destination. If New Jersey was not "their Object I fear for [Brig. Gen. William] *smallwood*," he wrote. Wayne's concern was due to the Marylander's "feeble Condition" in Delaware, including his lack of adequate transport for even his command's baggage. If, however, the British "should amuse us below" his own position at Haddonfield, Wayne intended to steal a march northward "whilst they are passing at Dunck's ferry," today's Beverly, in order to outflank and avoid them. Wayne's intent was to "push the Cattle for Trent town" while he and his detachment joined with the militia, which were estimated to be no more than three hundred strong, "to prevent the Enemy from Maroding too farr."[20]

Barry's sailors and makeshift marines had, meanwhile, set fire to the hay-stacks they encountered as they moved down the New Jersey shore, igniting one stack after another, all the way to Salem Creek. On 26 February, Barry notified Washington from Port Penn, Delaware, that "According to the orders of General Wayne I have Destroyed the Forage from Mantua Creek to . . . [Salem]; the Quantity Destroyed is about four Hundred Tons & should have Proceeded farther had not a Number of the Enemies Boats appeared in Sight & Lining the Jersey Shore Deprived Us of the Opportunity of Proceeding Far-ther on the Same purpose."[21]

By 25 February, the Continentals and New Jersey militiamen had amassed one hundred and fifty head of cattle. Wayne, who had by then shifted his headquarters northward to Haddonfield, wrote to Washington that he be-lieved that there was more livestock between Cooper's Ferry and Dunk's Ferry, which he expected to drive in within four days to bring the total num-ber of livestock to two hundred and fifty head of cattle and thirty horses for Captain Lee's dragoons. The owners, he noted, received certificates.[22]

Wayne's dispatch across the Delaware had roused Howe from his stupor, if only momentarily and in the most dilatory and distracted fashion. On the twenty-fourth and twenty-fifth, he launched a two-pronged movement into New Jersey. "We imagine," wrote Lt. Col. Francis Downman of the Royal Artillery, that "the intention is to make a junction with the light infantry and most likely by this manoeuvre they may surround Mr. Wane and his cattle" from above and below. Archibald Robertson, captain-lieutenant of the Royal Engineers, noted that the dispatch of so many soldiers was "to surprise" Wayne. Working to support the army's descent, the crew of Hamond's *Roebuck* had busied itself from about 3:00 P.M. on 24 February "fitting out the *Pembroke* (Tender) & [two] half Galley's with arms Provisions" and other supplies preparatory to making the assault. Capt. John Linzee of the frigate

Pearl commanded the naval contingent, which included his tender, the sloop *Zebra* (fourteen guns), two galleys, and "a Great No. of flatt Boats, Carrying the 2 Battns. of [the] Light Infantry" Brigade. Late on the night of 24 February, over twenty flatboats and escorts set out for Billingsport, carrying the infantry under the command of Lt. Col. Robert Abercromby ("Abercrombie"), Thirty-Seventh Regiment of Foot. They anchored there around 6:00 A.M. and disembarked the light infantry, nicknamed the "Light Bobs." From Billingsport, the light infantrymen were to "march on Salam." In Captain Muenchausen's words, they were to "have a slap at General Wayne, if possible." Captain Hamond of the Royal Navy ordered the flatboats to follow the brigade downriver in order to support the expedition and provide it with greater mobility. Just after noon, the flotilla again sailed, and "Rowd and Towd with flatt boats down the River," before anchoring off Wilmington, Delaware. Observers quickly ascertained Abercromby's objective, and, as Ens. George Ewing of the Third New Jersey Continentals recorded, in "Salem the Melita was cald to oppose them."[23]

Hamond's sailors ferried a second brigade around 10:00 P.M. on 25 February, when another contingent of flatboats and escorts carried Lt. Col. Thomas Stirling's ("Sterling") two-battalion strong Forty-Second Regiment of Foot (also known as the Royal Highland Regiment or the Black Watch), Maj. John Graves Simcoe's Queen's American Rangers, a Loyalist legion with cavalry and infantry, and "4 three po[unde]rs" to New Jersey. The ad hoc brigade mustered around a thousand soldiers. Stirling landed above Cooper's Ferry around midnight and quickly seized the ferry's wharves to land the artillery, being momentarily delayed "on accot. of a few shot fir'd . . . by a guard of militia," noted John Peebles, a captain-lieutenant of the Highlanders. The Scots' advance scattered the New Jersey Militia. Stirling then organized a field officer's guard of about a hundred and fifty men to escort supply wagons forward and then set off with the bulk of his force for Haddonfield, about seven miles east southeast. Given the proximity of Cooper's Ferry to Philadelphia, Hamond's squadron could easily support Stirling. Across the river in Philadelphia, Lieutenant Colonel Downman was confident that "by this manoeuvre they may surround Mr. Wane and his cattle." Tellingly, Howe did not assign a general to command the British response. Without a general officer to direct and coordinate the two brigades or orders to cooperate with one another, Abercromby and Stirling were left to their own devices. No matter how accomplished the two brigade commanders were, an operation of that size demanded a general to

George Romney (Britain, 1734–1802), *Colonel Robert Abercrombie* (1788, London, oil on canvas, 76.5 x 63.0 cm). Gift of Phillips and Henderson, Adelaide 1982, Art Gallery of South Australia, Adelaide, 823P9.

oversee it. It was an altogether appalling demonstration of Howe's seeming apathy. His soldiers and his monarch deserved far better.[24]

Ellis's scouts kept Wayne well informed about the British movements, if not their numbers. Wayne reported to Washington that about two thousand infantrymen had landed at Billingsport, where Abercromby divided his brigade to cover Wayne's most likely routes of march. In line with Wayne's imprecise estimate of British strength, the American commander stated that

Abercromby had sent fifteen hundred soldiers southward to Blessington (present-day Sharptown), where they "Encamped . . . within Seven Miles of Selem," and another five hundred northward along King's Highway. Unhappily, but not unexpectedly, the British had a decidedly easier time "Collecting the Cattle &Ca." than did Wayne. No doubt disappointed, as well as angered, Wayne reported that the "Inhabitants in that Quarter" gave the "Enemy exact Intelligence of our Numbers and Rout—in Consequence of which that body were thrown over [the river] below" Wayne's position to block his line of retreat to the south. Scouts to the north soon reported that two thousand British soldiers had landed at Cooper's Ferry "with four Pieces of Artillery and a Considerable body of Light Horse." Individually, Abercromby and Stirling easily outnumbered Wayne's scattered parties; combined, they had overwhelming strength. Encumbered by livestock, none of the Continental or militia detachments could outrun the Britons or Loyalists without first abandoning what they gathered, Doing so meant failing in their mission to feed Valley Forge. Standing and fighting meant sure disaster. Wayne faced a dilemma.[25]

After landing the light infantry at Billingsport, Cdr. James Watt, captain of H.M.S. *Delaware*, recorded that the "Flatt Boats & Gaily's" *Cornwallis* and *Pembroke* paralleled the Light Bobs' advance toward Salem and "follow[ed] them down the River." While moving downriver, Lt. Thomas Spry, commanding *Cornwallis*, observed Cdr. John Orde's sloop *Zebra* sailing in pursuit of Captain Barry's "6 [armed] boats" as they returned to Port Penn, Delaware. Spry supported Orde's pursuit by firing "two 24 pound shott at one of them." Unable to catch Barry's raiders, Watt and company continued and "Anchord off Sealam Creek in 5½ fathom water." Watt's choice of anchorage was astute. A mere five miles northeast of Port Penn, it allowed Watt to assist Abercromby's light infantry in and around Salem while he kept a watch over Barry's boats downriver. Should Barry depart Port Penn, the Delaware's current would increase Watt's speed while in pursuit. Barry would be a fool to venture upriver while Watt commanded his approaches.[26]

While Barry's flotilla had "amuse[d]" and attracted the enemy, Wayne and the soldiers who remained with him had, on 23 February, marched northeast toward Haddonfield via the King's Highway, passing through Blessington and on to Swedesboro (Raccoon Creek), where he spent the night at the Rev. Nicholas Collin's house. They had arrived around midnight. Just after Wayne bedded down, sentries fired "warning signals" alerting Wayne of a British approach, but it turned out to be a false alarm. Collin thought his guest "a well-bred gentleman [who] showed me great respect," and also noted the shabby appearance of Wayne's force, "the greater part [of which] were miserably clothed, some without boots, others without socks." Collin estimated their strength at "300 men." Wayne departed the next morning and none too soon, for, in the Reverend Collin's words, "on the morning [of 24 February] at 11 o'clock, a regiment of English infantry came to attack him, but he had already then escaped. These troops had come in running march the last [Swedish] half mile, and the militia in Swedesborough had hardly time to escape." Abercromby missed Wayne, but he captured "four or five Waggon[s] belonging to the Commy. which were on a back Rout[e] from Selem loaded with Spirits Brandy &Ca." as well as "a small guard of Seven men left to Conduct them."[27]

Abercromby's light infantry paused for a while in Swedesboro. Collin requested of the "Commander" that he "not to be in any way molested." After verifying that Collin was indeed the rector of the Swedish Lutheran church, the officer "posted guards at all the larger houses and also at my gate." Collin lost a few "hens and ducks" to the light infantry, but Abercromby's soldiers "plundered" many of Collin's flock and others. The Rev. Frederick Schmidt, pastor of the Moravian church at nearby Oldmans Creek confirmed some of Collin's experience. His "house was full of soldiers." Schmidt found them "polite, but [they] carry off trifles" like petty thieves. While the Continentals and militiamen may have appeared as armed ragamuffins, Reverend Collin found the redcoats "undisciplined" men who could not "always be controlled." Indeed, Collin believed the British soldiers' propensity to rob "both friend and foe . . . most despicable." From this time forward, until June, Collin observed around him that "Everywhere distrust, fear, hatred and abominable selfishness were met with" by one and all. The armies' hunger for New Jersey's bounty had set loose many of war's terrors upon the people.[28]

WAYNE AND HIS BAND of three hundred pushed northward to Haddonfield. Their stay there, like that at Swedesboro, was short. The night that Stirling landed, he set out to attack Wayne or block his escape. With Abercromby's light infantry to the south and Stirling's Highlanders and Simcoe's Rangers approaching from the west northwest, Wayne's range of options was narrowing, and his chances of success were lessening. After leaving behind a "Field officers Guard to come up with the Waggons," the Scot pressed on for Haddonfield, but, yet again, Wayne eluded capture. Wayne fretted that "from the Supiness and Disaffection of every part of this State which I have passed through (on my Present tour)—I don't expect a Single man of the Militia to turn out more than those already under Col Ellis, which don't amount to three Hundred." Nevertheless, Ellis' New Jersey men performed creditably. One of their number, Lt. Aaron Chew of the Second Battalion, Gloucester County Regiment, was patrolling the riverfront when he took note of Stirling's column. Chew galloped through a snowstorm to Haddonfield, arrived at 2:00 A.M. on 26 February, and warned Wayne of its approach. Wayne next ordered a drummer to beat to arms and then sent out scouts with Chew to confirm the report. As the enemy advanced, Wayne readied his roughly 550 Continentals and militiamen, decamped in the darkness of the early morning, and marched another fifteen miles or so northeast to Mount Holly. Wayne's mission, the small size of his command, and memories of the unhappy fate of his rearguard element that Maj. Gen. Charles Grey had manhandled at Paoli, Pennsylvania, on the night of 20–21 September 1777 likely hastened his departure.[29]

From Mount Holly, Wayne sent ahead to "Trent Town" forty barrels of gunpowder, a hundred and fifty head of cattle, and assorted other supplies with an escort of about a hundred and forty soldiers under Lieutenant Colonel Sherman, who had led the first contingent of cattle northeast from Salem. Sherman's detachment and the cattle had not accomplished Wayne's overly ambitious and tiring march expectations. Having set out on 22 February, Wayne had expected Sherman to be at Mount Holly by the twenty-fourth, a distance of around fifty miles. They had instead marched thirty-four wintry miles to Haddonfield. Because of the size of the herd, the need to maintain the cattle's weight, the number of wagons carrying forage and other foodstuffs, and the road conditions, Sherman's rate of march was likely limited to just over ten miles per day.[30]

Stirling may have missed Wayne, but he made the most of his stay in Haddonfield, the limit of his penetration, some six miles inland from Cooper's Ferry. Roughly forty families, mostly Quaker, "who seem heartily tired of this Contest," lived in the village. Captain-Lieutenant Peebles noted that the villagers "seem'd well pleased at our coming." Learning that Wayne and company had departed, Stirling posted guards and allowed his soldiers some rest and respite from the weather by ordering them "into barns." The day after arriving, details searched for wagons and forage and then transported back to the ferry the seized or purchased goods, including "some live stock," which, noted John Peebles, "we buy here pretty reasonable." During the excursions "some skulking militia" captured two soldiers from Stirling's regiment, while Simcoe's rangers brought in two or three hogsheads of rum

By his batman (after Benjamin West), *General Sir Thomas Stirling of Ardoch and Strowan*. The Black Watch Castle & Museum.

they seized "at a house a few miles off," no doubt welcome in the cold, wet weather. Within a day of landing, the character of Howe's incursion into New Jersey had changed; the search for forage and sustenance had trumped the hunt for Wayne.[31]

BRITISH AND HESSIAN JOURNALS, diaries, and letters emphasized that Wayne was the focus of both brigades. Many of them commented that foraging was a secondary priority. Abercromby's and Stirling's behavior, however, raises doubts about the clarity of their orders and their priorities, but especially the nature of Howe's command. Indeed, Howe's subordinates appeared more concerned with driving the rebels from contested sources of supply than with seizing an opportunity to strike at them while they were vulnerable and heavily outnumbered. The search for comestibles had supplanted seeking combat, as the relative ease of foraging evidently outweighed larger strategic considerations. Indeed, foraging had become the *raison d'être* of British strategy in occupied Philadelphia. Howe's command demonstrated a singular lack of effort, focus, forethought, or immediacy. Sloth ruled, and the same strategic and operational diffidence that marked British operations in Pennsylvania carried on unabated in New Jersey. Lieutenant Colonel Downman observed that after having been but a few days in New Jersey, "The light infantry returned without doing anything." Shortly after the light infantry's return, "without having been able to catch up with General Wayne," Captain Muenchausen sounded a dejected note, that "General Wayne had already received information about our expedition against him (as unfortunately almost always happens)."[32]

Wayne, however, could only guess at the British Army's climate of command. As far as he knew, two experienced, talented, and aggressive enemies were hunting for him. Because of the armies' small sizes and having fought one another for nearly three years, senior commanders' reputations were well-known by their opponents. With Abercromby and Stirling to the south and southwest, Wayne's immediate numbers reduced to just over half, and Sherman's rate of march severely circumscribed, Wayne feared that the British were about to check him. Facing what he believed to be an enemy force that outnumbered him dramatically, Wayne's options were limited. Although his remaining force was considerably more mobile than before the departure of Sherman's detachment, Wayne still had to try to block or delay any British attempts against the cattle and supplies under escort. Unable to return across the Delaware from Salem County as originally planned, Wayne elected to bypass the British positions by marching northward. He intended to sweep northeast and then northwest in a wide arc in order to cross the river safely above Philadelphia.[33]

Wayne recognized that he would "not be able to Prevent . . . [the British] from passing thro' the Country at pleasure—their Numbers being *Eight to one*—but in Order to Circumscribe them as much as Possible," he took the "Liberty to Call on [Brig.] Genl [Casimir] Polaskie for such part of His Horse as can Conveniently be spared and [are] fitest for duty." On 27 February, Wayne requested Pulaski, who was at Trenton with a troop of the First Continental Light Dragoons, to join him "this Evening." Because the "Regiments are dispersed at a great distance" for forage, billeting, and security, Pulaski had "but few of the Cavalry . . . at present." Only eighteen were armed and fit for duty; the "remaining part are sick & without arms." Although Pulaski wrote to Wayne that he would "always be ready to oblidge you in every respect," his correspondence with Washington that same day revealed his sensitivity to rank and presumptions regarding the seniority of cavalry officers to all others. Worried that an infantry brigadier general, whom he considered junior to him in branch of service ("General Brigadie plus Jeune que les autres"), but not date of rank, would presume to give him orders, Pulaski asked Washington to provide clarification. Washington did so promptly: seniority based on date of rank was the only "preeminence in our Service." In order to make sure that Pulaski fully understood, Washington added that "the Officer whose Commission is of prior date commands all those of the same grade indiscriminately whether of horse or foot."[34]

But even before Washington clarified the matter of rank, Pulaski took personal command of the eighteen light dragoons and set out to join Wayne. By the twenty-eighth, Pulaski was at Burlington with fifty horsemen, including five officers he had "collected together in the Country." At the same time, Ellis and two hundred and fifty militiamen were at Evesham Meeting House (present-day Mount Laurel), roughly equidistant between Haddonfield and Mount Holly. Meanwhile Stirling held at Haddonfield, from which he sent forth foraging parties to the south and west between Cooper's Creek and Big Timber Creek. Stirling's parties had been productive. Simcoe's rangers seized several boats and one hundred and fifty barrels of tar. The tar, useful for caulking ships' and boats' seams, was loaded in boats and sent off to Captain Hamond of the Royal Navy. Loyalist refugees manned the boats, which conserved Simcoe's troop strength. The rangers also seized "some cattle" and destroyed "some tobacco" on the road to Egg Harbor, near present-day Atlantic City. Simcoe "returned in the evening

Julian Rys, *Casimir Pulaski*. Courtesy of Independence National Historical Park.

with some few militia as prisoners." They had mistaken the rangers for "Wayne's rear guard."[35]

ON THE MORNING OF 28 FEBRUARY, boats from the armed ship *Delaware* carried Lt. Col. Enoch Markham and a "Field offrs. Detachment" of about a hundred and fifty soldiers from the Forty-Sixth Regiment of Foot to Cooper's Ferry "to collect forage in its vicinity." That same morning, around 10:00 A.M., Abercromby's brigade re-embarked at Salem and headed up-river, possibly "intended to intercept General Wayne, & his collected supplies." Thus, on the last day of February, Stirling was within striking range of Wayne, and Abercromby was sailing upriver (so far as Washington understood it) to join with Stirling or block Wayne's line of march north.[36]

Although Wayne was severely outnumbered and his options seemed decidedly limited, he acted wholly in character—on 1 March he turned back to confront Stirling's foragers and thereby seized the initiative. Heretofore, Wayne had successfully evaded the British, but he now saw an opportunity to "drive in or cut off some of these parties." From Mount Holly, Wayne made a "forced March" toward Haddonfield, "altho my Numbers were few." Around 9:00 P.M., he arrived at Capt. Joseph Matlack's house, four miles southeast of Haddonfield, where he was reinforced by Pulaski and his fifty light horsemen. Ellis and his New Jersey militiamen remained at Evesham Meeting House, at the juncture of the Egg Harbor and Mount Holly roads (today's Mount Laurel and Hainesport Mount Laurel roads in Mount Laurel Township). As Wayne approached Haddonfield, Pulsaki's impetuous behavior forced him to act earlier than planned. If that surprised Wayne, it ought not have. Earlier, Pulaski had asked what Wayne's intention was, and then revealed to Wayne that his own "intention is to attack the enemy by Night." To say that Pulaski was independent and headstrong would be an understatement. The problematic Pole believed that "as strong as they may be we can loose nothing but gain proper by them." Never one to miss the chance to correct an imaginary slight received, he closed by telling Wayne "The letter you wrote Yesterday was done without consideration in several Articles[.] I shall wait your answer by the bearer." Without principle to stand on, Pulaski intended to stand on injured pride.[37]

About 10:00 P.M., Pulaski attempted to surprise the Queen's "Rangers Picket across the Creek at Keys Mill," a half mile southeast of Haddonfield, "but [it] Miscaried." In large part, it failed to surprise the British because they had been forewarned by a local man with "credentials." Simcoe wrote that he thought that when Stirling received the intelligence, he should have advanced and ambushed Wayne as he approached. He expected that once Stirling and Howe had received the report, Markham would advance to Haddonfield, and he supposed it possible that Howe might order "a strong corps embarked, and passed up the Delaware, above Wayne." Thus, as he wrote his memoirs well after the event, Simcoe was disappointed in his superiors' timidity. Stirling understood that Wayne's force "had been so considerably augmented, [and] that it would be imprudent to remain at Haddonfield." The informer may have been a plant put forward by Wayne, or a Loyalist who had been fed false information, for, according to Wayne, his strength had been "Exaggerated to thousands." Wayne reported that Stirling believed American troops were "moving in three Columns—for his Right, left and Center," and because of this "the *North Brittain* thought it prudent to Retreat." Consequently, Stirling formed his brigade and departed for Cooper's Ferry at 11:00 P.M., where it arrived around 2:00 A.M. on 2 March. He left behind most of the supplies and livestock his brigade had seized. Left unexplained by Wayne, was how he deduced Stirling's determination of the American advance, whether it was from an informant, an assessment of the road network, or something he had conjured in his mind's eye.[38]

The constant marching and countermarching had fatigued his troops, so Wayne waited until late the next morning before acting. He first sent a patrol southward to Salem to discover Abercromby's location and intentions. Learning that there was "nothing to Apprehend from that Quarter," the light infantry having departed, "I went with Genl Pulaski to examine the position of the Enemy" before Cooper's Ferry. Having traveled the night before in "uncommonly severe" weather with "cold sleet . . . the whole way," Stirling's brigade had spent the "coldest night that they ever felt, [moreover] without fire," alongside the river. Likely exhausted from the move and the cold, Stirling was at "Coopers ferry in full force" waiting to be taken off by the navy. Hamond's boats, however, were unable to extricate the brigade because the weather had worsened to "Fresh gales and [was] squally with Frost and Snow." Nonetheless, Stirling's brigade, now supplemented by Markham's guard, and covered by the navy's heavy guns, meant he was "too well posted [for Wayne] to do anything." The dirty weather, however, obscured Wayne's force and made aiming and firing a risky proposition for the navy's gunners. Wayne exercised a needed degree of tactical patience and forethought as he elected to pause and wait for an opportune moment to strike at Stirling, although, as always, Pulaski was "Impatient & Anxious *to Charge*."[39]

In need of forage after having left his previous collection behind in Haddonfield, Stirling had sent out a few wagons and an escort of "fifty of the 42d and Rangers, under the command of Captain [James] Kerr" of the rangers along the road to Haddonfield. He also sent out a mounted patrol of "ten [Ranger] Huzzars . . . towards Haddonfield," which encountered Wayne's advance guard, fifty Continentals under Capt. John Doyle of the Eleventh Pennsylvania Continentals, about noon. The officer commanding the British patrol, Lt. Alexander Wickham, sent word to Kerr and to Stirling, who was now in the process of embarking his brigade. Loudly calling out a series of commands, Wickham deceived Doyle into believing he had a large force with him. It gave Kerr enough time to fall back and for Stirling to form a line of battle with the Forty-Second on the right, the Forty-Sixth in the center, and the Queen's Rangers on the left, while still under the cover of the navy's guns. The British had declined in bringing Wayne to battle, so now Wayne brought it to them.[40]

Doyle reported to Wayne that British reinforcements, "having Crossed from Phila . . . were Marching up Coopers Creek and were pushing for our Rear," headed for Ellis' militia. He knew, however, that the "Other part of the Detatchment under Colonel [Richard] Butler [was] to follow as fast as possible." The remainder of Wayne's command was about three miles to the rear. Doyle hastened forward to develop the situation and came upon Stirling's covering force, a picket line "whose numbers were about three times as many as our's when joined to the Horse." However, it appeared that the pickets' flanks were "Approachable" and that the ground fronting their center was "favourable for the Cavalry." After consulting with Pulaski, a courtesy the Pole had earlier failed to give to his senior, Wayne "Determined to Attack them—in Order to gain time for the main body to come up—as well as to amuse and prevent the Reinforcement of the Enemy from proceeding further up the Creek."[41]

Stirling's picket line held its position in anticipation of a Continental advance, but when it did not materialize the embarkation continued apace. Horses were put aboard boats, and, "as the enemy did not advance, Colonel Markham's detachment followed them." When the boats were "scarce half way over the Delaware," Wayne sent Doyle forward, and "soon Obliged the Covering party to Retreat." As Doyle approached, "pushing them hard," Stirling responded "in force to support" the covering party with the Forty-Second Foot closing the distance between the forces by advancing in line of battle. He next ordered Simcoe to have the "Queen's Rangers . . . advance, which it did, in column, by companies," securing its left on Cooper's Creek, near Spicer's Ferry Bridge (near the old incinerator at today's Federal Street Bridge). Wayne was quite pleased at drawing the British forward "from under Cover of their Shiping." He had Doyle maintain a "Constant and galling fire" as he fell back "by slow Degrees" in order to fall back on "Butler's Detachment."[42]

Stirling pressed forward with the rangers' light infantry company in the advance. Three three-pounder "grasshoppers," drawn by sailors "with their accustomed alacrity," followed. The ranger infantry continued on the left with the post of honor on the right held by the Highlanders (traditionally the senior-ranking officer or senior-ranking regiment occupies the right of

Jean Laurent Mosnier, *John Graves Simcoe*. Courtesy of Toronto Public Library.

the line, the post of honor). When some of Ellis' militia came into view on the "opposite bank of the Cooper creek," the Queen's Rangers' grenadier company under Capt. Richard Armstrong secured the British left by lining up along "a dyke on this side: an advantage the enemy had not." Stirling's Highlanders, meanwhile, kept up a heavy fire on the right. Facing Simcoe's infantry, "there was nothing opposed to the Rangers but some cavalry, watching their motions." Moving forward to gain the high ground to its front, Simcoe's battalion pushed Pulaski's light dragoons, "an officer excepted," into some woods. Not surprisingly, the officer was Pulaski, "who, reining back his horse, and fronting the Rangers as they advanced, slowly waved with his scimetar for his attendants to retire." Simcoe's light infantry was but fifty yards from him, when, according to Simcoe, one of his rangers called out to Pulsaki, "'You are a brave fellow, but you must go away.'" Pulaski failed to hear, heed, or understand the warning; Simcoe then ordered Capt. John McGill to fire on him "on which he retired into the woods." Pulaski, as Wayne put it, "behaved with his Usual Bravery having his Own with four Other Horse Wounded."[43]

Easily outnumbered by Stirling's and Simcoe's battalions, Doyle's little band gave way as the British advanced, until they "halted on the advantageous ground" about a mile from Cooper's Ferry. When Simcoe then noted about a hundred militiamen near the Cooper's Creek Bridge on his left, he dispatched the grenadier company and opened up with his three-pounders "at the entreaties of the sailors." It was "at this Instant," according to Wayne, when "Hessian Grenadrs attempted to force over Cooper's Bridge . . . but they soon gave up the Attempt." Ellis's New Jersey militiamen were busy destroying the bridge and posed no threat to the British left, thus "they were no longer interrupted."[44]

The "fireing from the Enemies Shiping, field pieces, and Muskettry now became General." Captain Doyle's "Little Corps of Infantry" had acted well, and "bravely Sustained" the enemy fire, "but we could not Draw Mr Sterling far." It was nearly 6:00 P.M., and Colonel Butler had not yet arrived; the skirmish ended as "the firing totally ceased," and Wayne withdrew a safe distance. The threat removed, Stirling continued embarking his forces. They returned to their quarters by about 8:00 P.M. With more than a bit of self-satisfaction and embellishment, Wayne declared that "thus ended the Jersey Expedition which was Conducted with *great Caution*—by two *North Brittains* at the head of full three thousand Troops and Eight field pieces—but they have saved themselves, and we have saved the Country for this time at least." Lieutenant Colonel Downman's account begged to differ. According to the British artilleryman, the Highlanders had driven off "Wane." They "pursued him a great way, but he ran too fast" for the Scots to catch him. However the action was decided, it lasted about four or five hours and was inconclusive. Stirling's Scots suffered three wounded, while Simcoe's rangers had three or four wounded and one killed. Wayne, on the other hand, lost three light dragoons wounded, four or five horses killed, and three lamed. All of the casualties were from Pulaski's command. Reporting to Washington, Pulaski claimed to have captured seven sailors, among whom was a ship captain ("parmis Le quels il se trouvs un Capitain d'un Vaisso"). There is, however, no mention in the Philadelphia squadron's records of any officers or sailors captured. Stirling's and Abercromby's brigades retuned to Philadelphia without any further incident.[45]

Continental victories had been as rare as food, forage, and other supplies that winter, so Isaac Collins, publisher of *The New Jersey Gazette*, made the most of it, and crowed about Abercromby's and Stirling's "most pompous parade in landing in two [places] several divisions to the great terror of the horned cattle, and no small peril of some undefended stacks of hay." He mocked them for the size of their forces, so overwhelming was their strength "with above two thousand men, when they knew we had not above a quarter of that number in arms in that part of the country." Collins ignored Pulaski's charges at Haddonfield and Cooper's Ferry, and instead celebrated the Pole as "determined." No matter, for "happiest was that Briton who had the longest legs and the nimblest heels." Even when facing the New Jersey Militia, Collins ridiculed the Britons who had "fled ten times as fast from the militia, as they pursued after the Count." The encounters at Haddonfield and Cooper's Ferry had been skirmishes, but every ray of hope from the smallest incident mattered.[46]

FOLLOWING THE ENGAGEMENT at Cooper's Creek Bridge, Wayne remained at Haddonfield until 6 March "to refresh the Troops and procure Shoes to enable them to March" for camp, his "Troops being almost barefoot." After resting and presumably obtaining shoes, the return march proceeded. Wayne "Detached Lieut. Morton of the Virginia Troops to Camp with 22 head of Cattle (one of them for your Excellencies particular use being the fattest beast in New Jersey)." Morton also had in his "Charge" two chests with thirty muskets, bayonets, and other items "for the use of my [Wayne's] Division" of Pennsylvanians. John Chaloner commented that Wayne had previously sent over some 126 head of cattle, and he expected more. As valuable as Wayne's activities were in New Jersey, Washington wanted him to return to camp to meet with some "Gentlemen of Congress" over the pending consolidation of Pennsylvania's Continental Line into ten regiments.[47]

By 14 March, Wayne was in Bordentown, New Jersey, after having destroyed or sent away from the river with local Whigs the forage he could not take. From there Wayne crossed over to Bristol, Pennsylvania, and as he returned to camp he continued disposing of "the Forage within the reach of the Enemy in the Counties of Philada and edge of Bucks," as well as driving "off the Horses Cattle &Ca fit for our service." He also requested that a portion of Captain Lee's light dragoons join him at Bristol, believing the cavalry would "be of the most Essential Service." The following day, Lt. Henry Peyton and a dozen cavalrymen joined Wayne, who made his way to Bensalem, about sixteen miles northeast of Philadelphia. He promised Washington that "you will be waited upon by your Excellencies Most Obt Huml. Sert" on Monday, 16 March. By 23 March, Wayne was back on rotation as the duty brigadier general in camp. That same morning, "All Officers that was in Command with General Wayne in the Jersies" met with him at his quarters that "at 10 O'Clock to Render and Account of the Horses they had in Charge." Sadly, no record of those accounts or of the full range of participants has been discovered.[48]

The foraging progressed even as Wayne returned to camp unmolested. Awakened to the possibilities in New Jersey, General Howe on 12 March dispatched another ad hoc brigade to the state, this time under Lt. Col. Charles Mawhood, who had his own Seventeenth Regiment of Foot as well as the Twenty-Seventh Regiment of Foot under Lt. Col. Edward Mitchell. Colonel Markham, his Forty-Sixth Foot, and the Queen's Rangers under Major Simcoe paid a return visit to New Jersey with the new expedition. Lt. Col. John Morris's Loyalist Second Battalion, New Jersey Volunteers, and Maj. John Van Dyke's West Jersey Volunteers completed the roster. Easily sweeping aside the New Jersey Militia, Mawhood had virtually unimpeded access to southern New Jersey until his departure on 29 March. The destruction and disorder Mawhood's forces spawned forced Washington to dispatch the Second New Jersey Continentals under Col. Israel Shreve to restore order to the area. As in so many other instances with the overstretched Continental Army, it was a case of too little, too late. The violence and disorder continued unabated until well past June 1778, when the armies met in battle once again at Monmouth Courthouse.[49]

While Wayne's men had trudged northward through New Jersey, Captain Barry had widened his operations to include harassing British shipping on the Delaware. On 7 March, well after Watt had sailed upriver from Salem, Barry's flotilla intercepted an army escort, the armed schooner *Alert* (eight guns), and her charges, the supply ships *Kitty* and *Mermaid*. Barry and his men boarded and seized all three. Putting in on the Delaware shore, he set his crews to unloading the supply vessels, but a Royal Navy patrol surprised him. Barry was able to save most of the captured goods before igniting the three vessels. If not decisive, the riverine actions boosted Continental morale and further burdened the Royal Navy's Philadelphia squadron.[50]

Wayne, and before him Greene, had scored some important successes in the contest for survival. They had forwarded several hundred head of cattle, dozens of horses, loads of forage, and unnumbered quantities of wagons, harnesses, and other items so necessary for the Continental Army's survival. Yet, even as Wayne's leg of the foraging concluded, the third and final portion continued under Capt. Henry Lee, Jr.

CHAPTER FOUR

The Zealous Activity of Captain Lee

While Maj. Gen. Nathanael Greene's column foraged through Chester County and he expanded his intentions for an American crossing into New Jersey by Brig. Gen. Anthony Wayne, Gen. George Washington also expanded his intentions for the February foraging. He noted on 16 February that his soldiers had been short of beef "for four days and many of them have been much longer without" it. As Greene considered the next moves for Wayne, Washington acted.[1]

On 16 February 1778, Capt. Henry Lee, Jr., commanding Fifth Troop, First Continental Light Dragoons, received orders from Washington to march his troop of light dragoons "immediately" to Dover, Delaware, and Head of Elk, Maryland. Lee was to work with the commissaries in Maryland and Delaware, and "exert" himself to drive to Valley Forge "all the flesh-prov[is]ions" held in the magazines in those states. Washington "empowerd" Lee to impress "any number of Waggons" he deemed necessary for the mission. He also directed Lee to "consult" with Brig. Gen. William Smallwood, commanding the Continental Army's First and Second Maryland brigades, at Wilmington, Delaware. Smallwood, Washington wrote, would "afford you ev'ry assistance" in emptying the magazines, and would assign him "proper officers" who knew the area.[2]

After forwarding the magazines' contents to Valley Forge and consulting with Smallwood on the countryside's livestock and forage, Lee was to get what "resources can be derived thence towards the relief of our distresses." Washington expressed his confidence in Lee by not ordering Smallwood to oversee Lee's operations, merely to assist Lee. In this stage of the grand forage, Lee reported directly to Washington even as he kept Greene and Wayne informed of his activities. Confident in Lee's abilities, Washington knew that he need not write anything more to "animate your Zeal on this occasion."[3]

Washington's sangfroid masked his distress over the army's condition and the state of its supply. He revealed his concern, however, to Col. Henry Hollingsworth, deputy quartermaster general at Head of Elk, Maryland, and to Brigadier General Smallwood. Washington confessed to Hollingsworth that Lee's impending journey was a "painful necessity." Although emptying the magazines had potentially serious implications for Smallwood's

Charles Willson Peale, *Henry Lee*. Courtesy of Independence National Historical Park.

command that winter and in the upcoming campaign season, the main army's wants necessitated Lee's forwarding the magazines' stocks as "expeditiously as possible." Washington thus "entreat[ed]" Hollingsworth to assist Lee with all his ability to "promote this very important and interesting work," while also remaining mindful of the "delicacy of this Subject and the propriety of Secrecy." Advertising the army's distress risked inviting a British thrust and exposed the weak foundations of the Continental and states' governments. Writing more fully to Smallwood, Washington told him that the "distress of this army for want of provisions is perhaps beyond any thing you can conceive." If the army's leadership failed to "strain every nerve to procure immediate relief" from want, Washington feared his soldiers might mutiny over the lack of provisions, or that he might be forced to disperse the army, and surrender the area near Philadelphia to British control. Washington "dreaded" the options. As if writing in confirmation of Washington's fears, Thomas Jones, deputy quartermaster general for issues, informed Col. Charles Stewart, the commissary general of issues, that "we are [in] ten times [the] worst Situation now then ever you knewe" before this. The army's situation was so precipitous that Brig. Gen. James Mitchell Varnum of Rhode Island believed it would soon melt away.[4]

The Continental Army held something of an existential middle ground in the War for Independence. It was an army of liberation in the eyes of many of its members, but also one of occupation and intimidation. Congress had charged it with defending American liberties and securing the nascent republic's independence. To accomplish that task, it needed at times to deprive or deny other Americans, including Loyalists, Indians, and the enslaved, of their liberties. As the army reinforced the states' revolutionary regimes, it also served as an adjunct for the rebel governments. Continentals helped bolster or reestablish congressional and state authority in the army's areas of operational responsibility; they assisted in suppressing Loyalism in disaffected regions; and they supported the states' militias, which, in turn, also suppressed Loyalists and acted as auxiliaries to the army and governments. At the heart of this paradoxical mission is what historian John Shy has described as the "triangularity of the struggle," the contest between the revolutionary armies (Continentals and militias) and imperial forces for the adherence or submission of the population. Popular affection, submission, order, and material support were thus among the key objectives pursued by both opponents in the larger contest for America."[5]

WASHINGTON'S ORDERS PLACED Lee at the center of the army's foraging actions in the upper Chesapeake and brought him into contact with senior officers of the Continental line and staff, the states' political and military leadership, and the people of Maryland and Delaware. As Capt. Johann Ewald, an experienced officer of Hessian *jägers*, put it, Lee was "to do on a small scale what a general does on a large scale." While Washington left unstated how Lee should conduct himself, the young officer was well-enough acquainted with Washington's mode of operation that the young dragoon exercised a restraint uncommon in the eighteenth century, even among many American soldiers. Lee's concept and execution of the operation—to borrow modern terms—and the foragers' conduct demonstrated a marked recognition of Delawareans' and Marylanders' property rights and a sensitivity to, and understanding of, civil-military relations that were in stark contrast to that of the British Army and its German and provincial auxiliaries in America. Lee's restrained, even scrupulous, behavior revealed an inherent appreciation of the long-term effects of his actions in a struggle for popular affections.[6]

General Washington selected well when he "intrusted" Lee for this "important business." Both of them coming from prominent Tidewater Virginia families, Washington had known Lee and his family for years. Indeed, Lee's close familial connections with Washington contributed to the young Virginian's initial preferment. Lee's battlefield acumen and performance, however, more than justified Washington's preferential treatment. Commissioned a captain in Maj. Theodorick Bland's Regiment of Virginia Horse on 18 June 1776, Lee and the now-renamed First Continental Light Dragoons mustered into the Continental Army on 31 March 1777 at Morristown, New Jersey. Lee soon showed himself a skilled officer and careful planner, capable in command, and noted by observers in both armies for his "zealous activity" and "boldness."[7]

A few days after the army had entered Valley Forge, Sgt. John Smith of the First Rhode Island Continentals noted that Captain Lee and his troop had captured thirteen enemy "Light horse[men]" and their mounts, and had brought the captives into camp. Lee once more made his mark when he detected an opportunity to strike at the enemy in late December, when Gen. Sir William Howe had led most of the British Army out toward Derby on a large forage. Captain Lee, "a party of his men," and some "Riflemen Advanced near Darby to Draw out a Party," and capture or kill them. The riflemen were from Col. Richard Butler's Ninth Pennsylvania Continentals, and may have also included some of Col. Daniel Morgan's Eleventh Virginia Continentals. Nonetheless, when Lee and Butler struck, the combined force captured several enemy soldiers, including, Butler noted, the quartermaster of the Seventeenth Light Dragoons and a handful of infantrymen. The following month, Col. Timothy Pickering reported with pride that Lee's troop had captured one-hundred and thirty of "ye enemy prisoners" since August 1777.[8]

Lee's troop had regularly challenged British patrols, maintained a watch against an enemy advance, harried British communications with Chester

County, and gathered intelligence for Washington, as he refined his grasp of partisan warfare. The young captain from Virginia (he was but twenty-one years old) was becoming a successful practitioner of *petite guerre*, the small war that was the province of active young officers and light troops. Indeed, Capt. Louis-Michel de Jeney, a French officer of Hungarian birth, deemed partisan warfare as the "most fatiguing, the most dangerous, and the most extensive" sort of war. Partisan officers, in de Jeney's estimation, required "extraordinary Talents," including "Imagination . . . , A penetrating Mind," and what the Prussian general and philosopher of war, Carl von Clausewitz later termed *"coup d'oeil,"* a gifted soldier's ability to grasp the essence of a situation and act with determination and resolve. Noting the tendencies of some *ancien régime* officers, de Jeney, also counseled against a partisan officer's attachment to "Women, Wine, or Wealth," all of them causes of "neglect . . . , perilous Indiscretions . . . , [and] Crimes without Number." While all of this awaited Lee in his future life of dissipation, impecunity, and disgrace, he was still the dashing light dragoon and partisan officer on the rise. Contemporary estimations of Lee certainly suggest as much.[9]

Captain Lee and his troop operated from an outpost at John Scott's Farm, about six miles due south of Valley Forge. His position was but one element in the army's extended screen line south of Valley Forge, and then east across the Schuylkill. Lee's post was one of three picket posts south of the encampment. It was about four miles west of Radnor Meeting House, itself some sixteen miles northwest of Philadelphia and eight miles southeast of Valley Forge, and another four miles northwest of Newtown Square. Radnor Meeting House served as a hospital for Valley Forge and as officers' quarters, while Newtown Square was an important communications junction where the roads from Haverford, Derby, and Chester converged. These three positions formed a triangle, with Scott's Farm and Radnor Meeting House the base, and Newtown Square the apex. Together, they were a small, mutually supporting network of outposts. Infantrymen manned the Radnor and Newtown positions, which limited their speed and mobility, whereas Lee commanded the sole Continental cavalry in the area.[10]

In mid-January 1778, Lee again demonstrated his skill when he and a small group of his light dragoons defended their outpost against two score of British light dragoons. Lee had galled the enemy to such an extent that the British had targeted him by name. According to Howe's aide, Captain von Muenchausen, Lee "has alarmed us quite often by his boldness." Lee may have been bold in action, but he was thorough in planning and anything but foolhardy. He had presented before Washington a thoughtful analysis of the security line in his area, recommendations for establishing new positions that would provide mutual support for one another while improving the encampment's security, and his thoughts on how best to maintain, or at least not worsen, relationships with local farmers as foragers went out into the countryside. Determined to deal with Lee, Howe dispatched forty light dragoons who "endeavoured to surprise" the American in the early morning of 20 January.[11]

Maj. Richard Crewe of the Seventeenth Light Dragoons made a "long roundabout way to seize a rebel dragoon captain by the name of Lee" on 19 January. Crewe and his dragoons departed Philadelphia at 11:00 P.M. Captain Lee and from six to ten officers, noncommissioned officers, and troopers manned the outpost at Scott's farm. At dawn, a few minutes before 7:00 A.M., Crewe attacked. In the excitement, Lee estimated his enemy at "near two hundd in number." Responding quickly, Lee's dragoons "manned the doors & windows" of Scott's stone house and prevented the British from entering and seizing it. While the "contest was very warm," Lee handled his men, whom he complimented for their "bravery," well. After suffering what Lee initially believed were two killed and four wounded, the Britons "desisted & sheered off."[12]

As Crewe's light dragoons fell back, Lee seized the initiative and counterattacked. In the action, Lee and his cavalrymen "drove them from the stables & saved every horse." He reported that "We have got the arms, some cloaks &c. of their wounded." Lee even reportedly had time to chide Major Crewe for his own men's indiscipline. According to Capt. Johann Ewald, Crewe's soldiers "began plundering instead of overrunning" the American position. A firm disciplinarian with no little sense of irony, Lee reportedly called out, "'Comrade, shame on you, that you don't have your men under better discipline. Come closer, we will soon manage it together!'" Although the British light dragoons had failed to capture or kill Lee, they did manage to capture his quartermaster sergeant, four privates, and their horses, and to wound Lt. William Lindsay ("Lindsey") and two privates. From civilians in nearby Derby, Lee learned that his men had wounded one officer, a sergeant, and three privates, and killed another three light dragoons. "The enterprize was certainly daring," wrote Lee, "tho' the issue of it very ignominious" for the British. "I had not [even] a soldier for each window," he wrote. As the British withdrew, Col. Edward Stevens of the Tenth Virginia Continentals "pushed a party of infantry, to rea[c]h their rear," but was unable to make contact and join in the contest. Nonetheless, Lee's conduct impressed Washington, who saluted the young captain as "My dear Lee," praised him in the army's general orders for the day, congratulated him for his "gallant behaviour," and offered his "sincere thanks to the whole of your gallant party." By these actions, his past regular performance of duty, and longstanding acquaintance with Washington, Lee had clearly impressed the commanding general as an officer of merit and enterprise, one worthy of Washington's trust. The gallant "Capt. Lee's vigilance baffled the enemy's design." Not all of the participants in the defense of Scott's Farm, however, earned praise.[13]

Lee's immediate superior, Maj. John Jameson, took part in the defense of Scott's Farm. Jameson commanded a severely understrength, ad hoc squadron of light dragoons that ranged north of Philadelphia and east of the Schuylkill. Brig. Gen. Casimir Pulaski, chief of cavalry had ordered Jameson to "repair to the West side of the Skuylkill and take the Command of all the Horse on the lines on both sides the River." Jameson rode to Scott's Farm to develop a sounder appreciation of the area and Lee's responsibilities, as well as to "know what sum of Money he might want for the expence of his party." During the fight, Jameson received a wound in his forefinger, which had prevented him from writing sooner to Washington. In obeying Pulaski's orders, Jameson inadvertently incurred Washington's displeasure. Pulaski had failed to notify the commander-in-chief of Jameson's absence from his assigned post. Jameson asked Washington to "believe" him. Had he thought that Pulaski would have directed him anywhere "without your Excellencys knowledge" or his authorization, Jameson "should not have been absent" from his post. Eventually the matter was clarified, and the cloud over Jameson disappeared. Pulaski had once more demonstrated his penchant for independent action, no matter the consequences. Misunderstanding had led to opprobrium, which took time, effort, and pen and paper to remove. As for Jameson, he was promoted in 1779 to lieutenant colonel of the Second Continental Light Dragoons.[14]

Lee became something of a celebrity in the army following the action at his picket post. Colonel Pickering wrote at length about it to his wife, Rebecca, and pronounced that "Capt. Lee is perhaps the greatest partizan in the army." Capt. William Bernard Gifford of the Third New Jersey Continentals praised Lee's "vigilance." It had "baffled" Major Crewe's "designs." Brig. Gen. George Weedon observed that "Captn Harry Lee of Bland's Light Dragoons having been thus the whole Campaign a troublesome neighbour to the Enemy, they have tried frequently to retaliate, but have generally got worstes in the attempt." Weedon deemed it a "stroke of Generalship." Exercising more restraint, and throwing some cold water on the effusive praise,

Gov. William Livingston of New Jersey wrote to Maj. Gen. William Alexander, Lord Stirling, that while "Capt. Lee is undoubtedly a brave young Officer, but I imagine that the account of the number of the Enemy which he obliged to retreat, like the first accounts of most other rencounters, is rather exaggerated." Livingston's cooler observations aside, Lee had clearly distinguished himself as a capable and rising officer, someone worthy of greater responsibilities. He was an obvious choice to command the final leg of the Grand Forage.[15]

TRUE TO FORM, after receiving his orders from Washington on 16 February, Lee, with fewer than fifty light dragoons, acted on them "vigorously and methodically." He called on General Smallwood the next evening. After making inquiries about the state of the country, Lee learned from Smallwood that the region "between Christiana-bridge & duck creek abounded in good teams" of horses. Smallwood "dispatch'd" Lee early on the morning of the seventeenth, accompanied by "four very active officers, well acquainted with the Country." General Smallwood thought these four officers were" best adapted to aid him [Lee] in the Execution of the *design*." Smallwood also wrote to President George Read, Jr., of Delaware; Maj. Gen. Caesar Rodney, senior officer of the Delaware Militia; Colonel Hollingsworth; and Capt. Allen ("Allan") McLane, commanding a company of Delaware Continentals in Patton's Additional Continental Regiment, all of whom were at Dover. Smallwood requested that they share whatever intelligence they possessed and lend whatever "aid necessary on so pressing an Emergency."[16]

As Lee and his troop prepared to set off for Maryland, Deputy Commissary General of Issues Thomas Jones was "almost Desti[tute]," having a mere fifty barrels of pork and forty of herring at camp. He was expecting "40 head of Cattle" by the seventeenth, but they might only "Serve for to pay 2 days Beef," and the soldiers had been without fresh meat for three or four days. Daily, he expected "nothing else but every moment a Whole Brigade of the Starv'd soldiers will Come to our Quarters & without Examining who is or what is not to Blame will lay Voilent hands on the whole of us." To Jones's south, General Smallwood had his own concerns.[17]

Lee's mission was intended to help remedy the Continental Army's supply crisis, but it depended upon stripping supplies from another army detachment for it to go forward. Still Smallwood was confident in his command's ability to respond to the needs of the main army. Indeed, he wrote to Washington that it was with "great Confidence & Pleasure," he assured Washington on 21 February, that "there will in a few Days be a plentiful

Charles Willson Peale, *William Smallwood*. Courtesy of Independence National Historical Park.

Supply forwarded," upwards, he believed, of "70 head of Cattle." Brigadier General Smallwood was sure that much more would follow, but not, however, without his own brigades suffering. Subordinates had informed Smallwood that the magazine at Dover held "several Hundred Thousand Wt of Pork, which with the Stores at the Head of Elk, I have made a point of not touching" in order to reserve for the Main Army's use. Already, however, Smallwood's Marylanders, Delawares, and the Second Canadians at Wilmington had "suffered many Times extremely" and he feared that they would suffer the same privations as their comrades at Valley Forge. As recently as 11 February, Smallwood had inquired through Captain McLane about the possibility of his obtaining "any more Beef or Pork" from Robert McGarmont, deputy assistant commissary of purchases.[18]

Washington apologized to Smallwood for the "inconveniences with respect to provisions," but was forthright in his explanation of the main army's "irresistible necessity." As painful as emptying the magazines was, it was unavoidable. As Washington had made clear more than once, he had "been obliged to exert every nerve to keep the Troops here together." Smallwood's concerns were honest, but his circumstances, while straitened, were nowhere as dire as those of his comrades to the north. Not yet. Like the situation in southeastern Pennsylvania, the winter in Delaware and Maryland was as much a struggle for the army's physical survival as it was for the nascent republic's political survival. The search for provisions laid bare some of the region's tensions.[19]

DELAWARE AND MARYLAND were on the periphery of local British and Continental power as British and Continental forces competed for the support or allegiance of the people. British power, centered in Philadelphia, had wrought tremendous secondary effects within southeastern Pennsylvania and southward into the Chesapeake Bay region, but the greater the distance from Philadelphia, the greater the opportunity for the exercise and strengthening of Continental authority. Gen. Sir William Howe's 1777 invasion of Pennsylvania and subsequent occupation of Philadelphia had forced Delaware's legislature to shift southward from New Castle to Dover, in Kent County. The erstwhile capital's proximity to Philadelphia, a scant thirty miles or so downriver, put the Delaware Assembly well within British striking distance. The move to Dover made good sense, but safety was not the sole motive. Delaware's legislators had an important secondary reason for transferring the seat of government. They did so, in part, to conciliate the conservatives from Kent and Sussex counties. Although it may have been necessary, and even astute, this decision entailed a risk. By moving south to Dover, the assembly put itself closer to Sussex County, where the Loyalists were strongest.[20]

Washington had recognized the complex military and political conditions on the peninsula. He had addressed these problems by dispatching 1,800 soldiers in two brigades of Maryland, Delaware, and Canadian Continentals to Wilmington, Delaware, in December 1777. Posting Smallwood's command at Wilmington simultaneously fulfilled military, political, logistical, and civil objectives. It demonstrated Washington's strategic intuition and understanding of the war's complex nature and requirements. Nonetheless, in Capt. Enoch Anderson's estimation, "Comparing our numbers with the British, our situation was critical and dangerous." Something of a "patizan" officer, Anderson, a Delaware Continental, grasped the nature of the operational environment into which he was thrust, perhaps almost as clearly as the commander-in-chief. By deploying two brigades into Delaware, Washington responded to several threats at once. He used the Continental Army, not only to maintain watch over the Delaware River and British movements along it, but also to reduce the logistical strain on Valley Forge. Moreover, through its presence in Wilmington, the army served as a proxy for the Continental and state governments. Hence Washington, through Smallwood and his Maryland and Delaware Continentals, maintained watch over a vital British line of communication and guarded against an enemy attack as the army supported and protected the rebel government and projected the authority of the Continental Congress from "within a hearth of popular disaffection."[21]

The Continental Army's support-of-government function was an important task, even in a place as small as Delaware, or a region as compact as the Delaware-Maryland-Virginia Peninsula. Harold Bell Hancock, a prolific historian of Delaware, attributed the depth of Loyalism in the state to its "backward, rural population . . . , its isolation," and its strong ties to the Anglican Church. Hancock believed that nearly 50 percent of the white population, some 17,000 out of 35,719, was Loyal. The allegiance of the 2,000 enslaved African Americans was more problematic and likely to shift to whichever force held out the greatest promise for personal freedom. Many contemporary observers considered Delaware a "Tory province." So problematic was it that Col. William Richardson, his Fifth Maryland Continentals, and 200 Delaware militiamen had spent part of the summer of 1777 chasing down Loyalists in Sussex County, while then-Brigadier General Rodney's militiamen in Kent and Sussex counties spent several months "ferreting out Tories." Neighboring Eastern Shore Maryland was no better. In one historian's estimation, it was "One of the most strife-torn areas" in the state; Maryland's State Council considered the state of affairs an "Insurrection," and deemed the Loyalists "Insurgents." In sum, the area's turbulent political makeup made for a dangerous field of action and called for astute and sensitive leadership.[22]

Despite this set of circumstances, the Continental Army's leadership did not treat or consider Maryland or Delaware as conquered or hostile provinces, British or Loyalist assertions notwithstanding. Whereas Maurice de Saxe, the famed Marshal of France, had counseled as recently as 1757, that an "experienced general" would relieve his prince of the obligation to support his army by living off of the enemy, the Continental Army's oft-stated *raison d'être* was the defense of American liberties, of which property was sacrosanct — even when operating among the ill-disposed. The army's respect for property was tested, however, in the winter of 1777 and 1778. Lee, despite operating in a region rife with Loyalists, deserters, and the disaffected, was constrained as much by the intent of Washington's orders as by his own predilections.[23]

Defending liberty in the Chesapeake Bay was no easy matter. The estuary was both a physical and a political boundary; Maryland's "Eastern Shore was maritime . . . and Tory," whereas the bayside grew tobacco and was Whiggish. Indeed, "With the possible exception of western Long Island, the Chesapeake peninsula had the highest proportion of Loyalists in the colonies," according to historian William H. Nelson. Moreover, Loyalists' population densities were "evenly distributed" throughout the peninsula, which dissipated their potential strength, but also forced state and Continental forces to disperse and weaken themselves when policing pockets of resistance. Washington was well aware of his army's delicate position. He noted as much to Maj. Gen. Nathanael Greene, his most trusted division commander, when Washington wrote that the "good People of the State of Pennsylvania living in the vicinity of Philadelphia & near the Delaware River having sufferd much by the Enemy carrying off their property without allowing them any Compensation, thereby distressing the Inhabitants — supplying their own Army & enabling them to protract the cruel & unjust war that they are now waging against these States." Consequently, Washington's orders sent Harry Lee into a chronically disaffected region, one plentiful with Loyalists, deserters, malcontents, and the disaffected.[24]

LEE AND HIS TROOP ARRIVED at Wilmington on the evening of the seventeenth. At less than thirty miles from Valley Forge, the town was a day's ride. Once there, he conferred with Smallwood, who penned and dispatched an introduction on his behalf to Major General Rodney, who had acted on Smallwood's request to assist Lee by assigning him some officers who were familiar with the "Country below" Wilmington (see tables 4.1, 4.2, and 4.3 for participants identified in the Delaware and Maryland foraging). The note was short, and had been written in "great haste," for Smallwood was also host

TABLE 4.1 Capt. Henry Lee, Jr., Fifth Troop,
First Continental Light Dragoons

Rank	Name
Captain	Lee, Henry, Jr.
Lieutenant	Lindsay (Lindsey), William
	Peyton, Henry
Cornet	O'Neill (O'Neal), Ferdinand
	White, John
Sergeant	Brooks (Brooke), William
Quartermaster Sergeant	Peake, William
Farrier	Willis, Zachariah
Corporal	Neal, Ferdinand
	Waters, John
Trumpeter	Benjamin, Joseph
Private	Ausbury, Coleman
	Bend, Joseph
	Bigbie, William
	Binward, John
	Champe, John
	Coone, Israel
	Dehaven, James
	Ferguson, Robert
	Fillinbuilt, William
	Guthery, George
	Hagen, Thomas
	Halbert, William
	Harman, John
	Hedman, Downing
	Howton, Mark
	Humphrey, John
	Langdon, John
	Leonard, Coleman
	Lewis, Stephen
	McCourins, Michael
	Newman, William
	Pointer, George
	Power, Robert

(continued)

TABLE 4.1 Capt. Henry Lee, Jr., Fifth Troop,
First Continental Light Dragoons (*continued*)

Rank	Name
	Rosamond, Robert
	Ruth, George
	Thesmain, Annanais
	Wright, John

OCA, 345, 352, 438, 420, 586; *Valley Forge Legacy: The Muster Roll Project*, "1st Dragoons," http://valleyforgemusterroll.org/muster.asp (7 May 2021). The entire roll of Lee's troop is given according to the listing in *Valley Forge Legacy*. The actual number of soldiers involved in the expedition was likely much smaller. Records list two members of Lee's troop sharing remarkably similar names, Ferdinand O'Neill (O'Neal) and Ferdinand Neal. Cornet O'Neill (O'Neal), who hailed from France, is listed in *OCA* with a commission date of 22 April 1777, while a Corporal Neal from Virginia is listed is listed in *Valley Forge Legacy* and in "Account of Cattle, & Provisions Collected," Howell Papers, Account Book, GCHS. Adding to the confusion, on Cornet O'Neill, see Woodruff, "Capt. Ferdinand O'Neal of Lee's Legion," 328–30 and *OCA*, 420. There may have been an error in transcribing ranks, but without a definitive answer both ranks and names are listed.

and aid to Brig. Gen. Anthony Wayne, who had recently arrived with his "five hundred men." Wayne, however, did not tarry in Wilmington. He and Capt. John Barry of the Continental Navy had an appointment in New Jersey.[25]

Lee next met with Colonel Hollingsworth, who had "Just retund from a tower down the Penensilo on a purchas for the Army." Hollingsworth informed Lee that "There is at present no supplys of meat of any sort at [Head of] Elk," although a supply of "Pork is expected daily." Lee found Hollingsworth a "very active officer" with a "just idea of the state of the army." Hollingsworth immediately sent "out two trusty Hands to seek out Cattle and Pork & requested them to informe me of the number of Cattle fit for Imediate use, and fit for fating [fatting or fattening] in their District." It was altogether likely that many of the cattle needed extensive fattening because of the winter. Hollingsworth also assigned his half-brother, Thomas Hollingsworth, a Baltimore merchant familiar with the area, to assist Lee.[26]

Lee was sensitive to the needs of local farmers, to their property rights, and to the army's conduct, image, and relationship with civilians. Indeed, as Lee promised Washington that he would pursue "every step . . . to drain this country of all superfluous forage & provision," he remembered his

TABLE 4.2 Other foragers

Rank	Name	Parent unit and immediate higher organization
Captain	McLane, Allen (Allan)	Delaware Regiment, Smallwood's Brigade
	Rumford, Jonathan, Jr.	Delaware Militia. Formerly captain, Delaware Battalion, Flying Camp, July–December 1776.
	Witherspoon (Wetherspoon), Thomas	Third Company, Col. Richard Cantwell's Battalion, New Castle County Militia
Lieutenant	Batten, James	Seventh Battalion, Chester County (Pennsylvania) Militia
	Quenouault (Quenowault), Paul	Delaware Regiment, Smallwood's Brigade
Ensign	McLane (McLean), Benjamin	Delaware Regiment, Smallwood's Brigade
Corporal	Casslon (?)	Unknown

OCA, 373, 477, 456; *Valley Forge Muster Roll*, http://valleyforgemusterroll.org/index.asp (7 May 2021); William Smallwood to George Washington, 21 February 1778, *PGW*, 13:634–35; "Account of Cattle, & Provisions," Howell Papers, GCHS; *PA*, 14:93; Hall's Regiment, Pay Roll of Pattens Company," Public Archives Commission, *Delaware Archives*, 1: 157, 158; "Delaware Militia, Arrangements," Public Archives Commission, *Delaware Archives*, 2: 851.

"Excellency['s] wishes . . . towards the inhabitants." He "furnished" himself with a roll of the "several hundreds that make up the township or county of Newcastle" before dispatching "partys of horse under proper officers" to supervise the foraging. They were to "call on the assessor of each hundred, whose office pointed him out as a guide & friend," and enlist the assessors' aid as they "collect[ed] all cattle fat for slaughter, [and] all horses suitable for draught or dragoon service." Lee ordered his foraging parties to explain to farmers that the British were about to launch their own foraging expedition and that by supplying the Continental Army, Delaware's farmers could help prevent it. But there was more to Lee's approach than appealing to personal security or patriotism. He "entreat[ed]" Washington for a "sufficient sum of money to pay off the people" before his troop left the area. Captain Lee was well aware of complaints over uncompensated losses to the army and he hoped to "please & oblige" Delaware farmers, or at least to avoid causing them greater "umbrage." In order to properly account for impressed property,

TABLE 4.3 Local commanders, staff, and agents

Rank	Name	Parent unit and immediate higher organization
Major General	Rodney, Caesar	Delaware Militia
	Smallwood, William	Smallwood's Brigade, Stirling's Division
Deputy Quartermaster General	Hollingsworth, Henry	Quartermaster General, Middle Department
Captain	Wilkinson	Unknown
Deputy Commissary General of Purchases	Hollingsworth, Thomas	Commissary General, Middle Department
Deputy Assistant Commissary General of Purchases	Howell, John Ladd	Commissary General, Middle Department
	Huggins, Thomas	Commissary General, Middle Department
	McGarmont (McGerment, McGarmet), Robert	Commissary General, Middle Department

William Smallwood to Caesar Rodney, 18 February 1778, Dearborn Collection, Houghton; George Washington to Smallwood, 16 February 1778, *PGW*, 13:563–64; Washington to Henry Hollingsworth, 16 February 1778, Hollingsworth to Washington, 18 February 1778, *PGW*, 13:558–59, 582; Henry Lee to John Ladd Howell, 19 February 1778, Reed Collection, VFNHP; Lee to Howell, 23 February 1778, Howell, *Book of John Howell*, 198, 200; Ephraim Blaine to Washington, 28 February 1778, Smallwood to Washington, 21 February 1778, *PGW*, 13:692, 634.

Lee assigned "persons in some centrical spot in each county to value every article that may be got," and ordered his foraging parties to maintain "Regular books." In closing, he promised Washington the delivery of fifteen wagons laden with barrels of beef and pork on Sunday, 22 February. It was an impressive start.[27]

The hundreds in which Lee concentrated his efforts constituted all of New Castle, the state's northernmost county, and the northeastern hundred of centrally-located Kent County. It was in New Castle County, however, that Lee focused his energies, although some of his foraging parties did enter Cecil County, Maryland. When Lee directed his foragers to work with assessors, he necessarily deferred to local knowledge. Nobody had a better idea about residents' wealth than these men, since it was they who assessed property values for tax collection.[28]

Middletown, in New Castle County, Delaware, served as the "centrical spot." Located in southern St. George's Hundred, Middletown was a road juncture near the Maryland line, which eased communications for Lee's foragers and was far enough removed from the coast to prevent a quick visit from the Royal Navy. John Ladd Howell, deputy assistant commissary general of purchases, oversaw the collection, inventorying, valuation, and transshipment of goods. Captain Lee "authorize[d] & empower[ed]" Howell, a Philadelphia merchant, to "superintend" the collection of supplies at Middletown, along with the "appraisements of each & every article that may be collected at this post," and to maintain an accurate and "just" account and to provide property owners with "proper certificates specifying the appraised value of each article." He enjoined Howell to "coadjute" Ens. Benjamin McLane ("McLean") of the Delaware Continentals in executing the orders Lee issued, and to organize the wagons into "brigades" for transporting supplies to camp. For security, Howell was to "urge" Capt. Thomas Witherspoon's ("Wetherspoon") "immediate compliance" in "furnish[ing] a Sufficient Guard for the Stores collecting at Middletown." Witherspoon's force was likely from his own Second Company of Col. Richard Cantwell's Battalion, New Castle County Militia. Backing up Howell's urging was an order to do so from General Rodney of the Delaware Militia. Lee "invest[ed]" Howell "with full powers to call on every subject of the United States to your aid & assistance" and gave him the authority "To nominate & appoint all & every necessary officers." Finally, Lee ordered Howell to "Acquaint" him with his progress at Middletown and "how the people comply with our orders; whether there is much discontent, [and] from what causes it may originate."[29]

Even as Lee wrote to Washington about his coordination with Smallwood, Hollingsworth, and Howell, and Lee's plan to prosecute the forage, he had already set in motion the early stages of the Delaware and Maryland expedition by going "out after Cattle" in Wilmington and the surrounding area. Within two or three days, Lee's light dragoons and the Delaware Militia had gathered nearly 100 head of cattle and by 20 or 21 February, he "expect[ed] to send off one hundd head of cattle from what I find already collected & those I expect to gather this day." By "sunday next," 22 February, Lee promised the arrival of over a dozen wagons carrying beef and pork. Indeed, so active and confident was Lee that he expected to collect at Dover all of the wagons and teams in New Castle County, "which will be immediately pushed on . . . to take in the salt provision."[30]

Washington approved of Lee's plan and the actions undertaken "for supplying our wants," and also of the "prospects which you have of success."

Lee's estimates buoyed Washington's confidence, and he deemed Lee's coordination with the hundreds' assessors "extremely judicious." Furthermore, Washington did not doubt that Lee's "activity and prudent management" would enable him to "avail [himself] of all the resources of the Country without giving unnecessary umbrage to the inhabitants." Despite the army's desperation, Washington and his commanders remained mindful of promoting and maintaining good civil-military relations. Indeed, Washington informed Lee that Col. Ephraim Blaine, deputy commissary general of purchases, would shortly be "setting out for the Neighborhood in which you are making collections of Cattle &ca," and that Blaine would "be as well provided as possible with Cash, in order to inspire the people with confidence and facilitate the execution of your plans."[31]

As active as Lee was, he could not be in two places at once. In order to increase the forage's productivity, he dispatched small parties of light dragoons, and Delaware Continentals and Delaware militiamen. Echoing Washington's trust in his junior officers, Lee entrusted noncommissioned officers with significant responsibility. On 22 February, he instructed John Ladd Howell to "Select Some of the likeliest youths of Capt [Thomas] Witherspoon's [Delaware Militia] Company—mount them on the horses you have collected," and then place them under the command "of my Sergt, [William Brooks] They are to do the duty of dragoons." A Corporal Casslon led impressment parties, too, as did Lt. James Batten of the Chester County (Pennsylvania) Militia, and Lt. Paul Quenouault ("Quenowault") and Ens. Benjamin McLean of the Delaware Continentals. Lee's account book suggests that he directed operations while delegating authority to subordinates, an indicator of the mutual trust, respect, and shared understanding of the mission before them.[32]

In addition to militia adjuncts, Lee benefitted from the activity of a gifted fellow partisan officer, Capt. Allan McLane, who had extensive experience in foraging and in reconnoitering and harassing the enemy. Before assisting Lee, McLane had been "empressing Waggons to transport any provisions purchased, or procured" and tracking down and "apprehending" deserters. Although McLane's company of Delaware Continentals was "naked," according to Lt. William Dennis Kelley of the Fourth Virginia Continentals, they had no other "complaint." Indeed, their condition was anything but unique. It was something "which must be endured, as it is a general Calamity." So adept was McLane at his duties, that his company was later transferred to the newly-authorized Lee's Legion as the Fourth Troop (Dismounted) in July 1779.[33]

Thus far, Lee had acted with the alacrity, zeal, and attention to detail that Washington expected from him. Within a day or two of receiving his orders, Lee had reported to General Smallwood, met with Colonel Hollingsworth, examined tax rolls for the Delaware hundreds, and addressed how best to maximize his efforts by combining local militiamen with his dragoons and delegating authority to junior officers and noncommissioned officers to lead foraging parties. Having taken property rights into consideration, Lee ordered his subordinates to maintain proper records for people's recompense and requested funds for payments. Comfortable in exercising independent command, Lee was also punctilious in keeping Washington and local commanders apprised of his actions and what he encountered. Capable in combat, screening, and intelligence gathering, Lee was now demonstrating his further talents as a forage master for the army, his promise for higher command, and as a practitioner of the full scope of *petite guerre*.

BY 21 FEBRUARY, however, Lee's optimism and hope began foundering on the realities of wartime Delaware and Maryland. As he moved southward through Delaware and further away from Philadelphia, Lee discovered that Loyalist sympathies were more pronounced and that the Continental Congress and Delaware's state government had little authority and exercised even less control or activity. Lee estimated that in south central Delaware alone the people harbored some 500 deserters from the Continental Army. Writing from Dover, in east-central Delaware, Lee reported that a lack of wagons would delay his transporting salt as "expidetious as could be wished." Nevertheless, his foragers were active, doing "business very regularly," calling upon "each & every farm," and impressing "every article" useful for the army. Lee observed that only the "notoriously disaffected" showed any discontent. One of the chief problems, he noted, was that Delaware was "void of all government, therefore we can meet with no aid from the civil. They have a form, but there is no spirit or energy." President Read as much as confirmed it when he decried the "Disobedience of Orders on the part of the Militia in New Castle County" to turn out in support of Smallwood. Thus, in the absence of proper or spirited civil government, Lee operated in something resembling a void.[34]

Delaware's "want of government," combined with the deceit and "artifice [trickery] of the friends to the British army," had created an "asylum to deserters from the continental army," wrote Lee. He was taken aback by the state of affairs. Lee reported that a number of militia officers were busily "apprehending deserters, but tho' very active they meet with little success because they have no aid from government." Lack of spirited government had hamstrung the army's ability to maintain its strength. So weak was the state's authority that Lee estimated that "there cannot be less than [mutilated] hund'd deserters who live on [mutilated] fruits of their labor in this country." He suspected that "Some men of power and influence encourage the abominable practice by their private countenance." Lee suggested that if Washington were to write to Delaware's legislators on the matter and also provide Lee with the "directions and authority to apprehend & deliver to [the] Provost [Marshal]" all of the deserters he encountered, "great advantages might accrue to the army." Lee was persuaded that these actions taken together would boost the army's recruiting.[35]

Not long after receiving Lee's missive, Washington importuned President Read to enact a law that was "adequate to the remedy of this abuse." He cited Lee's claim that hundreds of deserters lived in Delaware, and redoubled his call upon Read to lend all possible assistance to Lee in the "execution of the Business" he was about. Read corrected Washington by informing him that Lee was "mistaken in his Representation" regarding the absence of laws mandating punishment for those guilty of the "harbouring of Deserters." Delaware's legislature had addressed this the previous year. Read did, however, concede that the penalties were too low, and that the depreciation of currency had rendered them even less effective. He assured Washington that the General Assembly "undoubtedly will remedy the Defect." As to Lee's claim about the hundreds of deserters, Read challenged him once again. Read suspected that Lee's claims were "exaggerated," but assured Washington that he was not "otherwise chargeable than relying on the Information of some of the Military, that were here before him, who speak and act at Random." Delaware's rumor mill aside, Lee remained a careful observer of his surroundings.[36]

Delaware and Maryland, the breadbaskets of the Chesapeake, had met with the foragers' approval when it came to "collecting cattle," but much less so with horseflesh, little of which was "fit for the use of an army." Noting the temper of the people, Lee remarked to Washington that "friends" gave his men "every assistance," but the "opposite party, which is by far the most numerous in this state, are very sullen." Sullenness aside, the "wisdom" of compensating owners and the good conduct of the soldiers scouring the countryside for the army had paid off handsomely. Lee noted that "we have been troubled with no sort of discontent." This last assessment stood in marked contrast to Lee's previous message to Washington, in which he decried the mood of the people. Whether he realized it or not, Lee was discovering the scattered and complex patterns of Loyalism and disaffection in Delaware.[37]

Lee moved westward into Kent County, Maryland, "sweeping the marshes which abound in cattle," and reported even more pronounced Loyalist sentiments among the people living alongside the numerous watercourses. The people who lived by these waterways were "cheifly friends to the enemys of America," he wrote. Lee believed farmers were hiding their cattle around the Chester River for an anticipated British incursion in the spring, during which they hoped to be paid in specie. Their location and the "high price given for provision" by the British had these husbandmen making "great preparations for making fortunes in the ensuing spring." Furthermore, Lee believed that they had "not contented themselves with their old stock which is astonishingly large" and well fed, but had even "entered into a kind of league with the disaffected in the forests." He believed that farmers along the waterways working with the "disaffected in the forest" drove "great quaintitys of . . . heavy country oxen" into the marshes to fatten them for slaughter in the spring. Estimating that "not a less number than three-thousand head" were in Kent County, Lee also noted the countryside was fat in forage, fat enough to graze all of Maryland's marsh cattle, which were much smaller than the country oxen.[38]

Rather than surrender Kent County and the neighboring region to the enemy or to the disaffected, Lee suggested that Continental and state forces collect there "superfluous wheat and other forage . . . from the lower counties" of the peninsula and drive all of the cattle, save a "sufficient number of milch cows for the support of the respective familys" along the waterways, and create "large magazines of cattle for the American Army." As for "Cows with calf," Lee thought that they could be sold to farmers who might then "afford stocks" for future campaigns. If not total war, Lee's solutions certainly smacked of war's hard hand.[39]

Washington appreciated Lee's measures for acquiring supplies for Valley Forge, but decided against establishing a magazine on the Eastern Shore. The superior operational reach and mobility afforded to General Howe by the Royal Navy meant that any Eastern Shore magazine was but a short march from a lodgment on the Delaware shoreline or from an expedition up the Chesapeake. As Washington saw it, the peninsula's shallow breadth meant that an enemy foraging or a raiding party "would sweep what are collected before any force would be drawn together to oppose them." Indeed, Washington had received reports that Howe was considering just "such an excursion." Should the British "establish a post" along the Delaware River, something Washington thought not "improbable," it would "render it very difficult for us to draw our Stores from any magazines below Christeen" because of the ease with which British forces might march across the peninsula. Rather than Kent County, despite Lee's inducements, Washington determined that centrally located Chester County, Pennsylvania, was "fine Country for Forage and Grass, and being directly in our Rear is perfectly safe." Colonel Hollingsworth would select the actual location and inform Lee. In addition, Washington sent Colonel Blaine to the "lower counties" to assess the quantity of cattle and "other provision" that Lee was to remove.[40]

Complaints aside, foraging had been successful, albeit not without some difficulties. Following his initial grumbles about the poor horseflesh, Lee later learned that horses were available in Delaware, but they were difficult to come by. From Dover, he confessed to John Ladd Howell, then in Middletown: "I cannot suppose the reason why we want [for] them." Within two days of writing Lee's writing to Howell, Sgt. William Brooks had rectified the matter. Howell wrote back and reported to Lee that Sergeant "Brooks has under his charge three horses for the immediate use of your troop."[41]

Lee's Delaware counterpart, Captain McLane, faced a potentially greater challenge. Not long after signing over a "Drove of Cattle" in Dover to John Trump, who would "forward" it to the army, McLane received intelligence from Robert Porter, a merchant, and his associate, George Reynolds of New Castle. They had overheard George Manlove of Kent County on Sunday, 22 February, at the "Widdow Petersons." They reported that Manlove had "declared in their presence that he was then going to the Drawbrige with intent to Intercept Capt McLean and Rescue the Cattle from him which he had provided for the American Army." Manlove's intention was not due to his having lost any cattle to McLane. His willingness to join with his neighbors, a "Number of them Armed," was instead motivated by his opposition to impressment. Manlove had declared before Porter and Reynolds that the actions of the army demonstrated that it was "not Liberty but Slavery we were Contending" for in the struggle for independence. Fortunately, nothing came of Manlove's threats, and McLane continued foraging for the army. Indeed, he estimated that from January through March, "we passed out of the penesula 1500 fat Hogs 500 head of Cattle 200 head of Sheep and fifty head of horses for the army at Vally Forge and a full supply for Genl Smallwood at Wilmington."[42]

AS FEBRUARY CAME to a close, so too did Lee's time on the peninsula. Continental and Delaware foragers had succeeded in driving several hundred head of livestock and forwarding a goodly amount of flour and other supplies to Elk for valuation, consolidation, and eventual forwarding to the army at Valley Forge. The account book kept by Colonel Hollingsworth at Elk records the names of property owners, their "Places of abode," and their stock, wagons, carts, and drivers impressed for service. They had collected over two hundred head of cattle, impressed one hundred and sixteen horses and two oxen to draw twenty-nine wagons and one cart, and another nineteen horses aged between four to ten years old, with an average age of seven. The nineteen horses that were not wagon teams stood between thirteen and one-half to fifteen hands, averaging nearly fourteen and one-half hands, all within the recommended size for light cavalry horses according to Capt. Robert Hinde, a half-pay British officer and author of *The Discipline of the Light-Horse*. Their colors ran the gamut, and included gray, sorrel, iron roan, bay, black, brown, and piebald. Colonel Hollingsworth computed the total owed by the Continental Army at £3,815.10, although the actual computation comes out to £3,811.10. The currency was likely local, although whether it figured in Delaware, Maryland, or Pennsylvania currency cannot be determined.[43]

Drovers took their herds to Head of Elk, and from there to camp. John Ladd Howell recorded "one hundred & seventeen Head of Cattle" having left Middletown, Delaware "on their way to Camp." Slowly, they made their way to Elk, and from there to the main army. They may have stopped briefly at Oxford, Pennsylvania, where roads joined and good pasturage could be found. Sometime in March, John Chaloner, assistant commissary general of purchases, noted that Lee had "sent us two droves, consisting of more than 100 head each." As the cattle moved on toward camp, the wagons went off to collect and transport supplies. A brigade of nine wagons and teams under "Waggon master" James Simpson went to New London Cross Roads, Pennsylvania (today New London Township), on 23 March. Located just over the Maryland state line, west of the Delaware line, and six miles east of Oxford, and beyond the convenient reach of British forces.[44]

On 21 February, just four days after Lee's arrival in Wilmington, nine wagons under William Scott departed for Dover, while another six wagons and one cart under William Boyce left for that town the following day. Two more wagons made for Dover on 23 February. The disposition of two remaining wagons went unnoted. Most of the wagons, teams, and drivers were from New Castle County, although a pair came from Cecil County, Maryland, and another pair from Chester County, Pennsylvania. Foragers had impressed most of the livestock from New Castle, although thirty-eight head of cattle had been taken in Cecil County.[45]

Fourteen wagon owners served as drivers. The surnames of another five suggest a son or relative. Tax records in turn show most of these families to be of middling to lower-middling income. This was not the case, however, for wagon owners John Lewden, Thomas Couch, Capt. Thomas Witherspoon, Valentine Deshane, and Robert Haughy of New Castle County, and John Rollins and Sidney George of Cecil County. Evidence points to some of them belonging to the upper quintiles of wealth in their communities. When military authorities called upon these men for wagons, teams, and drivers, they dispatched "Negro Joseph," "Negro Sam," "Negro Harry," "Negro Cuff," "Negro Joe," "Negro Jack," and "Negro David." These drivers numbered among Delaware's enslaved; men without the surnames that would have afforded them some measure of identity and individuality, but all bore the signifier "Negro" before their given names. Their humanity must be recalled as much as their unwilling contribution to the army's survival and American independence.[46]

It is a bitter and uncomfortable irony that the unfree served unwillingly a cause dedicated to American political freedom and personal liberty. Enslaved people's labor contributed to the preservation and continuance of the all-encompassing political, social, and economic system that denied them their personhood, a system designed to exploit their unfree black labor for the benefit of white society. Unlike the farmers who unwillingly contributed to the army's survival through the impressment of their property for a cause they may not have supported, there was no personal compensation for the enslaved Joseph, Sam, Harry, Cuff, Joe, Jack, or David. They were but property, and their masters received the compensation for their labor. Like the soldiers who foraged to feed Valley Forge, they too were integral to the army's endurance.

FOLLOWING LEE'S RETURN TO CAMP, foraging by Smallwood's Continentals and the local militia continued. Lee and the foraging parties had forwarded much-needed livestock to Valley Forge and contributed to the army's survival. They had probably impressed the fattest and best animals, and had left the poorest specimens behind, although that was wholly relative to the location. Ephraim Blaine described the cattle collected by Lee and his "People" as "ordinary." He went on to note that the "Cattle in this Country in general are very small but numerous." Indeed, Blaine found the cattle so small, that he deemed it "almost a pity to remove any untill they have the advantage of the Marsh Pasture in the Spring which would make them early Beef." The army had to make do with what it could get, small as the cattle were. What remained was a sore disappointment.[47]

William Shannon, a deputy commissary general of hides, confirmed as much about the state of the area's livestock when he reported to Henry Hollingsworth that the soldiers posted at Wilmington had "suffered much by the badness of the Beef." He shared with Hollingsworth the fact that Smallwood had recently received intelligence about "good Cattle at the Cross Roads at Duck Creek," in northeastern Kent County. In response, Smallwood sent off Shannon and a team of foragers "to bring One hundred head to mix with our ordinary ones." Upon reaching the cross roads, however, Shannon met with disappointment. Instead of good cattle, he "found none good there." Shannon returned to Wilmington and reported his "surprise" to Smallwood. Taking what cattle Smallwood's command had, Shannon "had a quantity of the old Stock slaughtered" to feed the troops. Yet more disappointment followed. Cattle were dying on the hoof. They may have been stricken with rinderpest, or cattle plague, the greatest killer of cattle in the early-modern world. Cattle plague spread quickly and easily in herds and had a mortality rate near 80 percent. Whatever the cause, their meat was inedible. Inspectors had it "condemned and thrown into the River." Of the "near one hundred head" in possession of Smallwood's command, there was "not a single creature of them fit for use." Shannon pleaded with Hollingsworth to send "any Cattle fit for use . . . with all possible dispatch." It was not until spring that an adequate supply of fresh beef and other provisions began arriving in suitable quantities. Until then, soldiers continued their hand-to-mouth existence, even as quartermaster and commissary officers struggled to reconstitute the magazine at nearby Elk into a logistical hub to help reduce the reliance on more distant sources of beef and to maintain a source of supplies closer to the main army.[48]

LEE'S EXPEDITION, which had taken him into a region rife with Loyalists, likely sparked a short-lived, armed protest. Not long after the light dragoons' departure in late February or early March, Cheney Clow's ("Clough") Rebellion broke out. It lasted through April 1778. Although historian Wayne Bodle is "unclear" as to why Clow's Rebellion began, he suggests that it may have been the intrusion of the Continental Army into central and southern Delaware. The Continentals, bolstered by the handful of Delaware militiamen, had been too small a force to overawe the local Loyalists, but were large enough for their presence to be felt and to intensify existing tensions. Lee's dealings with civilians before and during the forage suggest that his conduct in itself was not the cause of the uprising.[49]

Restraint aside, it was altogether probable that the foragers' mere presence was, according to Bodle, the "one catalyst for popular resistance." Clow's rising brought out an estimated 600–700 Loyalists who "assembled on Jordan's Island at the Head of the Chester River," according to Col. Samuel Patterson of the Second Battalion, New Castle County Militia. Moving inland, Clow's Loyalists established a makeshift fort just over the Delaware line in Kent County, Maryland. Following an unsuccessful attack against the fort by Delaware militiamen under Lt. Col. Charles Pope of the Delaware Continentals in mid-April, Clow and his followers dispersed, and the militia burned the fort. Clow was eventually arrested and executed. If Clow's Rebellion failed to do much more than briefly excite Loyalist passions, it speaks, nonetheless, to the sensitive environment in which the foraging took place. The fact that Lee, his men, Continental staff officers, and the Delaware Militia took pains to avoid giving unnecessary umbrage speaks to their recognition of Delaware's and Maryland's complex operational environment. Washington's confidence in Lee's expertise at *petite guerre* and independent command was well placed.[50]

CHAPTER FIVE

A Most Proper Place to Remove the Stores to as They Arrive

Elk was nothing like the foraging columns under Nathanael Greene, Anthony Wayne, or Harry Lee. Yet, it was an integral element in Lee's activities and in the larger efforts at sustaining the army at Valley Forge throughout the winter encampment and beyond. Elk was the depot for much of what Lee's soldiers collected. It was a vital location for the reception, deposit, storage, and distribution of provisions and other supplies for the army. Although Elk was static, it was a hive of activity. Its warehouses and wharves, and the commissaries, quartermasters, sailing crews, and wagoneers who sought out, purchased, impressed, received, maintained, shipped, and distributed the provisions needed by the army were as much a part of the effort to overcome the fatal crisis of 1778 as was any forager.

When viewed from a strategic perspective, Elk's significance towered in its role as a collection and distribution hub in a much larger and more complex logistical system that foragers and purchasers fed. It was the southernmost magazine in what George Washington termed the "Line of Communication between [the] Delaware [River] and Hudson's River." Elk's importance to the Continental Army grew throughout the 1777 campaign. The collapse of the purchasing commissariat in New England magnified its importance. When George Washington sent Captain Lee into Delaware and Maryland, he reluctantly forbade Brig. Gen. William Smallwood from drawing upon the magazine's stocks, and forced Smallwood's division to rely its own foragers and some less-than-capable purchasing commissaries. Joseph Galloway, the Loyalist superintendent of police in British-occupied Philadelphia, recognized Elk's importance, when he observed that "Washington's supplies in great part were brought from Virginia and North Carolina up the Chesapeak bay, landed at Elk and carried in wagons to Valley Forge."[1]

BEFORE HE LED THE ARMY into winter quarters, Washington had believed that the Eastern Department (New England) would be able to supply it with beef, but due to Congress's reforms, and the consequent turmoil resulting from resignations and appointments of deputies, the department was unable to meet the army's needs. When Congress had adopted new regulations for the commissariat, including reducing commissions and dividing authority, Joseph Trumbull resigned as commissary general. In his place, Congress appointed Trumbull's least experienced deputy, William Buchanan, in August 1777. Buchanan was not up to his new job. Besides his lack of experience in commissary affairs, Buchanan's department was understaffed. Several deputies and assistant deputies had resigned in protest against the reforms, and many of those who remained were either inexperienced or inept. Moreover, Congress required Buchanan to attend its sessions, which meant that he was removed from the army as it maneuvered and fought in one of its most active campaigns. In his stead, Buchanan appointed Ephraim Blaine as deputy commissary general for purchases for the Middle Department. Blaine, in turn, appointed Philadelphia merchant John Chaloner as his assistant. He charged Chaloner with aiding him in his duties, and assuming them when Blaine was away from the army. However confused the situation was in the Middle Department, it was worse in the Eastern Department.[2]

In Congress's reorganization of the commissary general's department, it appointed Jeremiah Wadsworth of Connecticut as deputy commissary general for purchases in the Eastern Department in June 1777, a position he resigned two months later. It then offered the post to Peter Colt, a fellow Connecticut man, but upon receiving his commission Colt wrestled with the "propriety" of accepting it. Colt knew not the regulations, and the large size of the department—Massachusetts, Connecticut, and Rhode Island—gave him pause. After reading the new regulations and reflecting on them, Colt was even less sure about accepting the position. The new regulations, which, among other things, mandated that commissaries purchase cattle on their own credit, with their own funds, or with vouchers, met with resistance from farmers and purchasing agents alike. Payments were slow, Continental scrip was declining in value, Congress had no taxing authority to recall paper money and drive up its value, the states were loath to tax their citizens, and Americans were loath to pay taxes. Many Americans wanted the world, but few were willing to pay the price. Within the department, purchasing commissaries like Henry Champion refused to work under the new regulations and resigned. Colt had written to Buchanan several times since having first received the commission in August, but by October he had yet to hear back from Buchanan. Meanwhile, the purchasing commissariat screeched to a grinding halt in mid-September, and the soldiers suffered for it.[3]

It was not until the first week of November that Colt finally accepted his commission. In the interim, however, Colt's sense of duty had compelled him to assist in purchasing cattle and other provisions in the intervening months, but now that Congress had forwarded $200,000.00 to Colt for purchases he accepted the position. With money in hand, Colt and his deputies improved their ability to purchase much-needed supplies. From the time of Congress's proffered appointment until Colt finally accepted the commission, he had hammered away at Buchanan and anybody else who would listen to him about the restrictive and unworkable regulations laid down by Congress. Yet, even as he mulled over the offer and railed about the difficulties Colt still tried to assist in obtaining cattle and other supplies. In the meantime, Buchanan admitted to Washington that he had been inattentive to Colt's missives. Buchanan was not prepared for his role as commissary general of purchases. The amount of food needed by the army overwhelmed his senses and abilities. The job was simply too much for him. Moreover, he suffered from a lack of records and assistants. With the collapse of purchasing in the Eastern District, the army had to look within Pennsylvania, New Jersey, Delaware, and southward for sustenance, and thus the magazine at Elk assumed a crescive importance.[4]

WHEN THE BRITISH ARMY OCCUPIED ELK on 28 August 1777, it captured a vital base of supply for the Continental Army. The town lay at the head of navigation on the Elk River, the furthest reach that was navigable by shipping. The river was one of the major tributaries that flowed into and helped create the Chesapeake Bay, and was part of the estuarial and riverine transportation network so vital to communications along the Atlantic seaboard. Soundings of the river near the tip of Turkey Point—taken in August and September 1777 by John Hunter, sailing master of H.M.S. *Eagle* (sixty-four guns), flagship of the invasion fleet—indicated depths as great as twenty-four feet (four fathoms), enough for one of the Royal Navy's fifty-gun warships, which drew eighteen feet of water. Upriver, where the British Army landed at Elk Ferry on Oldfield Point, on the right bank, and at Cecil Courthouse on the left, the depths were a still respectable fifteen to sixteen feet, more than enough for the troop transports and escorts. Those soundings, however, suggest that the river was too shallow at Elk to admit any large ocean-going vessels. Indeed, they show the nearest a shallow-draft vessel could approach was about three to four miles downriver, where soundings pointed out depths of twelve feet. Beyond that, the chart points to a river channel that was so silted up that its depth was a mere four feet. Moreover, an island narrowed the approach.[5]

Hunter's soundings did not indicate the real trafficability of the Elk River to its head. The town of Elk had been a busy river port for decades, and continued so into the next century. In September 1781, Elk and other points downriver served as embarkation sites for elements of the Franco-American expedition advancing on Yorktown, Virginia, including some of its artillery. Shipping that tied up at Elk did so at today's Elk Landing near the confluence of Big Elk and Little Elk creeks, which indicates enough depth for at least shallower-draft vessels. As for the town, it sat to the north on higher ground above the lower-lying landing. Besides its convenient access to the Chesapeake Bay and coastal points, Elk's location at narrow and easily crossed portions of the streams, and proximity to roads leading eastward to Wilmington and northeast to Valley Forge, made it an ideal place for a magazine. Before the war, its central location had made it a convenient transit point for goods bound to or from Philadelphia, Baltimore, and New York. Elk was also a short march to Christiana Bridge, at the head of the Christiana River's navigable channel, which flowed into the Delaware River below Wilmington.[6]

Two weeks before the invasion force landed, commissaries reported 65 barrels of beef, 500 of pork, around 1,000 of bacon, another 2,000 of fish, and over 20,000 bushels of corn. Enough provisions remained in the magazines to worry Washington on the day of the British landing. On 25 August 1777, he wrote to John Hancock, president of the Continental Congress, about a "great quantity of Public and private Stores," which he feared would be captured by the British. Besides the foodstuffs there was also an all-important store of salt, vital to preserving food. Rather than allow the enemy to seize it, Washington determined that "Every attempt will be made to save that."[7]

Not all of Washington's worst fears materialized. Commissaries, militiamen, and others had been able to remove nearly all of the army's provisions "from thence, except about Seven thousand Bushels of Corn." As for those, Washington pressed the commissary, Col. Henry Hollingsworth, to remove the remaining corn. As usual, however, the "scarcity of Teams, in proportion to the demand, will render the removal rather tedious." Washington redoubled his efforts, and ordered the quartermaster to send more teams to "expedite the Measure." Ephraim Blaine joined in Washington's call to empty Elk's stores. He urged Zebulon Hollingsworth, Colonel Hollingsworth's younger brother, to "exert your utmost abilities to fetch off from the Neighbourhood of Elk, and the County Adjacent to the Enemys Encampments." Above all else, it was twenty to twenty-five barrels of preserved, salted provisions that needed Hollingsworth's attention. After that, his priorities were corn and then flour.[8]

James Johnston, adjutant of Col. John Hannum's battalion of Chester County, Pennsylvania Militia, recalled that he had "engaged" something like thirty to forty wagons to haul supplies away from Elk. According to Johnston, it took nearly two days to empty five hundred barrels of flour, one hundred of rum, a "great quantity of pork, salt, molasses, and other articles" from the warehouses, and transport them to his father's house and outbuildings in Chester County. William Welsh, who helped "transport considerable quantities of public Provisions," recalled that other stores went to Christiana Bridge by wagon. From there, the stores were transferred to boats, and then shipped to Philadelphia and Wilmington, and Trenton. Yet, their exertions notwithstanding, supplies still remained.[9]

Howe and the main body of his army set off from their initial lodgment around 4:00 A.M. on 28 August, while a smaller force under the command of Lt. Gen. Wilhelm von Knyphausen held back, and then crossed the river, and landed at Cecil Courthouse on 29 August. Knyphausen's command marched northward and rejoined the main army a few days later. As for the main body under Howe, it arrived at Head of Elk around 1:00 P.M. on 28 August, following a "most fatiguing march" of about twelve miles. After several weeks aboard ship, few of the soldiers had regained their stamina and many of the horses had died while in transit. Those horses that had survived were sickly and weak, hence the difficulty of the march. When the army arrived at Elk, Lt. William John Hale, Grenadier Company, Forty-Fifth Regiment of Foot, reckoned that some 1,500 "men were assembled to protect a large quantity of stores" there. The light infantry and grenadier brigades formed up in line of battle, and prepared to attack, but the opposing force "ran away without firing a shot."[10]

Entering the town, the British found a welcome sight in the large quantity of "stores remaining in the Town." Although the commissaries and militia had removed the greater part of the supplies, there still remained "100 butts of Porter . . . in one cellar, Madeira, Rum, Melasses, Tobaco, Yams, Flower, etc." Moreover, the British and Hessians found "a number of Sloops loaded with shoes, stockings, and rum, which had not time to escape." Howe's commissary general, Daniel Wier, estimated that the Americans had left behind enough food to feed the army with fresh provisions for two days, along with three hundred head of cattle of varying weights and six hundred sheep. Carl Levin von Heister, a Hessian cornet and aide-de-camp to Col. Carl Emil Kurt von Donop, estimated as many as "12 single-masted vessels" tied up at this "well-built village," while Capt. John Montresor of the Royal Engineers, counted "fifteen of the rebel sloops and Schooners." William Paca, a Maryland legislator, reported to Gov. Thomas Johnson that besides food and local shipping, the British had "taken above seventy slaves on our Bay side and the River Elk."[11]

After gathering up or destroying what supplies had not been removed by the Continental Army, the invasion force departed on 3 September, but it sent back to Elk the next day "what baggage could possibly be spared by the officers," and then the sick on the seventh for transportation to Philadelphia by sea. Reports confirmed the Britons' and Hessians' rich haul and their destruction of excess supplies. Writing from nearby Johnson's Ferry, to the west on the Susquehanna River, Charles Carroll of Carrollton, one of Maryland's congressional delegates, wrote to his father, Charles Carroll of Annapolis, of the "great waste at the head of Elk." He claimed that the wheat was "knee deep" in the streets, and more of it filled a mill race. Salt had been "scattered in the road," and that Howe's soldiers had destroyed about 400 hogsheads of tobacco. Washington wrote that most of the supplies at Elk, save the grain, had been evacuated. This, Howe's soldiers "either used or destroyed," and they "burnt some" of the vessels that Cornet von Heister had noted. Washington supposed the British "had no use for" them. Some of the destruction was due to Howe's orders, while other incidents were attributable to indiscipline. According to Maj. Charles Stuart of the Forty-Third Regiment of Foot, "A want of firmness in not enforcing orders, and a total relaxation of discipline" had been the hallmarks of the British campaign in America. Less than a week after the landing, Stuart had witnessed and rued the "plundering and irregularity of every kind" by British soldiers.[12]

MARCHING EASTWARD, Howe's troops skirmished at Cooch's Bridge in Delaware. Following the battle of Brandywine on 11 September, the so-called battle of the Clouds five days later, the night attack at Paoli on 20 September, and some inconclusive skirmishing, the British entered Philadelphia on 26 September. Once ensconced there, Elk was little more than a brief memory. In his Parliamentary testimony, Joseph Galloway opined that "Could Sir William Howe have remained a month at Elk or about Newcastle, [Delaware,] the counties from Elk to the [Virginia] Capes, about 200 miles, would in my opinion have risen in arms." Galloway clearly placed too much faith in Loyalism, and exhibited too little knowledge of recent history, British military capabilities, or the sentiments of the people. Howe did not have the forces to hold many strategic points, even if only to deny them to the enemy. As it was, holding New York and Newport had already stretched thin his manpower. Moreover, Howe likely had memories of December 1776 and January 1777, when Washington had struck back at Trenton and Princeton, and had mauled a Hessian brigade and then a British one in turn. The victories had forced the British to collapse the extent of their penetration and surrender most of New Jersey to the Continental Army and New Jersey Militia. After Trenton and Princeton, Howe no longer risked posting isolated forces. It was altogether too great a risk. Hence, Howe could not afford to retain Elk.[13]

Surprisingly, when Howe's army marched out of Elk it left behind quite a few supplies. In early October, Washington had enjoined Henry Hollingsworth to transport the remaining stores "some distance inland." Yet, less than a month after the British marched into Philadelphia, Continental forces reoccupied Elk, and commenced reestablishing it as a magazine. Supplies arrived haltingly as the commissariat and quartermasters adjusted to the new operational environment, wherein they operated in such close proximity to the enemy. Elk, part of a larger supply network, was one of several magazines in the region, each wanting for supplies and the wagons and teams with which to deliver goods to the army. The dispersal of supply sources and magazines mitigated Continental risk by broadly distributing the supply nodes. Thus, it lessened the impact on the army should one magazine fall to the enemy—others would pick up the slack.[14]

By 22 October, Maryland's Council of Safety was directing shipments of "Arms &ca to the Head of Elk." Two months later, on Christmas Day, a commissary, perhaps Ephraim Blaine, reporting on the "State of Supplies" anticipated the delivery of two thousand head of cattle over the next ten days to various magazines, including Elk. The "General return of this day" showed just over five days' rations of salted and preserved beef and pork, but only two days of flour for the army. Nearby, however, a forty days' supply sat in Lancaster, Wright's Ferry, and York, a whopping six thousand barrels averaging "26 Cwt [hundredweight in] each" location. Reality's brutal arithmetic quashed whatever hope there was in the commissary's report. He reported that it would require "250 Teams [of horses or oxen] each carrying 8 Barrels [per wagon] to supply the Troops with flour from the Magazines." Blaine estimated an average travel time of just under two weeks to complete the deliveries, but the trips would likely take longer because of the roads, the rain, and snow. As had been the case for months, the shortage of wagons, teams, and drivers compounded the problem.[15]

Reoccupying Elk was simple. It was little more than a matter of taking physical possession of the place once the British had departed. Reconstituting and rebuilding Elk as a magazine, however, proved more difficult.

Warehouses and mills had to be rebuilt, burnt hulks along Elk Landing had to be removed, provisions had to acquired, payments made, and wagons, drivers, and teams had to be found to transport provisions and other supplies to it and then to the army. Luckily, the physical damage was not too extensive. As had been the case throughout the war, however, systemic failures and shortcomings in the supply and transportation system dogged operations. As was the case throughout the winter, poor weather and "broken Roads" hampered transportation, but, as Washington stressed to Buchanan, it was "indispensibly necessary to form with all possible expedition ample magazines" to sustain the army during the winter, but also to support it in the 1778 campaign season. Throughout the fatal crisis of 1778, Elk magazine's operations represented in fine detail the larger realities of the Continental commissariat's operations in the Middle Department.[16]

There was a lag time between reoccupying Elk and reconstituting its stocks. Some of that delay was due to the transportation network. The roads being what they were, water transport was the most efficient and cost-effective manner to convey supplies from the southern states. Shipping, however, had to wait. V. Adm. Richard Lord Howe's fleet still lay at anchor in the Elk River on 13 September. Finally, the next day, it set sail, but "Progress down the Bay was considerably retarded by the State of the Weather and Intricacy of the Navigation, which did not admit of continuing under Sail during the Night." Howe's ships did not clear Cape Henry and "put to Sea" until nine days later. Once clear of the Virginia Capes, the fleet turned northward toward Delaware Bay, and then sailed upriver toward Philadelphia, where it joined the army in reducing the defenses along the Delaware River (Fort Mifflin on Mud Island, Pennsylvania, Fort Mercer at Red Bank, New Jersey, and Fort Billingsport, in present-day Paulsboro, New Jersey) and removing the iron-tipped *chevaux-de-frise* that lurked under the river's surface. Once the army and navy had cleared the river of its defenses, Howe left a powerful squadron under Capt. Andrew Snape Hamond as he led or sent the bulk of his command northward to New York and to Newport, Rhode Island. Although the British naval presence had lessened, frigates and sloops still cruised the Chesapeake Bay and Atlantic coast to interdict trade. So long as the Royal Navy was about, merchant vessels ran the risk of capture.[17]

Fully aware of the risks of coastal and riverine shipping, but also of the needs of the army, Virginia governor Patrick Henry ordered a galley from the state navy to transport "600 Bushels along the Western Shore to Elk" in January. This was done in conjunction with a Colonel Simpson, whom Henry had ordered to "seize two thousand Bushels Salt on the Eastern Shore &

send it to the Head of Elk for the grand Army." Henry also pressed Maryland governor Thomas Johnson, Jr. to fortify Elk: "otherwise a Barge or two [carrying British landing parties] may Destroy the Stores lodged there." Henry also begged the aid of one of Maryland's state navy galleys to convey supplies to Elk. In Henry's understanding, Elk was so important to the army's survival that its loss might prove "fatal" to the army's existence.[18]

After taking time to digest Henry's letter, Maryland's council replied to the governor and advised caution. The Continental Board of War had earlier proposed that Maryland's galleys might prove helpful in shipping provisions to Elkridge Landing on the Patapsco River, southwest of Baltimore at the head of that river. It was part of a larger congressional resolution for creating a "communication to transport provisions" from North Carolina to Maryland. While the council "had no Objection to risking the Gallies," it perceived more drawbacks than advantages to the "Scheme." Practicalities militated against the scheme. The council cited the expense and the "uncertain" prospect of the vessels' utility. When fully provisioned and "but tolerably manned," the galleys had little space left for stowing much else. Moreover, they drew as much as eight feet of water, a sure hindrance in the upper reaches of the Elk River. Maryland's council, instead, took a more combative stance. Rather than transporting supplies, the two Chesapeake Bay states' galleys would perform a greater service by "keeping this Bay clear or obliging the [Royal Navy's] Ships of War to keep together" by threatening them with attack. By using the galleys for transport, not combat, they became individually vulnerable to British frigates and sloops prowling the Chesapeake Bay. The number of British warships and "their Activity" in the Chesapeake threatened "Communication by Water" and made the prospect of galley transport altogether "too uncertain." Indeed, "in all Probability," the British would quickly discover the army's waterborne line of communication. Threatening and attacking the enemy was a higher priority for the council. Although overstretched, the Royal Navy dominated American waters. It took the French navy to finally challenge British maritime supremacy in American waters in 1779 and beyond. Until then, Britannia ruled American waves.[19]

DESPITE THE MARYLAND COUNCIL'S RELUCTANCE to employ its galleys as transports, commissaries expected a resumption of shipping to Elk. Washington also expected that Elk would receive provisions from the southern states. In early January 1778, he directed commissary and quartermaster officers about the expected arrival and transshipment of "Flour & Bread at Elk and hope[d]" that those much-needed provisions would either "be with the

Army or in the vicinity of it by the time they are wanted." Colonel Blaine, in his efforts to maintain an adequate supply at Elk and other magazines, ordered an assistant, John Lad Howell, to make every effort in forwarding by wagon or vessel to Elk all the provisions that he and Deputy Assistant Commissary of Purchases Thomas Huggins had obtained. To another deputy assistant commissary of purchases, Robert McGarmont ("McGarmant" or "McGermot"), Blaine urged him to "hurry forward all the Stores of Salt Provisions and Indian Meal [ground corn] without one moment loss of time . . . and what stores are Convenient to water Carriage." McGarmont was to get these supplies to the magazine at Elk as quickly as possible. Blaine promised to have wagons waiting to receive the provisions, along with spare barrels for other provisions.[20]

Blaine worked tirelessly in coordinating the efforts at restocking the magazine at Elk. Writing to Col. Henry Emanuel Lutterloh, the deputy quartermaster general serving with the main army, Blaine stressed that the great demand for provisions. He observed that the "principle part of our supplies for the army must come from the Head of Elk & Dover." As supplies arrived, the army tried to draw from them, but could not. The lack of wagons, teams, and drivers prevented the army from drawing provisions. Blaine requested that Lutterloh "may Immediately furnish me with four Brigades of good Waggons for the above purpose." Because of the army's inability to transport great quantities of flour, salted provisions, and other supplies, some inventory categories at Elk had still not reached the levels available in August 1777. Naturally, the stocks were fluid not fixed. They fluctuated according to shipments, droves, and herds that were received and dispatched. Given that Lutterloh was with the army at Valley Forge, he was more than aware of the state of affairs, and equally vexed.[21]

On 14 February, Blaine estimated that Elk held five thousand barrels of flour, two thousand of bread, five hundred of beef and pork, and another three hundred of "Indian Meal." Sixty hogsheads of rum, ten of whiskey, and another ten barrels of rum were on hand, along with six thousand bushels of wheat. Shortages in beef and pork were not too far off from the August inventory. The February 1778 stocks fell only sixty-five barrels short, but as for corn, the difference was a staggering fourteen thousand bushels. It was winter, so that was not unanticipated. In August, the warehouses had held one thousand barrels of bacon, whereas in February the commissaries did not even bother creating a column for it. There was no fish on hand in February 1778, compared to the two thousand barrels in August 1777. It was only in rum and whiskey that February's count exceeded August's. On the

"Estimate of Provisions," Blaine noted that "Large Quantities of Provisions [were] expected from the Southward, to the Head of Elk." No matter how large those shipments, there was no way to make up the shortfall when compared to the count in August without adequate transportation. Poorly-stocked larders or not, there was a "great Scarcity of waggons in Camp" at Valley Forge, not more than eight. No matter how well stocked was Elk, nobody would eat without the wagons to bring provisions to camp.[22]

AS THE PAINFULLY SLOW RECONSTITUTION of Elk proceeded, Buchanan suggested to Blaine on 15 January, that he consider establishing a magazine at Octorara, Pennsylvania, to serve as a collection site for supplies shipped to Rock Run, Maryland, and "other Landings, Charles Town and the Head of Elk." Octorara, located near Oxford, would put the new magazine about fourteen miles northwest of Elk, while Rock Run, on the left bank of the Susquehanna River, might enable deeper-draft vessels with larger shipments to deposit their cargoes and increase the stocks of provisions. Blaine mulled over his chief's recommendations and took them to heart. Sometime in February, he set off from Valley Forge to reconnoiter potential sites for magazines and port facilities and began riding toward Baltimore. Besides examining those locations, the ride southward would enable Blaine to assess the quantity and availability of provisions in the "Southern parts of my District." Blaine's itinerary, expectations, and observations point to his anticipation for renewed, even increased shipping—the Royal Navy notwithstanding. Americans had been practiced smugglers before declaring independence in 1776, so history may have buoyed Blaine's hopes for Americans avoiding British warships. Like Buchanan, Blaine's criteria touched upon a multitude of concerns, including the state and availability of port facilities, magazine sites' proximity to roads, sources of supply, the nature, quantity, quality, and availability of supplies, and proximity to the enemy.[23]

Blaine first scouted locations near the Chesapeake's head of navigation within Maryland, but after he arrived at the "Head of Elke . . . , [he] thought it prudent to look out if a place more remote, and secure from the Enemy, could not be found upon the Head of Chesepeak Bay." Colonel Blaine surely recalled that Elk was where the British Army had landed in August 1777. Its vulnerability to British seapower was well established, but that was a risk that could not be avoided at any river port in the Chesapeake basin. Journeying westward to the Susquehanna River, Blaine first stopped at "Johnstons Ferry," also known as Rock Run, but is today Port Deposit. Blaine discovered "no conveniency of Wharfe or Store Houses." The town sat at the foot of a range of hills, some with nearly vertical faces, and heights ranging over 200 feet. The post road, which ran to the ferry through a draw, gave the site access to larger magazines. Despite the river channel and road access, Johnson's Ferry would not do for receiving shipping. Across the river, "Opposite [Johnson's Ferry] at one Smiths, there is three Stores, but no Mills Convenient." Smith's lack of mills for grinding wheat into flour made Blaine drop it from consideration.[24]

Undeterred, Blaine made his way to today's Havre de Grace, then known as "Stephens or Harrisons Ferry," on the western bank, at the confluence of Susquehanna River and the Chesapeake Bay. Blaine noted that "large Ships may lay Opposite," which would enable deeper-draft, ocean-going vessels to approach the landing, but it too lacked warehouses to store offloaded goods and provisions. Smith's Ferry and Stephen's or Harrison's Ferry were also problematic because of their locations on the Susquehanna's right bank. Any goods landed at either of those two sites would have to be ferried across the river, adding to another delay in the movement of provisions. Turning eastward in his reporting, Blaine focused on Charlestown. Located on a post road on the western bank of the North East River, and situated on gently rolling terrain, Charlestown was more easily accessed by wagon traffic. There, Blaine found a "large building & Wharfe, [and] there I have Appointed a Person to receive such Stores as may be directed to his care." Charlestown's "Wharfe," built in the 1740s, was three hundred feet long, enough to accommodate six vessels at once, and wide enough to allow three wagons passage. The "large" warehouse boasted walls thirty-six inches thick, it stood three stories high, and was eighty feet long. Shipping approaches to the port were straight and open, unlike the narrow, twisting course of the upper Elk River approaches. Soundings taken in 1776 indicated that the North East River's depths ran from five to eighteen feet, with nine feet predominating. Across the North East River on Turkey Point, Blaine found the town of "North East . . . a poor & inconvenient Place, no Wharfe or Stores of any kind."[25]

Charlestown was clearly Blaine's port of choice. Because of the North East River's deeper channel and easier approaches, Charlestown was an improvement on Elk, which could not receive larger vessels. Yet, the shipping channel's shallow depth limited the size of vessels and, therefore, their carrying capacity. The average tonnage of a British transport during the war was 303 tons burden (sometimes expressed as burthen), which suggests a draft in excess of nine feet. In the mid-1740s, most of the vessels sailing the Chesapeake had ranged from twenty to two-hundred and fifty tons, with smaller schooners and sloops (most ranging from twenty to fifty tons) predominating in

Maryland's trade. Without significant channel dredging, the size of vessels sailing in these waters likely continued into the 1770s. Moreover, with a tidal rise and fall range of one foot in the upper Chesapeake Bay and up to three feet in the lower bay, nothing but coastal craft could tie up at Charlestown. Even so, the addition of a nearby port facility supplemented Elk's capacity for receiving and distributing supplies to the army. As such, Charlestown joined a regional supply network that included Elk, which in turn was part of the even larger system that connected the Continental Army with the American and European sources of supply that sustained the fight.[26]

Blaine closed his letter with a recommendation that Oxford Meeting House, close by Buchanan's earlier recommended site of Octorara, Pennsylvania, be used as "as a proper place to remove the Stores to as they arrive at Elke & Charlestown." Moreover, Blaine's observations on the cattle collected by "Capt. Lee and some of my people," and on the wheat and flour "in this neck or Penensula" reinforced the decision in his mind. Oxford, which was about fourteen miles equidistant from both Elk and Charlestown, and from there another forty miles to Valley Forge, recommended itself to Blaine as a good place to consolidate supplies before moving them on to camp. On the one hand, this made sense. By consolidating shipments, wagon brigades could more efficiently transport a greater number of goods in fewer wagons. On the other hand, however, it added another layer to an already creaky and struggling system. More commissary and quartermaster personnel would need to maintain Oxford, and Continental soldiers or militiamen would need to guard the stores and provide security against British and marauders' threats. This, of course, was "provided your Excellency approves of the same." Washington met the suggestion with silence, and there the decision on Oxford remained.[27]

BLAINE'S REPORT NEXT SHIFTED to his assessments of cattle, wheat, and flour. As for cattle, he reported that both Lee's soldiers and some of his own men had "collected a considerable number" of them. On the whole he deemed them rather typical for the area. Northeast Maryland and northern Delaware had quite a few head of cattle, but Blaine found they were small compared to other specimens he had seen. Clearly, he had not observed the much larger head of cattle that Captain Lee had seen. Rather than forwarding these small creatures to the army, Blaine suggested taking "advantage of the Marsh Pasture in the Spring which would make them early Beef." This, however, depended on the degree of "danger from the Enemy." Although Brigadier General Smallwood's two-brigade post at Wilmington provided a measure of security to the east, the enemy did not enter into this calculation. With the army's pressing need for meat, it had not the luxury of fattening the cattle into "early Beef." Small cattle would have to suffice. Soldiers had to eat.[28]

Wheat, that other necessary commodity, existed in "great Quantities . . . in this neck or Penensula." So much so, that Blaine assured Washington to "make not the least doubt, but [there is a] sufficient [amount] to maintain your Excellencys Army one Year," an astounding piece of news. Fifteen miles south of New Castle, Delaware, at Cantwell's Bridge, Blaine discovered large stores of wheat and flour. He estimated it "near Ten Thousand Bushels wheat & Two hundred & fifty Barrels of Flour." When Blaine questioned local inhabitants about the stores, they informed him that the stockpiles had been in place since the summer of 1777, and that there were even more "large parcels in sundry other places." Astonishingly, Blaine announced, "some Farmers have Two Years Crops in Stacks."[29]

Near the head of the Sassafras River, Blaine took note of more stocks of wheat held by business partners Samuel Canby and Thomas Stephens. Blaine counted "Five Hundred Barrels Flour, a Number of Empty Barrels, & three thousand Bushells of Wheat" in storage. The mill, likely located near Georgetown, Maryland, on the southern bank of the Sassafras, was about seventeen miles west of the Delaware River and the Royal Navy. In an interesting turn of events, a week before Blaine reported the news of Canby's and Stephens's stores, Brigadier General Smallwood had written to Washington with information about "one Canby's having contracted [to deliver] 1000 Barrells of Flour" to the British Army. Smallwood had earlier informed Washington that Canby was in Philadelphia, and that the delivery was to take place somewhere on the Delaware River. In response, Smallwood ordered some of his soldiers to seize the flour, which Washington approved, for he had "not the smallest doubt from your information, but it was designed for the Enemy." Naturally, Washington wanted Smallwood to note the quantity and quality of the flour seized.[30]

The stocks of flour seized by Smallwood's soldiers were likely part of the same store of wheat and flour identified by Blaine. If so, Canby and Stephens had a surfeit of provisions desperately needed by the army. On 1 March, Blaine instructed John Ladd Howell to proceed to "Canby & Stephens mill upon the Head of Sassafrass River," where he would find hundreds of barrels filled with flour and many more barrels waiting to be filled. Blaine instructed Howell to instruct Stephens to continue grinding wheat, "for which he shall be properly satisfied." All of the flour was to be shipped to Charlestown, "to the care of Mr. Patrick Hamilton," who was likely the "Person"

Imogen Robinson, *The Provision Train*. Anne S. K. Brown Military Collection, Brown University Library.

Blaine had appointed to receive shipping on behalf of the army. Once in Charlestown, it was a matter of getting the flour to the army. Blaine ordered Howell to "seize all Waggons which are passing and repassing with private property and load them all to Camp," bypassing the magazine at Elk.[31]

As always, transporting provisions or any other supplies to the army came down to wagons. Blaine requested that Washington send every spare wagon from camp to retrieve the stores. He assured the general that Howell would "stay at Middletown & direct the loading of them." Clearly, Blaine expected much of Howell's talents and energies. In closing, Blaine informed Washington that he had done everything possible to transport "Salt Provisions" to camp, and that "Mr McGarmont of this Place has been exceeding industrious, & procured a considerable Quantity of Pork." Once Blaine arrived in Baltimore, he promised to send Washington a full report on expected provisions from the "Southern parts" of the district.[32]

The fact that the Continental Army could have marched, maneuvered, fought, or even existed in such close proximity to such rich stocks of food since the summer of 1777, yet not discover them, attests not to farmers' or millers' skills at secreting their goods or deceiving the army, but to the operational environment and the army's limitations. Indeed, it said as much about the British Army's constraints. As Washington and his soldiers discovered, the region was rife with people who wanted to be left alone and at peace. These so-called disaffected people wanted nothing to do with either of the armies or with the war. Many of them had sequestered their goods, but this had not stopped foragers from ferreting out and exploiting some of their farms' and storehouses' bounty. No matter how active the foragers, however, it was impossible to uncover provisions and other necessary goods without adequate intelligence about the area. The poor intelligence picture spoke directly to the army's limitations in this arena.[33]

With four understrength and poorly-mounted regiments of light dragoons, the Continental Army did not have a large cavalry force. Moreover, some regiments had been dispersed across the Delaware River to New Jersey to show the army's presence and lessen the need for supplies at Valley Forge, while others patrolled the lands between the encampment and the British Army in Philadelphia. Traditionally, the cavalry was the arm most often charged with reconnoitering areas and the enemy, and assisting the commander in developing his understanding of the operational environment. Because of the expenses associated with horses, their feed and care, the equipping and training of cavalrymen, but also the often wooded and rugged terrain of tidewater and piedmont North America, there was no tradition and little understanding of how best to employ mounted forces. A fuller understanding of cavalry operations developed, but that was in the offing. Therefore, with only a handful of light dragoons, and a poorly-developed grasp of the region's fuller picture, foragers regularly relied upon local guides familiar with the countryside.

In relying on local guides, the army's commissaries and foragers entrusted the success of their operations to the guides' knowledge, honesty, and commitment to the cause of independence. In other cases, such as Blaine's reconnaissance, commissaries relied upon their own initiative, energy, and local knowledge, or that of their deputies. Most of them had been merchants before the war, and were familiar with the districts in which they served and the farmers, merchants, and others with whom they had done business. In their previous lives, supply officers had cultivated networks of personal and commercial relationships, which they now relied upon as purchasing commissaries. Intelligent and industrious commissaries exploited these elements as they did their best to provision Elk so that it in turn might provision the army.

WHILE MOST COMMISSARIES were active and diligent, others left much to be desired. One in particular, Thomas Huggins, stood out for his singular ability to regularly fall short in performing his duties and to raise the ire of his superiors and others. Huggins was not alone in fumbling in his duties or antagonizing people, although he did stand out for a time. Indeed, others such as Deputy Quartermaster General Robert Lettis Hooper in Pennsylvania, could also be notoriously difficult individuals, but Huggins's tale is suggestive of the commissariat's larger difficulties, albeit on an individual scale. More important, Huggins's story brings to the fore the importance of individuals within a larger system. Granted, the system that Congress had established to keep a check on power and corruption within the commissariat and the quartermaster general's departments worked against efficiency, yet even in modern, professional military forces, individuals make the difference in the conduct all military operations. Try as they might, modern doctrine and organizational theory will never account for, control, or eliminate personalities or unit cultures.[34]

The Ulster-born Huggins immigrated to Maryland sometime in 1772. Despite his short residency in Elk, he had impressed local business and political leaders enough to be appointed quartermaster of the Elk Battalion of Cecil County, Maryland Militia under the command of Col. Charles Rumsey, the county lieutenant, in January 1776. Lt. Col. Henry Hollingsworth was second-in-command. Huggins soon received an appointment as a deputy assistant commissary of purchases in the Middle District. This notwithstanding, Huggins was not well-enough versed in commercial affairs, nor did he have the extensive or intimate network of business contacts needed by purchasers. By the time of the Philadelphia Campaign, it had become manifestly apparent that Huggins also lacked other qualities necessary for his position, and was making a name for himself through the notable underperformance of his duties. On 15 October, just four days after the battle of Brandywine, Ephraim Blaine took Huggins to task for having failed to "wait upon Mr. Chaloner" when he had been in the "Neighbourhood of Camp," while Blaine was absent on other business. He reproached Huggins for having "been exceedingly neglectful as a purchaser for the Army," and in case Huggins failed to understand, Blaine told him that his performance in providing "our Supplys" was "Slack." Blaine directed Huggins to immediately "bring forward, all the Beef Cattle" he had purchased. He expected Huggins to deliver two hundred head of "good Beef" to camp by 20 or 21 October. Huggins delivered 198 head on the 21 October, not far below Blaine's expectations, and not enough of a shortfall to earn another reprimand.[35]

After having won a few weeks' reprieve for competent behavior, Huggins yet again incurred Blaine's wrath. On 18 November, little less than a month after he had delivered his herd of cattle to camp, Huggins sent 450 head of cattle, a shortfall of 750, and of barely acceptable quality in Blaine's eyes. Besides the problem with the cattle, Blaine was "much surprised" that Huggins wrote to him about salt. Blaine had given Huggins "special Orders to seize all within the limits of your district, especially from those persons who are known to be forestallers [who purchased supplies, created shortages, and drove up prices for their own profit] and Monopolizers." Do not, he enjoined Huggins let "one Bushell escape you." Blaine also expected Huggins to "salt up one Thousand Barrels of Beef and pork," and to keep an eye out for wheat and flour. Because mid-November was a bit late (early autumn was the time for slaughtering and preserving meat) there was no time to spare. Blaine's scolding was mild, but the message was still clear. Huggins needed to be more exacting and attentive in his duties. Unfortunately for Huggins, the clarity escaped him. The following month, Huggins managed to earn the ire of yet another commissary, Blaine's deputy John Chaloner. When Chaloner wrote Huggins, he admonished him for his sloppy record keeping. "Your method of doing business," Chaloner wrote on 29 December, "without invoice of Even a Memorandum of quantity or quality is by no means Excusable." Chaloner insisted that Huggins "must employ proper persons to Assist you and enable you to do business with method & propriety." Sloppy bookkeeping aside, it had been "A Long time since" Huggins had sent forward any supplies or cattle. Chaloner "flatter[ed]" himself by imagining that Huggins had sent some forward. In closing, Chaloner told the wayward purchaser that "If I am disappointed in this I shall be exceedingly unhappy."[36]

Corrected once more, Huggins's performance seemed to improve. Although the inattentive commissary had written to Chaloner "Complaining of the difficulty of procuring Waggons to forward Bread and Flour," he told Chaloner to expect "250 head" of cattle by 6 January. Chaloner urged Huggins to "Apply to the Governor and Council and Request their Assistance" in obtaining supplies. Things were looking up for Huggins, although Chaloner raged to Buchanan about Maryland's "Governor and Council" having called upon him to explain his having taken "Cattle from the Damn Quacker Torys." Most of the cattle, according to Chaloner were "in the hands of a disaffected" portion of the population. Chaloner was not alone in attracting the council's attention. Just as Huggins was emerging from his long-accustomed shadow of opprobrium, he stepped back into it, and widened his circle of offense, but in this instance, he was not alone.[37]

Only eight days into the new year, Maryland's council wrote to William Buchanan to register its concern about the conduct of the purchasing commissaries and their use of "Oppression or useless Violence" when they resorted to the "pressing Necessity for seizing Salt and Provisions within this State." The council claimed that it had not been informed of Congress's December resolution approving impressment, and then went on to accuse Ephraim Blaine of having "suppose[d] himself empowered to seize Salt imported into the Inlets or Stock in Somerset or Worcester County," in Maryland, and Blaine's having "left Mr McGerment at full Liberty, nay, to [have] require[d] him to seize all Salt imported there and all Cattle" without properly justifying the "Seizure of Property" or compensating owners for their losses. The council then turned to the matter of Huggins's "Unnecessary & wanton Violence, as stated to us, on Oath . . . on the Person and Property of [Englehard or Engelhard] Yeiser, of Baltimore Town."[38]

On 19 December, Col. Charles Rumsey wrote to the Maryland Council of Safety about Huggins's latest outrage. Yeiser, who had supplied the Maryland Militia with cattle and other provisions, "exhibited to us a Complaint, on Oath" sworn against Huggins ("Higgins") for "his forcibly and riotously seizing and putting him under a Guard by Violence with armed Men and taking from his Servants a Number of Cattle as they were driving to Baltimore." Huggins's behavior incensed Rumsey, who requested that the council deliver Huggins, "with a Guard, if necessary," to appear before him. Rumsey's letter on behalf of Yeiser had prompted the council to write to Buchanan in early January. The matter may have been more complex than Rumsey thought or Yeiser admitted. In writing to Buchanan, the council implied that Huggins's attack on Yesier resulted from a dispute over payments, whether payments had been made in gold or the "Paper currency of the States." As a result, "Huggins was obliged to appear before governor; [whereas] orders of [the] Commissary General prevent[ed] Yeiser from appearing." However the council settled the matter, Huggins returned to his duties, only to enlarge his circle of detractors, and attract unwanted attention from ever greater personages.[39]

In a letter dated 26 January 1778, Brigadier General Smallwood noted Huggins's indifferent performance of his duties. Soldiers, he claimed, had been "stinted 5 Days owing to Mr Huggins's inattention, who has really in many Instances been tardy, & subjected me to take upon me his Duty" as a commissary officer. While general officers of the Continental Army were far less removed from the daily workings, details, and minutia of their commands than their present-day counterparts, the fact that Smallwood felt compelled to act as his own purchasing agent points to the strains on the army's supply system, the inability or incapacity of some supply officers in performing their duties, and, no doubt, to Smallwood's great frustration. As if writing in tandem, George Read, president of Delaware, echoed Smallwood's complaint at length, noting that commissaries' shortcomings in general had forced Smallwood to spend an inordinate amount of time "supplying the defect of duty in others, particularly in the Commissary of Purchases Department, of which I believe he has great reason to Complain." Read "particularly allude[d]" to Thomas Huggins. Smallwood's interest in Huggins was due to Washington having instructed Smallwood not to draw from the magazine at Elk, as its stores were now dedicated to the main army at Valley Forge. Without Elk to sustain Smallwood's division, he relied more than ever on Huggins and his own foragers to feed his soldiers, and upon Huggins's trust among suppliers.[40]

Delaware's president noted that Continental "Credit among the Graziers was very low long before General Smallwood came to Wilmington; his Certificates, [and because of that] his Mode of pay, may be purchased at A considerable discount." Sadly, Read found, "this is such A discouragement that A great part of the Supplies lately are got by Stealth or Force—and it is the more so as A Mr McGarmont in the Neighbouring County of Kent, acting in the same line, pays regularly for the like Articles within his district." Huggins's presumably dilatory payments or the perceived meanness of them when compared to McGarmont's in neighboring Kent County point to Huggins's lack of credit among sellers, cash, the failure or inability to enforce uniform purchasing guidelines, the force of market pressures, or some combination thereof. No matter the reason, "the number of our Graziers," wrote Read, "will be greatly diminished in the ensuing Season as well from the Situation of many of our feeding Grounds, on the Shore of the Delaware, as the irregular Conduct of the purchasing Commissary and his Agents."[41]

Smallwood, yet again in great frustration, wrote to Washington that there "had [been] no other Supplies for the Troops here [other] than what I've had brought in by [foraging] Parties" and from "Prizes & Cattle intercepted on the way to Phila. except 27 head from Maryland." General Smallwood noted that of the twenty-seven head of cattle from Maryland, an unnumbered, but assuredly inadequate quantity, had been obtained by Huggins, "who was to have supplied us." He deemed that "scarce that number in the whole" was from Huggins and added that "there is no dependence in this Man." Giving vent to his frustration, Smallwood thundered to Washington that he had "repeatedly complaind of, & sent for & remonstated to him [Huggins], about the Sufferings of the Troops & his inactivity & inattention, but" it proved "all in vain." The brigadier general feared that if there were "no other dependance than on him, the worst consequences may be dreaded." In Huggins's stead, Smallwood proposed Capt. Jonathan Rumford, Jr., of the Delaware Militia, "an Active obliging Man" experienced in purchasing and with the promise of providing well for the army "if he was appointed to act & supplied with Cash."[42]

If not as near the source of complaint as Read or as involved in the commissariat's quotidian aspects as Smallwood, Washington was, nonetheless, deeply engaged as he took steps to "remedy [the evils] complained of" by Read and Smallwood. Washington assured Read that "orders shall be given" to Huggins's superiors. To Smallwood, Washington acknowledged that the "conduct of Mr Huggins has been much complained of," and that he had spoken to Colonel Blaine about Huggins's conduct. Blaine, who was "about Wilmington or the Head of Elk," was therefore aware of the complaints against Huggins, and likely none too pleased. Washington's patience was at an end. "I wish you to represent to him [Huggins] his conduct again," he informed Smallwood, "and get him removed" from the commissariat "If he neglects" to reform himself. Should matters come to that, Smallwood was to "appoint Captn Rumford to act in that line, and I'll direct Colo. Blaine to supply him with money."[43]

Washington's intervention through Smallwood and Blaine seemed to have worked the desired effect, although the matter ought not have gotten that far up the chain of command. On 10 February, Blaine wrote Huggins in great detail about his latest round of shoddy work. Huggins had neglected to forward provisions to Smallwood's division, "which you Assured me you had done before you left home." To what should not have any great surprise, the day after Huggins returned to Elk "complaints from the General [Smallwood] to his Excellency came to camp informing him that his people had been without meat two days." Naturally, there were other supplies that Huggins had neglected to transport to Smallwood, including "forty five head of beef Cattle." Expressing his barely restrained indignation and deep disappointment in Huggins, Blaine wrote that "such conduct and Neglect is [un]pardonable in persons who are appointed to purchase for and feed the army." Moreover, Blaine deemed Huggins "guilty of Neglect of Duty." In the future, Blaine "insist[ed] upon your [Huggins's] complyance with instructions from time to time." Smallwood's reproach, if there was one, was likely fiercer. In a letter to Capt. Allen McLane, he asked the captain to pass on his respects to Robert McGarmont, and to "tell him that chucklehead Scoundrel

Huggins will starve the Troops here—without he can forward Supplies to us now & hereafter."[44]

Following Blaine's upbraiding, Huggins's performance improved. Instead of complaints, reports noted what supplies Huggins had collected and his difficulty in acquiring wagons to transport the supplies to camp. Writing from Elk on 5 March, Howell informed Chaloner that Huggins had an impressive store of provisions, "26800 [pounds of?] Cod Fish," eighty barrels of beef, 150 of bread, 532 pounds of bacon, twenty hogsheads of "Rum from Baltimore & 2 Hhds Rum & one hhd Molasses purchased here." All he needed was wagons to get them to camp. Blaine also happily noted that "on my Arrival here I find Mr. Huggins has sent one hundred & sixty [head of cattle] off to Genl. Smallwood at Wilmington, the others with some he had before to the amount of about sixty are at feed in this Neighbourhood." By 26 March, Howell reported that Huggins had "engaged Waggons sufficient to remove all Stores" from Elk, which numbered "from 1500 to 2000 bls Bread & a large Qty. Rum, under his care in the course of this & next week. I am very glad of it." Huggins's inexperience, ignorance, ineptitude, indifferent performance, and violent temper were not the cause of the army's distress, nor even that of Smallwood's division. He was, however, emblematic of the larger systemic and organizational problems that hindered the supply system, and of one individual's impact on a debilitatingly inefficient system of supply. Huggins made a bad system worse, yet through experience, and frequent reproaches and perhaps coaching he finally seemed to have learned. By the spring of 1778, he no longer harmed Continental soldiers through his poor performance, but instead had become an active and energetic commissary agent. Huggins remained with the commissary general's department through at least May 1778, as the army prepared to march out of Valley Forge.[45]

COMMISSARIES AND FORAGERS reconstituted Elk and forwarded supplies even as they struggled against the administrative, physical, and other constraints that militated against them. Fresh meat, particularly beef, and flour were always in want, but as the seasons turned, the weather warmed, and roads improved, more supplies poured in, and the army was momentarily well-enough fed to enter the spring campaign season. The reality, however, was that the Congress and the commissariat in Delaware and Maryland failed the soldiers. As had been the case throughout the war, larger political and economic forces were at play. The same issues of political loyalties, weak Continental and state governments, near-worthless Continental scrip, a disorganized and malfunctioning commissariat, and the powerful inducement of British coin militated against the soldiery. Without an energetic, central government bolstered by popular support, delegates able to shake off some of their suspicions about centralized authority, and states willing to sacrifice some of their autonomy, there was little that could be done to reform the system and supply the soldiers their needs. It would time for those measures of trust to develop.

CONCLUSION

Making a Grand Forage

Small it may have been, but the Grand Forage of 1778 was great in its results. It contributed to the Continental Army's continued survival until the spring, the army's continued support of Continental and state authority, and its continued challenge to British authority. Moreover, the planning and execution intimated greater developments within the army's leadership, even as it struggled with a ramshackle logistical system that threatened the army's ruin on a regular basis.

Over fifteen hundred Continentals, militiamen, members of the commissariat and quartermaster general's offices, free and enslaved wagoneers, and others had foraged, driven, and transported the provisions and other supplies so vital to the survival of the main army encamped at Valley Forge. Foraging columns and purchasing agents had ranged across hundreds of square miles in southeast Pennsylvania, southern New Jersey, northern and central Delaware, and northeast Maryland in search of cattle, sheep, swine, wheat, flour, and more. The marching columns under Maj. Gen. Nathanael Greene and Brig. Gen. Anthony Wayne had skirmished with enemy forces in the process. They, and Capt. Henry Lee's light dragoons had encountered scores of civilians whose sympathies ran from active and enthusiastic support for the revolutionary regime to sullenness and open hostility to the cause of independence and overt loyalty to the crown. They had confronted people who simply wanted to be left at peace, the so-called disaffected who wanted nothing to do with the war. Throughout their foraging, Greene's, Wayne's, and Lee's soldiers had also come into close contact with the ethnic, religious, racial, and geographic diversity of the region and the complex military, political, and climatic conditions that all of those elements created as the foragers sought out the provisions and supplies so badly needed by the army.

The Grand Forage of 1778 was as much an act of desperation as it was a demonstration of George Washington's fortitude and strategic prescience. Washington faced a stark, unpromising, and uncompromising gamut of possibilities in February 1778. Without provisions, his best choice was dispersal somewhere into Pennsylvania's backcountry, beyond the reach of the British Army, and beyond its competing foragers. Feeding the army would become an easier task, but retiring westward would also cede control of southeast Pennsylvania to the enemy and completely undercut any pretenses to an independent American government. Moreover, it raised the specter of emboldened Loyalists rushing to the king's standard in defense of the crown.

As bad as dispersal was, an even worse possibility threatened: mutiny. Mutinies ranged from protests and the refusal by soldiers to perform their duties up through the overthrow of officers and violence against them. Generally, however, work stoppages and the refusal to obey orders or perform duties characterized most eighteenth-century mutinies. Arrears or stoppages in pay, the failure by the army to provide food, clothing, or other essentials in a timely manner or as guaranteed in enlistment contracts, the perceived or real violations of terms set forth in enlistments, or abusive treatment by superiors generally lay at the heart of soldiers' insubordination and the assertion of their claimed rights as soldiers, subjects, or citizens. Faced with these two extremes, Washington chose a third option. Determined to hold Valley Forge, challenge the British Army in Philadelphia, and uphold the revolutionary regimes of the Continental Congress and Pennsylvania, he launched the Grand Forage. It was a desperate act that ultimately succeeded and demonstrated Washington's burgeoning talents and those of many of his subordinate commanders and staff, even as it cast a pall over his opponent's performance, Gen. Sir William Howe, and some of his subordinate and associated commanders.[1]

WASHINGTON'S DEVELOPMENT AND PERFORMANCE as a tactician and strategist was a study in consistent if uneven growth and maturation. He was aggressive, but he learned how to exercise patience and tremendous restraint, and balanced risk against opportunity, as he had shown in the weeks following the standoff at Whitemarsh in December 1777. Rather than wage a winter campaign, as urged by some of the generals and a congressional delegation, he opted for winter quarters at Valley Forge. In the process, he squared the circle of civil-military relations and the competing and often contradictory needs of civil and military necessities. Tactically, however, Washington still favored complex plans that sometimes went awry and resulted in setbacks. In his attack against the Hessian outpost at Trenton in December 1776, a storm and ice floes on the Delaware River had prevented one of his three columns from crossing the river. Nonetheless, the attack was a success. At Germantown in October 1777, darkness, fog, fratricide resulting from Continental soldiers mistakenly firing on fellow Continentals, devoting too much effort against British defenders at Cliveden (Chew House), and a vigorous British counterattack combined to foil whatever success might have come to the attack. In later actions, such as Monmouth Courthouse in June 1778 and the Siege of Yorktown from September through October 1781, Washington proved himself a capable, if not brilliant tactical commander. Indeed, as late as the summer of 1781 he wanted to attack the British stronghold of New York City.

While Washington's tactical acumen often left much to be desired, it was in the strategic realm, his ability to select talented commanders, and his knack for getting the best out of average or even wanting officers that he showed his real mettle. Moreover, he was willing to forgive or overlook mistakes and serious misjudgments that might otherwise have cast an officer's reputation into shadows and his career into oblivion. His own probity notwithstanding, Washington could overlook the foibles of talented and trusted officers. He understood that the preservation of the Continental Army was one of the crucial elements for the success of the American cause — independence. It formed the disciplined, armed mainstay of resistance against British rule, and was a core around which the states' militias could mobilize. As an army in being, the Continental Army challenged British pretenses to authority. So long as the army existed, it functioned as both the proxy and safeguard of Continental authority. In the case of the Valley Forge encampment, it did as much for Pennsylvania's government. Thus, the Grand Forage of 1778, while wholly tactical in its execution, was thoroughly strategic in its conception and intentions.[2]

By sustaining the army at Valley Forge, the foragers' localized acts of impressment enabled the army to continue challenging British arms in and around Philadelphia. Valley Forge was an active post that hosted a combative field army, not a static quiescent garrison. Washington had grasped the nettle. He clearly understood the consequences of the foragers' smaller actions and the advantages to be wrought from them. Necessity and the anticipated advantages were worth the risk of sending over 1,200 soldiers beyond the protection of Valley Forge. Washington's actions, from his decision to enter to winter quarters at Valley Forge, maintaining the army's position there, continually challenging the British occupation, and launching the Grand Forage were the clearest expositions of military strategy in service to politics.

When Washington issued his orders to Maj. Gen. Nathanael Greene, Brig. Gen. Anthony Wayne, and later to Capt. Henry Lee, he gave them broad guidance, and did not tie their hands with overly detailed directions. This was as much an indication of his trust and confidence in Greene and

Lee as it was a recognition that he could not possibly mandate tactical actions from a distance. Time, space, and the nature of eighteenth-century communications limited Washington's ability to exercise much more than limited control. Hence, trust and confidence in subordinates was a cornerstone in Washington's exercise of command. Moreover, the autonomy he granted to trusted, talented commanders helped develop them for future commands and greater responsibilities. More immediately, however, with the foragers operating at a distance of twenty, thirty, or more miles from camp, trust and confidence were paramount, and Washington chose well.

FROM THE EARLIEST DAYS of the war, Washington had come to recognize and rely on Greene's abilities. Together, they had both matured into their responsibilities as general officers and were still developing during the Philadelphia Campaign and afterward. Washington respected the Greene's maturing judgment, despite some early missteps. His most serious error in judgment had been his convincing the commander-in-chief to defend Fort Washington in 1776 as the Continental Army withdrew from Manhattan following several losses against the British Army. Greene believed that the fort could be held, but also that the defenders could easily be ferried across the Hudson River to New Jersey. When Fort Washington fell to an assault by British and Hessian forces on 16 November 1776, nearly 3,000 American soldiers entered captivity on British prison hulks moored in New York Harbor. The disaster mortified Greene and stunned Washington, yet the Virginian maintained his faith in him. The disaster at Fort Washington was an expensive one that the Continental Army could ill afford to pay.[3]

Yet, Washington overlooked Greene's errors in judgement, as well his own, understanding that the army and its officers were learning their new trade under the most trying of circumstances—combat. Early on, Washington had perceived a steadiness and latent talent in the man, and over the years, Greene repaid Washington's trust more than amply. While foraging, Greene kept up a steady correspondence with him. He informed Washington of his intentions, the disposition of his forces, and the state of affairs and offerings of Chester County. Notified by Lee about Chester County's potential for foraging, Greene was not at all sanguine about his command's prospects. Nonetheless, he dutifully accepted the charge, and dove into it with his customary energy. Like Washington, Greene trusted his subordinate commanders' judgment, and gave them orders similar to those Washington had issued to him. Greene specified the mission and geographic locale but left the detailed execution to the officers in charge. As was the case with

Washington, the limitations imposed by distance, but also the nature of command within the Continental Army dictated that Greene could do no less for his subordinates.

The bounty of the lands targeted by the foragers was as varied as their peoples. All held cattle, swine, sheep, wheat, horses, and other supplies. Their chief distinction, however, was in the quantities available for foragers. Both armies had exploited Chester County from the earliest days of the British campaign for Philadelphia; thus its offerings were less than in nearby New Jersey, Delaware, or Maryland, and demanded all the more effort and skill at ferreting out sequestered supplies. The closer the proximity to Philadelphia, the greater the chances that foraging parties had exploited the most easily discovered holdings. Because of this situation, the foragers in Greene's column had to act with great diligence and imagination. Circumstances forced them to employ harsh measures such as the outright seizure of property without any promise of compensation, and physical coercion to halt the transportation of supplies into Philadelphia. As Greene, the apostate Quaker, noted to Washington on 15 February 1778, he had heard "The Inhabitants cry out and beset me from all quarters, but like Pharoh I harden my heart."[4]

Greene's soldiers scoured Chester County from as far south as Derby, to as far west as the branches of Brandywine Creek. An infantry force, the column lacked the superior mobility, speed, or reach of cavalry as it fanned out in search of provisions. Moreover, the lack of wagons also hampered the foragers. Besides hunting for provisions, they spent their days seeking out vehicles and teams to transport wheat, flour, and forage back to camp. Without account books, inventories, or receipts, it is difficult to determine the quantity or valuation of the supplies impressed by Greene's soldiers. It is difficult to assess Greene's actual contribution to the Grand Forage. Yet, it is possible to render some judgment on his performance in planning and executing the mission assigned him. Washington had given Greene what was perhaps the most difficult assignment of the three columns. He had sent Greene into a countryside with little to offer and without the necessary transportation to bring back to camp whatever supplies Greene's soldiers impressed. They had been out for ten or eleven days, and at the conclusion of the expedition Greene had written to Brig. Gen. Henry Knox with some satisfaction, but not much evidence, his pride in having helped sustain the army with what his soldiers had gleaned from the countryside. The adjutant of the Ninth Pennsylvania Continentals sounded a note gratitude and hope on 1 March 1778, writing ""Thank Heaven our Cuntry abounds with Provisions &

with prudent management we need not apprehend want for any length of time, defects in the Commisaries department, Contingencies of weather & other temporal Impediments have subjected & may again Subject us to deficiency for a few days."[5]

Not long after his return from foraging, Greene grudgingly accepted the position of quartermaster general. For a brief moment, the department functioned well enough to support the army, but he longed for command and distinction. As he complained to Washington in April 1779, "No body ever heard of a quarter Master in History as such or in relateing any brilliant Action." In spite of his irritation, Greene subordinated his own desires to Washington's wishes and the larger needs of the army and served as quartermaster general until 1780. It was then, because of more pressing strategic needs in the Southern Department, that Greene's wish to return to command was fulfilled.[6]

Following Maj. Gen. Horatio Gates's crushing defeat at Camden, South Carolina, in August 1780, Greene replaced the hero of Saratoga as commander of the Southern Department. Under Greene, able subordinates like Brig. Gen. Daniel Morgan, and with the assistance of local militia leaders, Continentals and state forces fought and wore down British strength at Cowpens, in the Race to the Dan River, and at the battles of Guilford Courthouse, Hobkirk's Hill, Ninety-Six, Eutaw Springs, and in dozens of other actions. By 1782, forces under his command, which included those of Brig. Gen. Anthony Wayne, Lt. Col. Henry Lee, and local militias, had forced the British Army to surrender its hard-fought gains in the Carolinas and Georgia. As Greene's forces attacked British outposts and threatened their extended lines of communication, they forced the British to collapse their vulnerable posts in the South Carolina backcountry, and concentrate forces in Charlestown. Greene proved an aggressive, if unsuccessful tactical commander. He lost more fights than he won, but more than ably demonstrated his strategic acumen and ability to work well enough with militia forces to accomplish his mission. Greene's direction of the Southern Campaign was a masterful demonstration of strategy, resourcefulness, and tenacity.[7]

At first glance, there is little to suggest a direct comparison between Greene the forager and Greene the field army commander. In the first instance, Greene's charge was to glean all that could be had from southeastern Pennsylvania and put to the army's use. He was to avoid combat. His force was altogether too small fight and prevail against a larger British column. Moreover, Greene's absence from Valley Forge had stripped some of the most combat-ready soldiers from the encampment and had left the position vulnerable to a British attack. As the commander of the Southern Department, however, Greene's sought out the enemy and waged a relentless and constant campaign against British and Loyalist forces. He left his bases of supply exposed and poorly defended, so that he might commit as many Continentals and militiamen as possible against the enemy. In both instances, Greene took measured risks, made the most of his limited strength, and carefully arranged his tactical actions to accomplish larger strategic goals. While commanding his foraging column and planning for Wayne's follow-on operations, Greene demonstrated his growing aptitude for independent command.

At Valley Forge, Greene's purpose was to feed the army so that it could maintain its position and continue challenging the British occupiers in Philadelphia, as it also supported state and Continental governments. In the Southern Department, his objective was the defeat of British forces, which would enable the restoration of the revolutionary regimes in the southern states. The only way to accomplish that was through combat. Continentals and militiamen raided and attacked British lines of communication and their isolated outposts. Greene's command only infrequently massed its strength to face the British Army; when it did, Greene's forces more often lost the battle. The constant pressure and never-ceasing threat of attack by Greene's soldiers and local militia commanders, however, won the day. The countless actions waged by Continentals and militiamen forced the British to collapse their exposed posts and extended lines of communication and surrender the countryside and population to the revolutionary forces. By 1781, after pursuing Greene's army across North Carolina and winning a pyrrhic victory at Guilford Courthouse in March, Lt. Gen. Charles Lord Cornwallis had turned from the Carolinas to Yorktown, Virginia, where he surrendered his army on 19 October. The following year, Britain held little more in the south than Charlestown, South Carolina, and Savannah, Georgia. In December 1782, Greene, accompanied by his foraging comrades Anthony Wayne and Henry Lee, liberated Charlestown, and restored South Carolina to state and Continental control. Greene's promise, shown during the Grand Forage, paid dividends in the Southern Campaign. He acted as had his chief. Military strategy ably served politics.

Greene best summed up his army's conduct of the Southern Campaign in a line to the Chevalier Anne-Cesar de la Luzerne a few days following the American defeat at battle of Hobkirk's Hill, South Carolina. "We fight, get beat, Rise, and fight again," he wrote. Perhaps nowhere more than in the Southern Department did the War for Independence resemble the civil war that it was, for, as Greene continued, "The whole Country is one continued scene of blood and slaughter." Lost battles aside, Greene had won a major campaign and helped end Britain's last desperate hope to salvage some portion of its American colonies and eke out something that did not resemble a complete defeat. Greene had more than repaid Washington's faith in him. After the war, Greene, his wife, Catherine Littlefield Greene, and their family retired to Mulberry Grove, a plantation upriver from Savannah. The state of Georgia had awarded the formerly Loyalist-owned plantation to Greene as a thanks for his decisive role in the Southern Campaign. Greene's life ended prematurely in 1786, aged forty-four years.[8]

AS HE HAD DONE when he ordered Greene to command the initial foraging column, Washington had also selected well when he appointed Anthony Wayne as Greene's second-in-command. Wayne, who hailed from Chester County, was unsurpassed in his knowledge of the area. On 26 December 1777, he had proposed to his "Excellency the practicability as well as necessity of making a grand forage in the Vicinity of Chester and Derby as soon as the Hutts are perfected" at Valley Forge. Indeed, Wayne can be credited with sketching out the broader concepts and some of the finer details for the Grand Forage. In the draft of a letter from December 1777, Wayne spelled out some of the actions and locations for the suggested forage, some of which Greene acted upon in February. Washington concurred with Wayne's assessment, but held back from issuing orders until February. Once Washington issued the orders, Greene set in motion the detailed planning for his column. Because of his ongoing commitments with Congress's Committee at Camp, he delegated the detailed work to Wayne and Col. Clement Biddle, commissary general for forage. It only made sense.[9]

Wayne, seconded by Biddle, drew upon his earlier recommendations to Washington and presented them to Greene. While smaller detachments scoured the countryside, the main body concentrated around Springfield Meeting House, and another detachment foraged around Derby, similar to Wayne's earlier proposal. Biddle, in the meantime, oversaw the issue of warrants and certificates for farmers whose goods the army impressed. Not long into the foraging, on 15 February, Wayne suggested that Greene expand the scope of the operation, to include "destroy[ing] all the forage upon the Jersey Shore." Greene agreed, and decided to dispatch a portion of his column under Col. Richard Butler to New Jersey, which met with Washington's approval to extend the scope of the foraging. Less than two days later, Greene reconsidered his original decision to detach Butler. Instead, he selected Wayne. Greene had mulled over his original decision, and while he had not lost faith in Butler, it seems likely that Greene thought Wayne best suited for what would surely be a more extensive operation in which local knowledge combined with higher rank would pay greater dividends.[10]

Wayne excelled in his new mission and excelled at independent command. His coordination with Capt. John Barry of the Continental Navy was faultless. Wayne's proposals accorded well with Barry's ongoing harassment of British shipping, and Barry readily accepted Wayne's request that he ferry Wayne's 300 or so soldiers across the river. Once in New Jersey, Wayne's ability to work well with other fellow commanders and local officials, including the prickly Brig. Gen. Casimir Pulaski, Brig. Gen. Joseph Ellis of the New Jersey Militia, and Justice Thomas Sayre, stood out, and served him and his soldiers well.

Like Greene, Wayne had also suffered battlefield humiliation. In Wayne's case, it had been the British night attack at Paoli in September 1777. Prideful and eager to clear his name, Wayne insisted upon a general court-martial. A board of thirteen field-grade officers, led by Maj. Gen. John Sullivan, heard evidence and formally cleared Wayne on 1 November 1777. Still, the sting remained, and Wayne had his own measure of revenge in a meticulously planned and daringly executed night bayonet assault against the British post at Stony Point, New York on 15–16 July 1779. Attacking with unloaded muskets and fixed bayonets in the manner of Maj. Gen. Charles Grey at Paoli, Wayne put paid to that earlier debacle. In a short follow-up note to Washington about the attack, Wayne complimented one of his comrades from the Grand Forage, when he acknowledged that he was "very much indebted to Major [Henry] Lee for the quick and useful intelligence he repeatedly gave me which contributed much to the success of the enterprise."[11]

Wayne was prideful but also exercised tremendous patience when needed—and even empathy. When the main army camped at Morristown, New Jersey, over the winter of 1780–1781, it was destitute once again. Soldiers' grievances at Morristown echoed those voiced by soldiers at Valley Forge, but the situation was different. The war had now entered its fifth year. As had been the case three years earlier, food was in short supply or of inferior quality, and the soldiers' uniforms, when they had them at all, were ragged. Soldiers felt neglected, indeed even abused when they learned of politicians' debates over their pay and enlistment bounties. Many had not been paid for upwards of a year. Many were angered over differing interpretations of their enlistments, whether they were bound for three years' service or service until the end of the war. Wayne paid close heed to the Pennsylvania Line, and pleaded with the Pennsylvania Assembly for his soldiers' relief. Wayne was sympathetic to his soldiers' travails, but his best efforts at intervention and mediation on their behalf were to no avail. On 1 January 1781, soldiers of the Pennsylvania Line mutinied.[12]

Try as they might, Wayne, Col. Walter Stewart of the Second Pennsylvania Continentals, Col. Richard Butler from foraging days, and other officers were unable to prevent the mutiny. Appeals to pride, discipline, duty, and examples of personal bravery fell on deaf ears. The mutineers would have their say. Led by a committee of sergeants, they negotiated with Wayne. For nearly two weeks, Wayne listened, cajoled, and implored mutineers, politicians, and fellow officers, including Washington. In the end, the mutineers surrendered their arms. Over 1,200 soldiers of the Pennsylvania Line received discharges, and over 1,100 were furloughed until the spring. Wayne had played a central role in bringing the affair to an end, which afforded Washington "great satisfaction" for its speedy resolution.[13]

Wayne later went on to command in Georgia and played an instrumental role in the reduction of Savannah, which surrendered to him in July 1782. Shortly thereafter, Wayne, however, made a rash and inhumane decision. Following what might have been the crowning achievement of his career in the Continental Army, receiving the surrender of Savannah, Wayne's temper overrode his better sense when he ordered the execution of twelve Creek prisoners of war in June 1783. Despite Wayne's tarnished honor, Washington put him into uniform once more when he ordered him to take command of the Legion of the United States in 1792. Still a meticulous and demanding trainer of soldiers, Wayne drilled the Legion until he deemed it ready for battle. He led it to victory over the Western Confederacy of Shawnees, Ottawas, and their allies at the battle of Fallen Timbers in August 1794. Wayne then helped negotiate Treaty of Greenville in 1795. He died in 1796 at the age of fifty-one.[14]

Washington had clearly discerned Wayne's abilities as a thoughtful planner, leader, and talented combat commander, and, as had been the case with Greene, he understood that while Wayne's errors had cost soldiers' lives, he too was learning the lessons of higher command while engaged with the enemy. Hence, even before selecting Wayne as Greene's second-in-command on the Grand Forage, Washington had recognized the man's latent talent and promise for greater responsibility. Like Greene, Wayne more than repaid Washington's faith through his accomplishments. Wayne's conduct in New Jersey fully demonstrated his aptitude for independent command and his ability to work cooperatively with what remained of the Continental Navy, and also with Joseph Ellis's New Jersey Militia, and the ever prickly and contentious cavalryman, Casimir Pulaski. For Wayne, the foraging expedition was both a proving ground and preparation for his future.

HENRY LEE COMMANDED the third column in the Grand Forage. Unlike either Greene or Wayne, he had never held high command, but that did not mean that he escaped Washington's eye. Lee had entered Virginia service as a captain in June 1776, and then mustered into the Continental Army in March 1777, in which he remained a captain until April 1778. In February 1778, as Washington finalized his plans for the Grand Forage, he selected Lee for this important mission. Having known Lee and his family for years, Washington was well acquainted with the young dragoon's character and temperament. While but a captain, Lee may have had the strongest personal relationship with Washington of all the foraging commanders. The young Virginian balanced audacity and dash in battle with prudent judgement and careful planning. Accounts of his performance while on the army's picket line and in battle confirmed Lee's innate talent. Moreover, Lee also possessed a temper, and it was only later, following his well-deserved promotions, that his audacity overrode his judgement. All of that, however, lay in the future.

Following the Grand Forage, Washington invited Lee to join his military family, a sign of Washington's regard for Lee's intellect, and a quick path to promotion. Lee, however, refused the offer, confessing to Washington that "I am wedded to my sword, and that my secondary object in the present war, is military reputation." Washington graciously accepted Lee's decline and expressed his appreciation for the "undisguised manner in which you express yourself [for it] cannot but strengthen my good opinion of you" as a soldier. Shortly thereafter, Lee received a much-deserved promotion to "Major-Commandant" and command of his own "separate corps" of three troops of light dragoons, which grew to four troops on 13 July 1779 when Capt. Allen McLane's company of Delaware Continentals was formally incorporated into the corps as a dismounted troop. McLane had been serving under Lee's command since June. Both were talented partisan officers. They were well acquainted from having served together during the Grand Forage, when they had had the opportunity to take the measure of one another and discern each other's talents. It was a good combination that paid dividends later in the war.[15]

In the summer of 1779, Lee's squadron was operating in the Hudson River Valley and around Suffern, New York, about thirty-five miles northwest of

New York City. Washington described the area as a "very disaffected country." Lee was "entirely detached and unsupported." Nonetheless, Washington ordered Lee to "countenance the militia, plague the enemy—and cover the country from the depredations of their light parties, as much as possible," all within the province of a practiced partisan officer. While on this duty, Lee's soldiers had apprehended deserters from the Continental Army. In an effort to stamp out this pernicious behavior, Lee suggested to Washington that deserters should be executed, their corpses decapitated, and their heads sent to the Continental "Light Troops" as a warning. Washington approved of the suggested executions, provided they were performed "with caution and only when the fact is very clear and unequivocal." As for beheadings, it "had better be omitted," for it was best to avoid the "appearance of inhumanity otherwise they give disgust and may exite resistment rather than terror."[16]

It was too late. The day after Washington had counseled Lee against beheadings he learned of the event, and he feared for the consequences, "both in the Army and in the Country," should word of the decapitations spread. Lee was not at all contrite, although he was "sorry it [Washington's letter] did not reach me previous to the execution of the deserter." Indeed, the tone of Lee's letter suggests pride in the results, and thus the act. He wrote, "Altho' from what I observe here it has had a very immediate effect for the better on both troops & inhabitants." Lee's self-assured, even cocksure tone intimates an overconfidence born of privilege, position, and success. Nonetheless, he refrained from summarily executing a deserter from the Tenth Pennsylvania Continentals, who was instead "sent up unhurt." The executions, however, Lee promised to continue. Rather than putting to death the lot of them, Lee followed the "spirit of your Excellcys directions," and determined "that only one instead of the whole be executed of such as may be apprehended." Harshness aside, Lee continued demonstrating his daring and tactical acumen. In August 1779, he led a surprise attack against the British outpost at Paulus Hook, New York. Like Wayne at Stony Point, Lee at Paulus Hook gave further proof of Washington's discernment of talent and of the Continental Army's maturing tactical aptitude.[17]

By October 1780, Lee's small command had been redesignated the Second "Partisan Corps," better known as Lee's Legion, and in November, he received a promotion to lieutenant colonel. He continued demonstrating his tactical prowess and ferocity in combat throughout the Southern Campaign and served with distinction until the war's end. To say that Lee's life after the

1783 Peace of Paris was one of contrasts would be an understatement. Without the war, Lee was adrift in unfamiliar waters. Although he was briefly commissioned major general in 1798 during the war scare with revolutionary France, Lee never again commanded American soldiers. His better-known son, Robert E. Lee, commanded rebel forces in the American Civil War, attempting to destroy the union of states his father had helped create. Following a postwar life of politics and debt, Lee died in 1818 at Dungeness Plantation, on Cumberland Island, Georgia. Lee's death was more than simply his passing. It marked a poetic closure to that which had given his life so much meaning, the War for Independence. Henry Lee died under the care of Louisa Catherine Greene Shaw, daughter of his old comrade, Nathanael Greene. Lee's sixty-two years on earth had been full ones. In retrospect, Lee's performance as a commander of light dragoons and on the Grand Forage were but the merest suggestions of his capacity for higher command, his moments of poor judgement notwithstanding.[18]

WASHINGTON DID NOT intentionally select all of the subordinate commanders who played roles in the Grand Forage. While he had placed some of them and their commands in certain locations before the Grand Forage, he had not done so with the foraging operation in mind. Therefore, with so many of them in position when the foraging began, it fell to them to support or participate in it. Unsurprisingly, some performed well, even exceptionally so, while others fell short in the performance of their duties. Capt. John Barry, easily one of the finest officers in the Continental Navy, played a key role supporting Wayne's operations in New Jersey. Judging by the correspondence, Barry and Wayne were cut from the same cloth. Both were fearless, ambitious, and combined daring with thoughtfulness. Barry also shared Lee's aptitude for partisan warfare, albeit in a riverine environment.

Having scuttled his frigate *Effingham* to prevent capture by the Royal Navy in 1777, Barry was without a command. That, however, did not last long. After assuming command of a collection of whale boats, Barry began a campaign of riverine raiding and attacking British transports. In this, Barry was masterful. He struck at British weakness and consistently evaded the Royal Navy, despite its best efforts. Barry's burning of "Hay along the Shore from Billings Port" to Salem, however, was a mixed success. While it denied the British valuable feed for their animals, British accounts make plain that it did not distract them from Wayne's foraging. Nevertheless, Barry and his sailors contributed to the success of Wayne's foraging by transporting the command across the Delaware River, burning hay, and keeping the Royal Navy busy as they attacked transports. Following the war, Barry captained merchantmen, sailed in the China trade, and returned to naval service in the 1790s as its senior captain. The Irish-born Barry completed his last voyage on 12 September 1803, when he died at his estate, Strawberry Hill, in Philadelphia's Northern Liberties, aged fifty-eight.[19]

Barry was the ideal partner to support Wayne's foraging in New Jersey. He demonstrated commendable energy and activity by ferrying Wayne's brigade across the Delaware River and destroying marsh hay along the New Jersey bank. Moreover, the scheme fit in well with his ongoing raiding and harassment of British transports on the river. Most important, Barry cheerfully subordinated himself and his pride so that the larger objective of the Grand Forage might be met. It was his greatest feat during the operation, and the one most worthy of emulation.

WAYNE'S TACTICAL SKILL and local knowledge notwithstanding, he and his ad hoc brigade needed assistance once they landed in New Jersey. They were fortunate to have that of Col. Joseph Ellis, commanding the New Jersey Militia's Second Battalion, Gloucester County Regiment. Ellis was an active and intelligent officer whose militiamen served as foragers, scouts, and sources of local intelligence. The performance of Ellis's soldiers exhibited what Continentals and local forces were capable of accomplishing when led by competent officers who knew their soldiers' strengths and weaknesses and knew not to ask of them more than they could accomplish. That working relationship also extended into the ranks of local magistrates whose knowledge of local matters was unmatched. These local officials also held positions of responsibility in their county militia regiments, which conjoined civil authority with local military authority. Fortunately, Wayne, Ellis, and the magistrates worked well together; none stood on punctilio, nor did any let their egos or sensitivities interfere with the larger mission. Ellis, who had stood at the center of New Jersey's militia actions during the Grand Forage, was also a prominent local politician. He had been sheriff of Gloucester County, had served as a county representative to the New Jersey Provincial Congress, and had voted for independence. After the war, Ellis continued his public service as a county judge and member of the state's legislature. In the middle of his sixth decade, Ellis died in 1796 following a life of service to Gloucester County and to New Jersey. Ellis's local knowledge and ability to muster and maintain the militia in support of Wayne's command had proved invaluable to the success of the foraging in New Jersey and the Continental Army's survival at Valley Forge.[20]

REGRETTABLY, BRIG. GEN. CASIMIR PULASKI, Wayne's fellow Continental brigadier general, was one to stand on punctilio, and to bring his ego and sensitivities to the forefront. A patriot who had struggled against Russian encroachment into Polish affairs, Pulaski fled his homeland, and, like so many foreign officers, found a commission in the Continental Army. Pulaski's bravery and daring were beyond doubt, but his willingness or ability to accept or understand seniority predicated upon date of rank escaped him. When called upon for assistance by Wayne, Pulaski answered the appeal, gathered as many light dragoons as he could, and quickly made for the Pennsylvanian. Yet, Pulaski, protested to Washington about the effrontery of a mere brigadier general of infantry presuming to issue orders to a brigadier general of cavalry. Despite Washington's polite, but forceful reminder about the supremacy of dates of rank, the seniority they awarded, and the senior-ranking officer's right to command, Pulaski tested both Washington's and Wayne's patience. Notwithstanding Wayne's cautious approach when he turned on his British pursuers, Pulaski launched impetuous attacks at Haddonfield, and again at Cooper's Ferry. Fortune had momentarily favored the bold.

In 1779, however, Pulaski's good fortune ran out when in command of his own legion during the Franco-American attack against Savannah. The Pole died at the age of thirty-four while leading his horsemen in an attack against Springhill Redoubt on 9 October. Charles-Henri, comte d'Estaing, who commanded the French expeditionary force, deemed the charge rash, and noted that Pulaski was in the wrong place at the wrong time. Pulaski's intemperate words and battlefield impetuosity had raised hackles during the foraging in New Jersey. He had tried Washington's temper, annoyed Wayne to no end, and had tempted fate, but, nonetheless, he had briefly benefited before his luck ran out in Georgia. Pulaski's former commander, Wayne, whom he had so blithely disregarded in New Jersey, symbolically reunited with the Pole when he took possession of the town that now held the cavalryman's remains. Pulaski had learned nothing from his time serving with Wayne on the forage, nor afterward.[21]

AS A BATTLEFIELD COMMANDER, Brig. Gen. William Smallwood was of middling quality, and as a colleague he often left much to be desired. Hailing from Charles County, Maryland, Smallwood, like Washington and Lee, belonged to the Chesapeake Bay's tidewater gentry. A member of the Maryland Assembly before the war, Smallwood assumed command of the First Maryland Battalion in January 1776 and was promoted to brigadier general in October. He distinguished himself in the battles for New York but performed poorly at the battle of Brandywine on 11 September 1777, and again at Germantown on 4 October 1777. In the first instance, Smallwood commanded poorly trained Maryland militiamen, about whom he complained before the battle, and in the second, he was a victim of circumstances when heavy fog and Washington's complicated plan conspired against him.[22]

Like many American-born officers, Smallwood resented the rapid rise of foreign-born volunteers, and was overly sensitive about rank, seniority, and real or perceived slights. Smallwood could also be hypercritical and often quarreled with or sniped at fellow officers, including Col. Otho Holland Williams of the Sixth Maryland Continentals, Maj. Gen. Horatio Gates, and others. Ambitious, and as the senior officer of the Maryland Line, Smallwood longed for promotion to major general. Charged with commanding the southernmost outpost of the Continental Army at Wilmington, Smallwood did well. He likely derived some small measure of satisfaction at the autonomy. His sensitivity to rank aside, Smallwood cheerfully "afford[ed]" to Captain Lee "ev'ry assistance" while foraging in Delaware. Left to shift for itself as Lee's light dragoons emptied magazines, Smallwood's division competed with Lee and thus the main army for scarce supplies. Despite his soldiers' want, he gave Lee every assistance possible.[23]

When the focus of the war shifted to the southern states, Smallwood found himself in South Carolina. At the battle of Camden in August 1780, he commanded the army's reserve, the First Maryland Brigade. While trying to rally the broken militia to his front, Smallwood was separated from his command. Unfortunately for Smallwood, his brigade followed suit, and also broke. Recriminations followed the disaster at Camden, and Smallwood earned a left-handed compliment from Nathanael Greene, who commented to Lt. Col. Alexander Hamilton, that Smallwood had earned a "great reputation" for gathering some 150 soldiers at Salisbury, North Carolina, "which was no thing but accident." Greene also took note of the "great parties prevailing in the Maryland Line and [conceded] perhaps his merit is not a little diminished on that account." As it happened, Camden was Smallwood's last action, although he did receive his promotion to major general on 15 September 1780. Greene's elevation to command of the Southern Department irked Smallwood, who had hoped to assume command following Gates's demise. Furthermore, Smallwood refused to serve under Maj. Gen. Friedrich

Wilhelm de Steuben. Instead, Smallwood journeyed north to "Maryland with a view of forwarding the troops & supplies from that State, and to settle the matter with Congress respecting his right of promotion" and seniority. Following the war, Smallwood returned home. He served as first president of the Maryland Society of the Cincinnati and devoted his time to increasing his holdings in land and slaves, but also his debts. Smallwood served as governor of Maryland from 1785 to1788, and as a state senator in 1791. In February 1792, at the age of fifty-nine, Smallwood, a lifelong bachelor, died indebted, owing his creditors £17,500, Maryland currency. The chancery court ordered the sale of some of Smallwood's lands to satisfy the debts, his last wrangles settled.[24]

The army's Grand Forage of 1778, which had demanded such high degrees of energy, imagination, cooperation, teamwork, and the subordination of oneself to the greater good seemed to have escaped Smallwood afterward. He had had his shining moments, to be sure, but in the aggregate, he left much to be desired. In the end, Smallwood's dedication to American independence and his loyalty to Washington were not enough to enable him to rise above his own injured pride and self-interest.

WITH SO MANY OF WASHINGTON'S BEST ARMED, equipped, and uniformed soldiers away from camp, Valley Forge made a tempting target, but Gen. Sir William Howe did not act. Instead, he tarried, and sent out his own foraging detachments—constantly. When he did act, it was against Wayne in New Jersey, and that effort was less than half-hearted. Well aware of the difficulties the Continentals faced at Valley Forge and Wilmington, Howe still chose not to risk his forces in battle. Upon his return to England in July 1778, Howe blamed Lord George Germain, secretary of state for the American Colonies, for having failed to support him while in command. His correspondence with Germain previous to that indicated that the general was not about to shoulder any responsibility for the failure of British arms in America. In his defense, Howe pleaded a variety of reasons for not attacking Valley Forge, chief among the "entrenched situation of the enemy . . . [and his] continued . . . remonstrance for more troops." Sir William, having "judged it imprudent" to attack until the spring, decided against that too. He had it on "good information . . . that the enemy had strengthened the camp by additional works," but Howe was confident of "moving him from thence when the campaign should open," and therefore "dropped all thoughts of an attack."[25]

In pleading his paucity of forces, Howe suggested that Germain had "deemed [the requests for reinforcements] nugatory: and that, of course,

I had lost the confidence of those, who were in the first instance to judge of my conduct." Instead of telling Howe that he was unable to send more troops, Germain left him in the dark, signaling his "loss of confidence" in the general. Howe complained of not having been adequately reinforced, of having had his recommendations for officers' promotions denied, and, most tellingly, of having lost the ministry's confidence. However, historian Piers Mackesy makes plain that Howe's requests for reinforcements were extravagant and that Howe treated the ministry's refusals to accede to them as personal affronts. In the matter of rebuffed recommendations for promotions, the ministry denied just two of them. As for Howe's claims that Germain had lost confidence, Mackesy attributed it to Howe's sensitivity to Germain's requests for more frequent and fuller communications and his urging Howe and his elder brother, V. Adm. Richard, Viscount Howe, commander of British naval forces in America, to disrupt rebel trade through coastal raids, a tighter blockade, and less lenience with pardons.[26]

Although Germain and his purported ill treatment were at the heart of Howe's accusations, he broadened them to include the Loyalists who had been slow "to assist offensively in compelling his Majesty's revolted subjects to their duty." It was only after repeated victories and the British Army's demonstration of its "apparent ability to retain our advantages, [that] induced the inhabitants at last to be less reserved." Yet, it was too little, too late, despite Howe's best efforts. Finally, there was the French alliance and the orders to abandon Philadelphia. Before this, Howe argued, Britain's occupation of the city "convinced the country of the superiority, and persuaded them of the established power, of his Majesty's arms." Congress and the Continental Army were failing in their efforts to raise supplies or recruits. The rebellion's demise "then indeed became real, and had the appearance of being unsurmountable," but, without mentioning names, Germain had lost heart over the French alliance, and ordered Philadelphia evacuated. Germain's fecklessness was a "sudden and melancholy change in our affairs," which breathed new into the rebellion, as well as disheartening "the friends of government."[27]

More than Germain's supposed slighting conduct, lack of manpower, and his other given reasons constrained Howe. On 22 October 1777, a little more than a fortnight after his victory at Germantown, Howe offered his resignation, through Germain, to George III. Howe saw no hope of victory without another "ten thousand men" and another campaign. He complained of the "little attention" that Germain had given to his "recommendations." Howe's despair deepened as he reported on 30 November, news of the "misfortune" of Lt. Gen. John Burgoyne, who had surrendered over 5,000 soldiers at Saratoga on 17 October. Any thought of future offensive operations "for effecting any essential change in their [Americans'] disposition, and the re-establishment of the King's authority" was beyond the realm of consideration without extensive reinforcements. Until then, it was all Howe's command could do to "maintain its present possessions." On 11 December, the colonial secretary informed Howe that the king had "received . . . [Howe's] request with concern" and was considering it. The matter, however, remained that the ministry had no details about Burgoyne's debacle, nor had Howe "finished" his campaign, a sharp rebuke by Germain that Howe needed to complete what he had started.[28]

On 17 January 1778, Howe reiterated his desire to resign. As the vessel carrying his missive sailed for London, Germain's response was making its way to Howe aboard the "*Mercury* packet," a literal case of two ships passing in the night, albeit separated by hundreds of miles of sea. On average, the communications between the men from October 1777 to April 1778 took 56.25 days, 48 days from Philadelphia to London, and 64.5 days from London to Philadelphia. Germain had written to Howe on 4 February and informed him that the king had given his "royal acquiescence in your request of leave to resign your command." Gen Sir Henry Clinton would assume command. Thus, when Washington had sent forth his foragers on 13 February, Howe had long ago given up the fight. He saw no chance of reconciliation between Britain and the rebellious colonies, much less victory. Rather disingenuously, Howe claimed in his defense, "It is not necessary for me to say much of 1778. — Very early in April I received my orders to return home — The conduct, therefore, of the campaign of 1778 was to rest upon my successor." Howe had shrugged off all responsibility for the failed campaign.[29]

Surprisingly, news of Howe's desire to quit the theater remained a closely held secret within the army. Lt. Col. Thomas Stirling, commanding the Forty-Second Regiment of Foot, expressed his surprise, that "we have now received such heartbreaking news of the recall of Genl Howe" in a 13 April letter to his brother, Sir William Stirling. All of this, however, was unknown to Howe's soldiers. Thus, it is perfectly plausible that Howe was preoccupied with quitting the American theater while Greene's and Wayne's foraging took place, and that however subtly, Sir William's diffident conduct influenced the conduct of his forces when he finally dispatched them into New Jersey. Howe's correspondence, in both tone and substance, strongly suggest that Howe recognized the scale, scope, and complexity of subduing the rebellion and that well before his descent on Philadelphia in the summer of 1777, he was discouraged about British military prospects. Following his return to England, Howe never again commanded in battle. Nevertheless, for a man who had failed to wring victory in America, Howe's life following his Philadelphia denouement was anything but disgraceful. He was appointed a member of the Privy Council in 1782, served as lieutenant general of the ordnance from 1782 to 1804, and received the colonelcy of the Nineteenth Light Dragoons in 1786. In 1793, Howe was promoted to general. He succeeded his brother, Richard, Viscount Howe, as the fifth Viscount Howe in 1799. Following a long, often distinguished and sometimes frustrating military career, Sir William died in 1814, childless, at the age of eighty-five.[30]

Washington had presented Howe with the last great opportunity of his tenure as commander of the British Army when he launched the foraging expeditions. Yet, Howe sat fast. Consumed with his resignation, defending his reputation, and feeding his own army, Howe declined the opportunity of bringing Washington to battle while the Continental Army and its fortifications at Valley Forge were at their most vulnerable. To be sure, Howe needed to husband his most precious resource, his soldiers, and success in an attack against Valley Forge was an uncertain prospect.

If Valley Forge was altogether too daunting, then Nathanael Greene's exposed column offered Howe a less challenging, but still promising opportunity for a signal victory. Attacking Greene's command presented fewer difficulties than the earthworks to Howe's northwest. Defeating Washington's most trusted subordinate, and perhaps even destroying the foraging column would have had a tremendous effect on both armies' morale, but Howe chose not to act. Instead, he waited until Anthony Wayne had crossed the Delaware River, and then sent two sizable formations against him without a general to direct their actions. Howe had quit. His indifference, inaction, and lethargy were inexcusable. Whether Howe could have won a decisive victory is beside the point. Rather than act, Howe let slip his last chance, and instead sulked and wallowed in self-pity.

HAVING LEFT GREENE to his own devices in Chester County for nearly two weeks, Howe finally roused from his torpor, and ordered the Light Infantry Brigade under Lt. Col. Robert Abercromby to pursue Anthony Wayne and his band of Continentals. After landing at Billingsport on 24 February, Abercromby deployed the Light Bobs northeast and southwest along the King's Highway, and descended on Wayne's location at a rapid pace, very nearly capturing him. Following this burst of energy, Abercromby and the Light Bobs settled into a smaller version of what had become the British Army's modus operandi while in Philadelphia—foraging and making themselves obnoxious. Although unknown to Wayne, Robert Abercromby no longer posed a threat to the American foragers. Like his chief, Abercromby had surrendered the initiative in favor of the well-worn, but altogether more comfortable path of least resistance. Like his chief, he settled for the pursuit of provisions over combat. Previous to this, nothing in Abercromby's record suggests that he was anything but a typical regimental officer—dependable and brave, but not exceptional.

Biographer Raymond Callahan describes Abercromby as coming "from one of those Scottish landed families that were to play an important role in British military and imperial history over the next two centuries." Having first volunteered for service in the Seven Years' War, Abercromby had earned a commission for gallantry in action in the aftermath of the disastrous assault against Fort Ticonderoga on 8 July 1758. In 1775, he was major of the Sixty-Second Regiment of Foot, after having spent some fifteen years as a captain on half-pay. The following year, however, found Abercromby as lieutenant colonel of the Thirty-Seventh Foot. War in America proved Abercromby's path to advancement. When the seat of war shifted to the Southern Theater in 1780, Abercromby too went south, where he developed a lasting connection with Lt. Gen. Charles, Earl Cornwallis, and surrendered with him at Yorktown on 19 October 1781. Rising to colonel in 1782, Abercromby followed Cornwallis to India in 1786. He eventually rose to lieutenant governor and command of the army in Bombay, which Cornwallis, in Callahan's words, reckoned "was probably the limit of Abercromby's abilities." Following a turbulent decade in India, which included promotion to major general, and a knighthood, Abercromby returned to Scotland, where he died in 1827, at the age of eighty-seven, having risen to become the senior-most general in the army—an accomplishment due more to dedicated service and longevity, than to any great or discernable acumen or talent. Abercromby's mediocre performance in New Jersey was but another unremarkable moment in an unexceptional career.[31]

ONE DAY AFTER landing the Light Infantry Brigade, flatboats and escorts landed Lt. Col. Thomas Stirling, his two battalions of the Forty-Second Foot, Maj. John Graves Simcoe and his Loyalist legion, the Queen's American Rangers, and supporting artillery at Cooper's Ferry. Like Abercromby, Stirling advanced; like his fellow Scotsman, he came close to falling upon Wayne;

and like him, Stirling then turned to foraging. When pressed by Wayne and Pulaski at Haddonfield, Stirling, suffering from poor intelligence about his enemy, took counsel of his fears, abandoned the supplies and livestock that his soldiers had gathered, and withdrew to Cooper's Ferry. Pressed once more by the Continentals, Stirling briefly stood and skirmished with them before reembarking for Philadelphia. At best, it was an ignominious end to a half-hearted attempt.

Stirling's conduct was revealing. It displayed the contradictions of British military efforts that he had railed about. In a November 1777 letter to his elder brother, Sir William, the younger Stirling had given vent to his frustrations about the conduct of the war. In it, he declared that "this Conflict cannot last either much longer either Britain must tire of the waste expence & withdraw her troops or the Americans be subdued by a spirited exertion next Campaign in either case one year more must end it." Stirling's half-hearted pursuit of Wayne was anything but a "spirited exertion." Indeed, Stirling's decision to shift his energies into foraging mirrored the larger state of British military affairs in Philadelphia. Sustaining the British Army had overridden subduing the Continental Army. In retrospect, it was a remarkable moment for an officer who had heretofore shown great promise.[32]

A soldier since 1747, Stirling had seen action in Europe, Canada, and the West Indies. He had served in the Illinois Country following the Seven Years' War and had been lieutenant colonel of the Forty-Second Foot since 1771. The regiment returned to Britain in 1767 but departed once more for North America in 1776. Once in America, Stirling reorganized the Highlanders into two battalions, and then instituted a training regimen inspired by his experience "in the former war with the Indians and French bushmen," and devoted personal attention to training the regiment's noncommissioned officers. In the New York Campaign, Stirling distinguished himself in the assault on Fort Washington, and in taking an enemy post at Elizabethtown, New Jersey in 1779. He was promoted to colonel and made an aide-de-camp to George III in 1780. That same year, American fire at Connecticut Farms, New Jersey, struck and broke Stirling's thigh, splintering, but not shattering it. The injury troubled him for several years thereafter, and although his last field command was in 1780, he eventually rose to the rank of general in 1801. Stirling had succeeded his brother as fifth baronet of Ardoch in 1799. After a full career in imperial service, Stirling, who never married, died in 1808, having lived seventy-five years. His title expired with him. Like Abercromby, a fellow Scot, Stirling, had demonstrated little initiative and no discernable aptitude for higher or for independent command. His brigade easily outnumbered Wayne's band and was unencumbered by livestock and supplies. Personally brave, Stirling was unsuited for his mission. Indeed, to deem Stirling's performance in New Jersey as uninspired would be an understatement.[33]

SIR WILLIAM HOWE depended on the Royal Navy's Delaware River Squadron when he dispatched Robert Abercromby's and Thomas Stirling's commands in pursuit of Anthony Wayne and his foragers. Accustomed to working closely with his brother, V. Adm. Richard, Viscount Howe, Sir William Howe did as well with Capt. Andrew Snape Hamond of the Royal Navy. Without a formal command structure that united both the army and the navy under a single chief, personal relationships were the central component to joint army-navy operations. In this realm, Hamond stood out for his competence and energy providing riverine support for the army. The performance of his captains and crews working directly with the army more than amplified these qualities.

Hamond kept his squadron, particularly the shallower-draft vessels, busily employed supporting Howe's forces in New Jersey, responding to Captain Barry's attacks, trying to bring Barry to battle—but failing—and improving the navigation to Philadelphia. Hamond's sailors manned the sweeps on flatboats and galleys, while others worked the halyards and sails of the other vessels that landed Abercromby's light infantry at Billingsport and paralleled its advance southwestward. For Stirling's shorter trip to Cooper's Ferry, it was a matter of dispatching boats directly across the Delaware. Combatting Barry's raiders, however, was a different matter. Barry's smaller craft had the advantage of greater maneuverability, so Hamond deployed his "Ships of War . . . [to] form a Chain down the River." Near the close of March, and long after his sailors had reembarked and returned Howe's soldiers, Hamond reported that his crews "have already taken and destroyed most of the Enemys Armed Boats that infested the Mouths of the Creeks," and as for improving the navigation on the river, "Buoys are laid to mark the Obstructions, and Shoals; so that the Navigation to Philadelphia is rendered as practicable as it can be, untill more of the Chevaux de Frizes are either removed, or destroyed, which is about to be undertaken." Without a clear shipping channel, resupply for British forces was impracticable, if not impossible. In the captain's estimate, "The Town has been well Supplied with Provisions during the whole Winter, and the Army has been remarkably healthy; but the Seaman in the Ships of War have not been quite so fortunate." His sailors' health was likely due to their damp and cold living conditions aboard ship, and their constant exertions.[34]

Captain Hamond had learned his craft well from his patron, Lord Howe. They had become acquainted in 1759, and from that point forward, Howe took Hamond under his wing. During the War for Independence, Hamond saw extensive action enforcing the blockade, scouting the enemy, taking soundings, and doing whatever else he could do to prosecute the war. Following a return to England in December 1778, Hamond was knighted in January. He sailed once more for America in June 1779 and earned lavish praise from V. Adm. Mariot Arbuthnot for his "ever ready, animated, and forward" conduct during the siege and capture of Charlestown, South Carolina, in the spring of 1780. Following his return to England in 1780, Hamond sailed for Nova Scotia, where he served as lieutenant governor and commissioner of the Halifax Navy Yard. Later, Hamond became comptroller of the Navy Board. Yet, despite all of his accomplishments, Hamond never attained flag rank. Biographer Roger Knight concluded that Sir Andrew "was a vigorous naval officer, who never quite fulfilled his potential." Whether the causes for Hamond's unfulfilled potential were his own, those of others, or some combination, are difficult to determine. In 1828, age of eighty-nine, Sir Andrew crossed the bar. Among all the senior British officers who took part in the belated pursuit of Wayne, Hamond outshone all of them. His squadron, charged with maintaining British communications along the Delaware River and supporting the army, provided rapid and timely support when it crossed the river into New Jersey, and remained nearby, ready to render assistance. Hamond alone demonstrated competence in the British response to the Grand Forage of 1778.[35]

THE ARMY THAT SURVIVED the Valley Forge winter did so because of George Washington's determination to hold the post and his officers' and soldiers' willingness to endure the privation and suffering. They were not the passive victims of popular memory, and Valley Forge was not a traditional setting for winter quarters. Instead, the encampment was the home of a field army that vigorously patrolled, skirmished, and sought out provender to sustain itself. The engineers who designed the encampment's network of mutually supporting fortifications and the soldiers who built the earthworks transformed the place into a military stronghold. Valley Forge was a hub of military activity, a fortified camp from which the Continental Army projected power and sustained local and Continental government.

The Continental Army had denied the British Army victory in Pennsylvania through its stubborn survival at Valley Forge. Howe and his political master, Germain, had hoped for a quick, decisive victory, but that was not to be. Instead, the war in America was a long, slow, grinding affair. The American War for Independence was a war of attrition; the Continental Army's survival at Valley Forge was but one step on the road to independence. One of the central elements in the army's survival was the Grand Forage of 1778. While everyone at Valley Forge was aware of the army's poor condition and the difficulties of the commissariat, few knew the degree to which its survival was threatened. Washington had shared few details beyond a select circle of officers and politicians. Therefore, most of the foragers did not recognize the greater significance of what they had undertaken. Washington's Continentals had become so inured to want and privation that for most soldiers it was but another forage.

Like so many of the smaller and more mundane acts in the American War for Independence, the Grand Forage of 1778 quickly faded from memory. In this, it was like so many actions before and after in every war. When veterans and observers reminisced about the war, their memories gravitated toward larger, more momentous events. Campaigns, battles, and individual heroism dominated historical remembrance and commemoration. Stories of individual adventures that celebrated feats of derring-do and morality tales that suggested higher national purpose were more fitting for audiences in the Early American Republic. Foraging was altogether too prosaic. It was a matter of gathering food and supplies, the everyday stuff of any army's existence. To be sure, there had been dramatic moments, but like the forage itself, they faded from memory. Instead, it fell to antiquarians and local historians to tell their communities' stories. Biographers and professional historians picked up on the chroniclers' works and incorporated them into their own. Still, their larger stories subsumed the story of the Grand Forage, which is as it should be, for they had greater matters at hand.

The army that George Washington commanded was as much his creation as it was the states' and the Continental Congress's. It embodied the characteristics of its still-developing parent societies and those who led it. Hence, the army was as much an evolving and maturing institution as were the newborn United States of America. Indeed, the army of 1777–1778 and beyond was the third iteration of the Continental Army, its first two incarnations having ended with the expiration of soldiers' enlistments on 1 July 1776, and once more at the end of 1776. Over its short lifetime, the army had lost more battles than it had won and retreated as often or more than it had advanced, but gradually it learned how to hold its ground, to fight, and give a good account of itself in combat. Some of the same evolution and maturation had taken place within the army's senior ranks. Washington's plan for the forage, admittedly an act of desperation and improvisation, his choice of commanders for the foraging, and the wide latitude he afforded them all point toward that growth, but also to the mutual trust between them. The structural problems underpinning the fatal crisis, however, were beyond Washington's purview. No amount of planning, trust, or competence on the part of the army's senior officers could remedy that, for it was solely within the realm of congressional and state politicians.[36]

Washington confronted the fatal crisis of 1778 with a steadiness and determination that had become characteristic of him by 1777. His calm exterior masked deep concerns about the state of supplies and the army's ability to hold its position at Valley Forge. Washington's faith in Greene, Wayne, Lee, and others—in some cases because he had no other choice—resulted from his judgement of character, talent, and temperament. He had cultivated not just trust, but his subordinates' autonomy through his judicious delegation of responsibility. Washington made mistakes throughout his tenure as commander-in-chief of Continental forces, but from them he developed a profound strategic acumen through which he subordinated military decisions to higher political affairs. He learned when to take risks and when to exercise restraint and patience. Washington amply displayed these qualities, and more, in the Grand Forage of 1778.

Acknowledgments

Historians most often write in isolation, but none work alone; this book is no exception. I owe countless thanks to many individuals and institutions. Their support and generosity were instrumental in the book's fruition. Pride of place goes to my old colleagues on the Staff Ride Team, Combat Studies Institute, at Fort Leavenworth, Kansas. Kevin E. Kennedy, my then–team chief, enthusiastically championed my research for the Philadelphia Campaign staff ride that led to this book. Many thanks, Kevin. Teammates Charles D. Collins and Curtis King, who joined in on the so-called japery and wool gathering, were part of the early staff ride site visits ("recons") and initial executions of the ride and its refinement, including a February 2009 nor'easter that closed Valley Forge and made the drive to and from Paoli a white-knuckle experience. Their advice, expertise, and fellowship were invaluable. Many thanks to the U.S. Army Program Executive Office Command, Control, and Communications-Tactical, which funded the initial research and execution of the staff ride.

Deb Gershenowitz, my editor at UNC Press is owed a special appreciation. Her advice, counsel, and championing of this work cannot be underestimated. While Deb has also been exceedingly patient, she failed to make me cry. Thank you.

Numerous historians have generously given of their time to read or listen, and comment on the various drafts or papers delivered, and have offered their continued and much appreciated support, some without even being aware of it. All errors are my own. Many thanks to Wayne K. Bodle, Stephen A. Bourque, Mark T. Calhoun, Anthony E. Carlson, Benjamin Carp, John M. Curatola, Huw J. Davies, John M. Grenier, Bryan Hockensmith, G. Stephen Lauer, Mark Edward Lender, Wayne E. Lee, Edward G. Lengel, Brian McAllister Linn, Paul D. Lockhart, Christopher P. Magra, James Kirby Martin, Holly A. Mayer, Mark D. McGarvie, Matthew Muehlbauer, Amanda Nagel, Charles Patrick Neimeyer, Jill S. Russell, Craig Bruce Smith, Barry Stentiford, Ellen D. Tillman, Gregory J.W. Urwin, Janet G. Valentine, Bruce Vandervort, Glenn F. Williams, and Donald P. Wright. A special recognition goes to Barry Norcross, who inspired in me a serious interest in military history in his Alhambra High School history class, "Americans at War," in 1975. Thank you, Mr. Norcross.

Nothing much happens in the U.S. Army without the support of one's bosses. G. Scott Gorman and Richard Dixon, the civilian leadership at the School of Advanced Military Studies (SAMS), have fought more bureaucratic battles on behalf of the faculty and serious scholarship than I or any of my colleagues are aware. Colonels (ret.) Henry "Hank" Arnold, Jr., James Markert, and Kirk Dorr, former directors of SAMS, deserve special recognition for their support of scholarship and its role in teaching. Thank you, gentlemen. The ladies of SAMS, Candace Hamm, Anna White, Ashley Caudle, and Jackie Kania deserve special thanks for their assistance with army adminstrivia, their good humor, their harassment, and their friendship. Thank you, ladies.

As much as I enjoy teaching, research and writing are close seconds. The research for this book took me to over thirty libraries, archives, and historic locations associated with the Grand Forage of 1778. Without librarians, archivists, fellow historians, and the public who appreciate the past, none of this work would have been possible. My gratitude goes out to the librarians and archivists of the American Antiquarian Society in Worcester, Massachusetts; the American Philosophical Society in Philadelphia; the Chicago History Museum; the William L. Clements Library, University of Michigan (thank you for keeping up the tradition of morning tea); the Connecticut Historical Society in New Haven; the David Library of the American Revolution, now part of the American Philosophical Society. Meg McSweeney, chief operating officer, and Kathie Ludwig, librarian, made my time at the David memorable. Thank you to Peter Harrington of the Anne S.K. Brown Military Collection, Brown University Library; the Detroit Public Library; to Jen Peters, Special Collections Librarian, Fenimore Art Museum, for her help with the Col. Charles Stewart Collection; the Gloucester County Historical Society, New Jersey; the Historical Society of Philadelphia, an underfunded gem; the Houghton Library, Harvard University; the Library of Congress; the Massachusetts Historical Society; Morristown National Historic Park Library, New Jersey; the National Archives in Kew, Surrey; the National Archives of Scotland and the National Library of Scotland, both in Edinburgh; the National Archives and Records Administration in Washington, DC; the New Jersey Historical Society in Newark; the New-York Historical Society; the New York Public Library; the Princeton University Library; the Rhode Island Historical Society in Providence; the Ike Skelton Combined Arms Research Library at Fort Leavenworth. Ellen McCallister Clark, library director, Society of the Cincinnati, has graciously aided me on projects since I was a graduate student.

Thanks to the University of Houston Libraries; to archivist Dona M. McDermott, Valley Forge National Historic Park Library, for her hospitality and assistance, and Ranger David J. Lawrence, Park Guide, Valley Forge National Historic Park, for his questions and suggestions regarding Anthony Wayne in New Jersey. Douglas Bradburn, founding director of the Fred W. Smith National Library for the Study of George Washington and now president and CEO for the Mount Vernon Estate and Gardens, was an early and enthusiastic proponent of my work, and exceedingly generous with his time. Thank you to Samantha Snyder, librarian at the Washington Library, and to Joseph Stoltz, director of Leadership Programs. At the Washington Library, Sean Thomas, former director of Leadership Programs, and Melissa Robertson, formerly manager of Leadership Programs, were great supporters of this project. Thanks also to the Wisconsin Historical Society in Madison. Thank you to Joseph Williams for his kind permission to read from Abraham Williams's letter. I owe a special debt to Joseph Lee Boyle for his yeoman work in compiling the weather data for the entirety of the Philadelphia Campaign through the Battle of Monmouth and for sharing his copious notes on the Continental Army's provisioning. Lee's scholarship is exceeded only by his generosity.

Generous support from the U.S. Army Command and General Staff College, the Society of the Cincinnati, the David Library of the American Revolution, and the

Fred W. Smith National Library for the Study of George Washington made the research for this book possible.

I owe a special thanks to my students and colleagues at SAMS. You have no idea how much you have taught me, or have contributed to my development as a historian.

John Couture and the staff at the Bier Station in Kansas City, Missouri, provided a welcoming atmosphere and allowed me to homestead a table where I wrote about Light-Horse Harry Lee.

With this book, I think my mother, Rosalie M. Herrera, finally understands (mostly) what it is that I do for a living. Despite decades of wondering what exactly it is that I do, why I do it, or how I came to be a historian (we're still working on that), she has always been there for me as a voice of support, encouragement, and curiosity. Thanks, Mom. I love you.

Most of all, Dolora deserves my love, thanks, and gratitude for her years of support in all that I do, and have done as a historian and more. Without her, this book would not have come about. Thank you, I love you.

Portions of this book have previously appeared as "'[T]he zealous activity of Capt. Lee': Light-Horse Harry Lee and *Petite Guerre*," *The Journal of Military History* 79, no. 1 (January 2015): 9–36; "From Small Things: How a Staff Ride Became Two Articles and a Book Project," *Reflections on War and Society: Dale Center for the Study of War and Society Blog*, University of Southern Mississippi, 11 September 2015; "Foraging and Combat Operations at Valley Forge, February–March 1778," *Army History* 79 (Spring 2011): 6–29; and "'[O]ur Army will hut this Winter at Valley forge': George Washington, Decision-Making, and the Council War," *Army History* (Fall 2020): 6–26. They reappear through the permissions of *The Journal of Military History*, *Army History*, and the Dale Center for the Study of War and Society.

Notes

Abbreviations

Archives and Collections

AAS	American Antiquarian Society, Worcester, Massachusetts
APS	American Philosophical Society, Philadelphia, Pennsylvania
CHS	Chicago Historical Society, Illinois
CTHS	Connecticut Historical Society, Hartford
DHS	Delaware Historical Society, Wilmington
DPL	Detroit Public Library, Michigan
FAM	Fenimore Art Museum, Cooperstown, New York
GCHS	Gloucester County Historical Society, Woodbury, New Jersey
GMD, LC	Geography and Map Division, Library of Congress, Washington, D.C.
GWP	George Washington Papers, Library of Congress, Washington, D.C.
HEH	Henry E. Huntington Library and Art Gallery, Department of Manuscripts, San Marino, California
Houghton	Houghton Library, Harvard University, Cambridge, Massachusetts
HSCC	Historical Society of Cecil County, Elkton, Maryland
HSP	Historical Society of Pennsylvania, Philadelphia
LC	Library of Congress, Washington, D.C.
MAHS	Massachusetts Historical Society, Boston
MDHS	Maryland Historical Society, Baltimore
MNHP	Morristown National Historical Park, New Jersey
NAM	National Army Museum, London, UK
NARA	National Archives and Records Administration, Washington, D.C.
NAS	National Archives of Scotland, Edinburgh
NJHS	New Jersey Historical Society, Newark
NLS	National Library of Scotland, Edinburgh
NYHS	New-York Historical Society, New York
NYPL	New York Public Library, New York
PCC	Papers of the Continental Congress, National Archives and Records Administration, Washington, D.C.
PUL	Manuscripts Division, Department of Rare Books and Special Collections, Princeton University Library, Princeton, New Jersey
RIHS	Rhode Island Historical Society, Providence
Rutgers	Special Collections and University Archives, Rutgers University Libraries, New Brunswick, New Jersey
SCL	Society of the Cincinnati Library, Washington, D.C.

Small	Albert and Shirley Small Collections, University of Virginia, Charlottesville
Swem	Special Collections Research Center, Swem Library, College of William and Mary, Williamsburg, Virginia
TNA	National Archives, Kew, UK
UHL	University of Houston Libraries, Houston, Texas
VFNHP	Valley Forge National Historical Park, Pennsylvania
VHS	Virginia Historical Society, Richmond
WHS	Wisconsin Historical Society, Madison
WLCL	William L. Clements Library, University of Michigan, Ann Arbor

Published Sources

Army List
    A List of the General and Field Officers, as They Rank in the Army. . . . London: J. Millan. Various Publication Dates.

JCC, 5
    Ford, Worthington Chauncey, ed. *Journals of the Continental Congress, 1774–1789.* Vol. 5, *June 5, 1776 to October 8, 1776.* Washington, D.C.: Government Printing Office, 1906.

JCC, 6
    Ford, Worthington Chauncey, ed. *Journals of the Continental Congress, 1774–1789.* Vol. 6, *October 9, 1776 to December 31, 1776.* Washington, D.C.: Government Printing Office, 1906.

JCC, 9
    Ford, Worthington Chauncey, ed. *Journals of the Continental Congress, 1774–1789.* Vol. 9, *3 October–31 December 1777.* Washington, D.C.: Government Printing Office, 1907.

LDC, 8
    Smith, Paul H., ed. *Letters of Delegates to Congress, 1774–1789.* Vol. 8, *September 18, 1777–January 31, 1778.* Washington, D.C.: Library of Congress, 1981.

LDC, 9
    Smith, Paul H., ed. *Letters of Delegates to Congress, 1774–1789.* Vol. 9, *February 1–May 31, 1778.* Washington, D.C.: Library of Congress, 1982.

LMCC, 2
    Burnett. Edmund C., ed. *Letters of the Members of the Continental Congress.* Vol. 2, *July 5, 1776—December 31, 1777.* Washington, D.C.: Carnegie Institution, 1923.

LMCC, 3
    Burnett. Edmund C., ed. *Letters of the Members of the Continental Congress.* Vol. 3, *January 1, 1777–December 31, 1778.* Washington, D.C.: Carnegie Institution, 1926.

NDAR, 10
    Crawford, Michael J., ed. *Naval Documents of the American Revolution.* Vol. 10, *American Theater: October 1, 1777–December 31, 1777, European Theater:*

October 1, 1777–December 31, 1777. Washington, D.C.: Naval Historical Center, 1996.

NDAR, 11

Crawford, Michael J., ed. *Naval Documents of the American Revolution*. Vol. 11, *American Theater: January 1, 1778–March 31, 1778, European Theater: January 1, 1778–March 31, 1778*. Washington D.C.: Naval Historical Center, 2005.

NDAR, 12

Crawford, Michael J., ed. *Naval Documents of the American Revolution*. Vol. 12, *American Theater: April 1, 1778–May 31, 1778, European Theater: April 1, 1778–May 31, 1778*. Washington, D.C.: Naval Historical Center, 2013.

OCA

Heitman, Francis B., ed. *Historical Register of Officers of the Continental Army During the War of the Revolution, April 1775, to December, 1783*. New, rev., enl. ed. Washington, D.C.: Rare Book Shop Publishing Company, 1914.

ODNB

Oxford Dictionary of National Biography Oxford Dictionary of National Biography, ed. H. C. G. Matthew and Brian Harrison. Oxford: Oxford University Press, 2004. Online ed., ed. Lawrence Goldman, January 2008.

PA, 5

Hazard, Samuel, ed. *Pennsylvania Archives*. Ser. 1. Vol. 5. Philadelphia: Joseph Severns, 1853.

PA, 6

Hazard, Samuel, ed. *Pennsylvania Archives*. Ser. 1. Vol. 6. Philadelphia: Joseph Severns, 1853.

PGW, 10

Washington, George. *The Papers of George Washington: Revolutionary War Series*. Vol. 10, *11 June 1777–18 August 1777*. Edited by Frank E. Grizzard, Jr. Charlottesville: University Press of Virginia, 2000.

PGW, 11

Washington, George. *The Papers of George Washington: Revolutionary War Series*. Vol. 11, *19 August 1777–25 October 1777*. Edited by Philander D. Chase and Edward G. Lengel. Charlottesville: University of Virginia Press, 2002.

PGW, 12

Washington, George. *The Papers of George Washington: Revolutionary War Series*. Vol. 12, *October–December 1777*. Edited by Frank E. Grizzard Jr. and David R. Hoth. Charlottesville: University of Virginia Press, 2002.

PGW, 13

Washington, George. *The Papers of George Washington: Revolutionary War Series*. Vol. 13, *December 1777–February 1778*. Edited by Edward G. Lengel. Charlottesville: University of Virginia Press, 2003.

PGW, 14

Washington, George. *The Papers of George Washington: Revolutionary War Series*. Vol. 14, *March 1778–April 1778*. Edited by David R. Hoth. Charlottesville: University of Virginia Press, 2004.

PGW, 21

Washington, George. *The Papers of George Washington: Revolutionary War Series*. Vol. 21, *1 June–31 July 1779*. Edited by William M. Ferraro. Charlottesville: University of Virginia Press, 2012.

PGW, 22

Washington, George. *The Papers of George Washington, Revolutionary War Series*. Vol. 22, *1 August–21 October 1779*. Edited by Benjamin L. Huggins. Charlottesville: University of Virginia Press, 2013.

PMHB

The Pennsylvania Magazine of History and Biography.

PNG, 2

Greene, Nathanael. *The Papers of General Nathanael Greene*. Vol. 2, *1 January 1777–16 October 1778*. Edited by Richard K. Showman, Robert E. McCarthy, and Margaret Cobb. Chapel Hill: University of North Carolina Press for the Rhode Island Historical Society, 1980.

PNG, 3

Greene, Nathanael. *The Papers of General Nathanael Greene*. Vol. 3, *18 October 1778–10 May 1779*. Edited by Richard K. Showman, Robert E. McCarthy, and Elizabeth C. Stevens. Chapel Hill: University of North Carolina Press for the Rhode Island Historical Society, 1983.

PNG, 8

Greene, Nathanael. *The Papers of General Nathanael Greene*. Vol. 8, *30 March–10 July 1781*. Edited by Dennis M. Conrad, Roger N. Parks, Martha J. King, and Richard K. Showman. Chapel Hill: University of North Carolina Press for the Rhode Island Historical Society, 1995.

PWR

Lynn, John Blair, and William H. Egle. *Pennsylvania in the War of the Revolution, Battalions and Line: 1775–1783*. Vol. 1. Harrisburg, Pa.: Lane S. Hart, 1880.

WGW, 21

Washington, George. *The Writings of George Washington from the Original Manuscript Resources, 1745–1799*. Vol. 21, *December 22, 1780–April 26, 1781*. Edited by John C. Fitzpatrick. Washington, D.C.: Government Printing Office, 1937.

WMQ

The William and Mary Quarterly

Preface

1. Herrera, "Foraging and Combat Operations at Valley Forge," 6–29; Herrera, "'[T]he zealous activity of Capt. Lee'," 9–36; Herrera, "'[O]ur Army will hut this Winter at Valley forge'," 6–26; Herrera, "From Small Things: How a Staff Ride Became Two Articles and a Book Project."

Introduction

1. Mackesy, *War for America*, 214, reports that the British Army's returns for March 1778 give a total strength in Philadelphia, including Germans and provincials, of 19,350, of whom 14,700 were fit for duty. Bodle, *Valley Forge Winter*, 169, estimates the strength of the force led by Nathanael Greene at between fifteen hundred and two thousand soldiers. The February 1778 returns for Washington's army put the total at 22,283 total strength. Lesser, *Sinews of Independence*, 59.

2. For examples pointing toward the centrality of logistical efforts and military operations, see Bowler, *Logistics and the Failure of the British Army*; and Syrett, *Shipping and the American War*.

3. For a more complete discussion of the historiography, see Herrera, "Foraging and Combat Operations at Valley Forge," 6–29; Herrera, "'[T]he zealous activity of Capt. Lee'," 9–36; and Herrera, "'[O]ur Army will hut this Winter at Valley forge'," 6–26. Joint Chiefs of Staff, *JP 3-0*, xx, II-1; Huber, "Compound Warfare,", 1–9; US Army, *FM 3-0*, 3-1. See also Murray and Mansoor, *Hybrid Warfare*.

4. See Lockhart, *Drillmaster of Valley Forge* for Steuben in myth and reality.

5. Bodle, *Valley Forge Winter*, 2–7. Bodle's is the most through and recent examination of the encampment. The correspondence between Washington and his subordinates was constant. Washington's instructions allowed for substantial latitude in the accomplishment of his subordinate commanders' missions.

6. Nathanael Greene to unknown, 5 January 1778, Greene Papers, AAS; Greene to Alexander McDougall, 25 January 1778, *PNG*, 2:261.

7. George Weedon to John Page, 17 December 1777, Weedon Papers, CHS.

8. Timothy Pickering to John Scammell, 17 February 1778, Pickering Papers, MAHS.

9. William Buchannan to Thomas Wharton, 4 November 1777, 24 November 1777, Buchanan Letters, NYPL.

10. 6 October 1777, 24 November 1777, JCC, 9:775, 961–62; Carp, *To Starve the Army at Pleasure*, 78–79.

11. Samuel Tenny [Tenney] to Peter Turner, 18 February 1778, Turner Papers, WLCL; General Orders, 3 February 1778, *PGW*, 13:442.

12. Risch, *Supplying Washington's Army*, 17–20; Buel, *In Irons*, 43–46.

13. Resavy and McNichol, *Continental Army*, [1]; Capt.-Lt. John Peebles, Forty-Second Regiment of Foot, noted on 3 February 1778, "deserters coming in frequently & in parties—12 Serjts. & 1 Corpl. of their artily came in today who say their army at Valley forge are in great destress for want of Cloathing Shoes &ca.—and yesterday or today some country men brought in one of their militia Colls. prisoner, & some people from the Jerseys brought in a Committee-man—well done my lads keep it up," in *John Peebles' American War*, 162.

14. Bodle, *Valley Forge Winter*, 168; Thibaut, "In the True Rustic Order," 153–54; 6 February 1778, Angell, "Diary," 128; 9 February 1778, Marshall, *Diary*, 167; James Varnum to Greene, 12 February 1778, *PNG*, 2:280.

15. Risch, *Supplying Washington's Army*, 82–87, 18–20, 180, 221, 228; Bodle, *Valley Forge Winter*, 167–69; Ephraim Blaine to Thomas Wharton, Jr., 12 February 1778,

Boyle, *Writings from the Valley Forge Encampment*, 1:49; "Congress printed $241,000,000 between 1775 and 1779. Continentals traded at par in 1775, rose to $1.5 per dollar of specie by the end of 1776, and reached a of five to one by the end of 1777," according to Kulikoff, "The Economic Crisis of the Revolutionary Era," http://www .librarycompany.org/Economics/PDF%20Files/kulikoff.pdf, (7 May 2021).

16. 26 January 1778, Muenchausen, *At General Howe's Side, 1776–1778*, 47.

17. Walter Stewart to George Washington, 18 January 1778, Washington to Stewart, 22 January 1778, *PGW*, 13:276–77, 317.

18. Simcoe, *Military Journal*, 34; John Lacey, Jr. to Thomas Wharton, 24 January 1778, *PA*, 6:202; Washington to Lacey, 8 February 1778, *PGW*, 13:477–78; Jackson, *With the British Army in Philadelphia*, 162–64; Risch, *Supplying Washington's Army*, 82–87, 18–20, 221, 228; Bodle, *Valley Forge Winter*, 6, 9–10, 167–69; Blaine to John Howell, 10 February 1778, Howell, *Book of John Howell*, 197.

19. Jedidiah Huntington to Jabez Huntington, 20 December 1777, Huntington Papers, CTHS.

20. Pickering to Rebecca White Pickering, 13 December 1777, Pickering Papers, MAHS.

21. Jackson, *With the British Army in Philadelphia*, 162–64; Risch, *Supplying Washington's Army*, 82–87, 18–20, 221, 228; Bodle, *Valley Forge Winter*, 6, 9–10, 167–69. Living a hand-to-mouth existence in while campaigning in North America was not new to the British Army. See Yagi, "Surviving the Wilderness," 66–86.

22. Washington to Greene, 12 February 1778, *PNG*, 2:281; Stewart, *Foraging at Valley Forge*, 16.

23. Washington to Greene, 12 February 1778, Greene to Washington, 15 February 1778, *PNG*, 2:281, 285; John Laurens to Henry Laurens, 17 February 1778, Laurens, *Army Correspondence*, 127–28; Bodle, *Valley Forge Winter*, 169, 176; 17 February 1778, Stoudt, *Ordeal at Valley Forge*, 137, 138; Lesser, *Sinews of Independence*, 58–62.

24. Bodle, *Valley Forge Winter*, 178, 180–82; Wharton to Lacey, 9 January 1778, Pennsylvania Supreme Council to County Lieutenants, 9 January 1778, *PA*, 6:168, 169.

25. Richard McAlester to Wharton, 22 January 1778, 2 February 1778, William Coats to Wharton, *PA*, 6:169, 227; Dorland, "The Second Troop Philadelphia City Cavalry," 288.

26. Lacey to Wharton, 24 January 1778, 2 February 1778, 15 February 1778, *PA*, 6:202–203, 226.

27. Lacey to Wharton, 24 January 1778, 2 February 1778, William Coats to Wharton, 2 February 1778, Lacey to Wharton, 15 February 1778, *PA*, 6:202–203, 226, 265; Washington to Lacey 8 February 1778, Lacey to Washington, 11 February 1778, Washington to Lacey, 13 February 1778, *PGW*, 13:477–78, 510–11, 521; John Armstrong was major general of the Pennsylvania Militia.

28. Bodle, *Valley Forge Winter*, 140–42. The authorized strength for a troop was seventy-six officers and men, Loescher, *Washington's Eyes*, 9, 35–36, 67, 109, 148; Washington to Casimir Pulaski, 31 December 1777, Pulaski to Washington, 9 January 1778, *PGW*, 13:89, 192–93. Capt. Henry Lee's troop of the First Continental Light Dragoons was posted at Scott's Farm, about six miles south of Valley Forge, and an ad hoc squadron with elements of the First, Second, and Fourth Continental Light

Dragoons under Maj. John Jameson, First Continental Light Dragoons, patrolled southeast of Valley Forge in Bucks County.

29. Washington to Pulaski, 14 January 1778, *PGW*, 13:239–40; 19 December 1777, *JCC*, 9:1036; Bodle, *Valley Forge Winter*, 140, 142.

30. Bodle, *Valley Forge Winter*, 136, 138–39; Lacey to Washington, 19 February 1778, *PGW*, 13:592–93.

31. Washington to Buchanan, 7 February 1778, *PGW*, 13:465.

Chapter One

1. Risch, *Supplying Washington's Army*, 6, 17–18; Carp, *To Starve the Army at Pleasure*, 5, 6, 19–20, 21; Doerflinger, *A Vigorous Spirit of Enterprise*, 167–242. Thibaut, "This Fatal Crisis," is the authoritative study of the army's logistical state.

2. Risch, *Supplying Washington's Army*, 9–10, 11–12; Carp, *To Starve the Army at Pleasure*, 20; Kortenhoff, "Republican Ideology and Wartime Reality," 189–90.

3. Risch, *Supplying Washington's Army*, 14–16, 34, 35–36, 42.

4. Kortenhoff, "Republican Ideology and Wartime Reality," 189; Risch, *Supplying Washington's Army*, 36–37.

5. Carp, *To Starve the Army at Pleasure*, 38, 41, 43; Risch, *Supplying Washington's Army*, 169–73; James Duane to Robert R. Livingston, 19 June 1777, *LDC*, 7:223.

6. Carp, *To Starve the Army at Pleasure*, 42–44; Risch, *Supplying Washington's Army*, 172–73.

7. Kortenhoff, "Republican Ideology and Wartime Reality," 201–3; Risch, *Supplying Washington's Army*, 25, 36; Graydon, *Memoirs of His Own Time*, 299.

8. Carp, *To Starve the Army at Pleasure*, 32; Risch, *Supplying Washington's Army*, 37, 40.

9. Kortenhoff, "Republican Ideology and Wartime Reality," 202–4; Risch, *Supplying Washington's Army*, 38–41; Lender, *Cabal!*, 116.

10. George Washington to Thomas Johnson, 6 November 1777, Orders to Peter Adams, 7 November 1777, *PGW*, 12:144, 150; William Smallwood to Johnson, 6 November 1777, Browne, *Journal and Correspondence of the Maryland Council of Safety*, 413. Smallwood's letter is dated 6 November 1777, but was printed as 8 November 1777. As 1777 ended, Brig. Gen. Anthony Wayne wrote of the "Wretched situation of our soldiers . . . , our poor naked fellows—feel their own misery—and are Concious of Meriting better treatment." Anthony Wayne to Richard Peters, 30 December 1777, SCL.

11. Washington to William Livingston, 1 November 1777, Washington to George Read, 8 November 1777, Washington to Patrick Henry, 13 November 1777, *PGW*, 12:88, 145, 150, 174, 241–242; Livingston to the Assembly, 5 November 1777, Livingston, *Papers of William Livingston*, 100.

12. Richard Peters to Washington, 18 October 1777, *PGW*, 11:546; Board of War to Thomas Wharton, 18 October 1777, *PA*, 5:686.

13. Resolution of Council, 21 October 1777, *PA*, 5:691.

14. Henry Beekman Livingston to Francis Lewis and William Duer, [n.d.] Dearborn Collection, Houghton.

15. Richard Peters to Washington, 7 November 1777, Washington to Peters, 11 November 1777, *PGW*, 12:158, 212. Washington also had to address the matter of

Maj. Gen. Israel Putnam's practice of seizing for his forces in New York clothing supplies destined for the Main Army. See Washington to James Mease, 12 November 1777, *PGW*, 12:227–28.

16. Ruddiman, *Plows, Plagues, and Petroleum*, 121, 123–24; Fagan, *Little Ice Age*, xii, xiii, xv, 160.

17. Ludlum, *Early American Winters*, 101; Washington to William Buchanan, 28 December 1777, *PGW*, 13:29. See Boyle, "'Up to our Knees in Mud'," APS, for a detailed study and daily recordings of the weather. For a comparative look at the Valley Forge and Morristown encampments, see Bailey, "Two Winters of Discontent," 306–34.

18. 11, 12, 14 December 1777, Armstrong, "From Saratoga to Valley Forge," 256, 257; 14 December 1777, Brigham, "Revolutionary Diary," 15; 11 December 1777, Dearborn, *Journals*, 117; 12 December 1777, Waldo, "Diary," 305; 12 December 1777, McMichael, "Diary," 157; Jedidiah Huntington to Jonathan Trumbull, 14 December 1777, *Trumbull Papers*, 204, 205; John Laurens to Henry Laurens, 12 December 1777, Laurens, *Papers of Henry Laurens*, 190. On the selection of Valley Forge and decision making, see Newcomb, "Washington's Generals and the Decision to Quarter at Valley Forge," 309–29; Bodle, "Generals and 'Gentlemen'," 59–89; Bodle, *Valley Forge Winter*, 11–12; and Herrera, "'[O]ur Army will hut this Winter at Valley forge'," 6–26.

19. John Chaloner to Peter Aston, 17 December 1777, Blaine, *Letterbook*, 57; 19 December 1777, Armstrong, "From Saratoga to Valley Forge," 258; 1 November 1777, *JCC*, 9:854; 18 December 1777, Dearborn, *Journals*, 118.

20. 19 December 1777, Angell, "Diary," 121; 19 December 1777, Brigham, "Diary," 16; 19 December 1777, McMichael, "Diary," 157; Hurd, Diary, VFNHP; Johnson, *Record of Connecticut Men*, 159, 158, 157.

21. 19 December 1777, Angell, "Diary," 121; 19 December 1777, Brigham, "Diary," 16; 19 December 1777, McMichael, "Diary," 157; Hurd, Diary, VFNHP.

22. 20 December 1777, Weedon, *Orderly Book*, 160–61; 20 December 1777, Armstrong, "From Saratoga to Valley Forge," 258; From a Committee to Inspect the Beef, 20 December 1777, *PGW*, 12:648–49; *OCA*, 438, 592, 204.

23. Marshall and Reade, "Massachusetts at Valley Forge," 270, state that Capt. Michael Farley was the assistant commissary of issues for Learned's Brigade, but he appears as lieutenant and quartermaster for the Ninth Massachusetts Continentals, per *OCA*, 222; 4 November 1775, *JCC*, 3:322.

24. Robert Lettis Hooper to Horatio Gates, 11 April 1779, RG 93, M859, NARA.

25. John Chaloner to ?, 16 December 1777, Society Collection, HSP.

26. Azariah Dunham to Ephraim Blaine, 17 December 1777, Blaine Papers, Force Collection, LC.

27. Dunham to Blaine, 17 December 1777, Blaine Papers, Force Collection, LC. Wagon brigades had no fixed table of organization, equipment, or manning. They might have as many as thirty teams, or as few as seven. Two or four horses, or two oxen constituted a team. See Risch, *Supplying Washington's Army*, 84, 311, 429.

28. 20, 21, 23, 25, 26 December 1777, Armstrong, "From Saratoga to Valley Forge," 258–60.

29. Thomas Jones and John Chaloner to Thomas Wharton and Council, 24 December 1777, *PA*, 6:130.

30. Jones and Chaloner to Wharton and Council, 24 December 1777, *PA*, 6:130.

31. Lender, *Cabal!*, 149–52.

32. Risch, *Supplying Washington's Army*, 171–72, 38; Jones to Wharton, 19 December 1777, *PA*, 6:107–8.

33. George Ross to Jones, 6 December 1777, *PA*, 6:69–70.

34. Committee at Camp to Laurens, 12 February 1778, *LDC*, 9:79, 80.

35. Carp, *To Starve the Army at Pleasure*, 44; Council to Pennsylvania Delegates in Congress, 20 December 1777, *PA*, 6:116.

36. Council to Pennsylvania Delegates in Congress, 20 December 1777, John Bull to Wharton, [23 or 24 December 1777], *PA*, 6:116–117, 129; *PWR*, 258–59.

37. Risch, *Supplying Washington's Army*, 21–22, 83–84; 17 September 1777, *JCC*, 8: 752–53; 6 October 1777, 14 November 1777, 10 December 1777, *JCC*, 9:775, 905, 1013–15; 25 February 1778, Muhlenberg, *Journals*, 133; Council to Deputy Wagon Masters, *PA*, 22 December 1777, 6:124.

38. 10 December 1777, *JCC*, 9:1013–15.

39. 10 December 1777, *JCC*, 9:1013–15.

40. Buchannan to Wharton, 4 November 1777, Buchanan Letters, NYPL.

41. Elisha Clark to Jeremiah Wadsworth, 6 December 1777, Wadsworth Records, CTHS.

42. Charles Stewart to John Davis, 22 December 1777, Davis Papers, LC; Stewart to Blaine, 23 December 1777, Blaine Papers, Force Collection, LC; 23 December 1777, Barnard Diary, HSP.

43. Capt. Stephen Olney's Account, Smith Papers, RIHS.

44. 21 December 1777, Smith Diaries, AAS.

45. General Orders, 26 December 1777, *PGW*, 13:1.

46. The new constitutions of Pennsylvania and Delaware replaced the governor and lieutenant-governor with president and vice-president. Penn. Const. (1776), sec. 1, 19, 20; Del. Const. (1776), art.7. Washington, "Proclamation on Market at Valley Forge," 30 January 1778, *PGW*, 13:415–16; Montgomery, *History of Berks County*, 237–38.

47. John Lesher to Wharton, 9 January 1778, *PA*, 6:170.

48. Lesher to Wharton, 9 January 1778, *PA*, 6:171.

49. Thibaut, "This Fatal Crisis," table between 126 and 127; Trussell, *Birthplace of an Army*, 21; Risch, *Supplying Washington's Army*, 191; Friedemann, Kraybill, and Consolazio, "The Uses of Recommended Dietary Allowances in Military Nutrition," 1008.

50. Risch, *Supplying Washington's Army*, 221; Biddle to Washington, 25 January 1778, *PGW*, 13:339–40.

51. "During the last week in February, 15,903 rations per day were required by the army at camp. Allowing 140 rations per barrel and 8 barrels per wagon, over 113 wagons would be required," Risch, *Supplying Washington's Army*, 221; Biddle to Washington, 25 January 1778, *PGW*, 13:339–40; Tylden, *Horses and Saddlery*, 179; Bowler, *Logistics and the Failure of the British Army in America*, 56–57. A barrel of flour,

corn, or oats weighed about 196 pounds, of wheat 280 pounds, of fish 290 pounds, of beef 240 pounds, of fresh or salted pork 220 pounds, of beer, whiskey, or rum 32–34 gallons (211–224 pounds). A keg of fish weighed roughly 40–50 pounds. Tare weights of barrels varied. English butter barrels generally weighed in at 256 pounds gross weight, 26 pounds tare weight, while soap barrels weighed in at 280 pounds and 32 pounds respectively. The weights and measurements given are rough estimates because of the lack of strict uniformity by American coopers. Compounding this imprecision, Americans used the terms cask and barrel interchangeably. A modern, 30-gallon, white-oak whiskey barrel weighs about 78 pounds tare. US Bureau of the Census, *Historical Statistics*, 750–51, 755; Zupko, *Dictionary of Weights and Measures*, 32, 27–28; 27 January 1781, "An Act for Raising One Million & Four Hundred Thousand Pounds Weight of Beef Towards the Support of the Continental Army," Metcalf, *Laws of New Hampshire*, 356; "Whiskey Barrels," *The Barrel Mill*, https://www .thebarrelmill.com/barrels (7 May 2021); For larger measurements, most states used the English hundredweight of 112 pounds. Virginia, the Carolinas, and Georgia, however, measured in quintals of 100; Kelly, *Universal Cambrist and Commercial Instructor*, 11.

52. The permanent Board of War did not assume its duties until January 1778. Gerry had previously served on the Committee at Headquarters, formed by Congress to look into the army's condition and prod Washington into a winter campaign. Reality dampened Congress's exercise of authority, and the army marched into Valley Forge. 7 November 1777, 17 November 1777, 27 November 1777, 28 November 1777, *JCC*, 9:874, 936, 971, 972; Committee on Emergency Provisions to Wharton, 30 December 1777, *LDC*, 8:499, 501, n. 1.

53. Syrett, *Shipping and the American War*, 128.

54. Bowler, *Logistics and the Failure of the British Army in America*, 41, 48–49, 68, 70–71, 9, 72.

55. Bowler, *Logistics and the Failure of the British Army in America*, 94–95, 56–57, 109, 92–93; Mackesy, *War for America*, 66; Syrett, *Shipping and the American War*, 126; Jackson, *With the British Army in Philadelphia*, 162–63; 6 January 1778, Peebles, *John Peebles' American War*, 161; Charles Stuart to Earl of Bute [John Stuart], 10 July 1777, 29 March 1777, Bute [Stuart] *A Prime Minister and His Son*, 112–13, 101–102.

56. 22, 24 October 1777, 8 December 1777, Morton, "Diary," 22, 23, 34–35; 10 December 1777, Robertson, *Diaries and Sketches*, 161; Timothy Pickering to Rebecca Pickering, 13 December 1777, Pickering Papers, MAHS; 13 December 1777, Peebles, *John Peebles' American War*, 154–55.

57. 28, 29 September 1777, 23, 24 October 1777, 14, 8 December 1777, Morton, "Diary," 9–10, 22, 23, 37, 34–35.

58. 18 December 1777, Howe Orderly Book, WLCL; 1 October 1777, Morton, "Diary," 10–11.

59. 21, 22 December 1777, Howe Orderly Book, WLCL; 22, 23, 24, 25 December 1777, Robertson, *Diaries and Sketches*, 162; 22 January 1778, Extracts from Various Standing Orders, NAM.

60. 28 December 1777, Peebles, *John Peebles' American War*, 157; Howe to George Germain, 19 January 1778, Military Despatches, TNA; Carl Leopold Baurmeister to

Friedrich Christian Arnold von Jungkenn, 20 January 1778, *Revolution in America*, 23, 148; Master's Journal of H.M.S. *Roebuck*, 29 December 1777, *NDAR*, 10:825.

61. 22, 27 December 1777, Howe Orderly Book, WLCL.

Chapter Two

1. George Washington to Nathanael Greene, 12 February 1778, *PGW*, 13:514.

2. Washington to Greene, 12 February 1778, *PGW*, 13:514.

3. Washington to Greene, 12 February 1778, *PGW*, 13:514–15.

4. Washington to Anthony Wayne, 9[–12] February 1778, *PGW*, 13:492–93; Greene to Clement Biddle, 12 February 1778, Greene to Wayne, 12 February 1778, *PNG*, 2:282–83. Biddle's appointment as commissary general for forage did not carry a military rank. He was, however, addressed as "colonel" out of respect for his previous service and rank in the Pennsylvania Militia. Risch, *Supplying Washington's Army*, 102, n. 16.

5. Washington to Greene, 12 February 1778, *PGW*, 13:514–15; Greene to Wayne, 12 February 1778, *PNG*, 2:282–83; 10 January 1778, *JCC*, 10:39–41.

6. Bodle, *Valley Forge Winter*, 5, 6, 9; McGready, "Contested Grounds, 33–35; Olsen, "Food Animals," 506–9; Revolutionary War Documents of Supplies Gathered, Howell Family Collection, GCHS; Purvis, *Colonial America*, 55, 68; Gaylord and Tucker, *American Husbandry*, 184; Washington to James Duane, 26 December 1780, *WGW*, 21:60.

7. Ewald, *Diary*, 80. The literal translation for *jäger* is hunter. *Jägers* were light infantrymen, although some units were mounted on horseback. They "were recruited from foresters and huntsmen," whose "individual fieldcraft and marksmanship were reckoned to be of special importance in America." Unlike most British and some American light infantry, *jägers* were armed with rifles, which had greater accuracy and longer ranges than smoothbore muskets but were much slower to reload. Atwood, *The Hessians*, 45

8. State of Pennsylvania, Simcoe Papers, WLCL; Bodle, *Valley Forge Winter*, 8–9; Sullivan, *The Disaffected*, 130.

9. State of Pennsylvania, Simcoe Papers, WLCL; Bodle, *Valley Forge Winter*, 9. The "Low dutch" were of Dutch descent, and typically members of the Dutch Reformed Church, whereas "High Dutch" referred to Germans. See Maar, "High Dutch and the Low Dutch in New York," 317–29; and Purvis, "Patterns of Ethnic Settlement," 107–22.

10. State of Pennsylvania, Simcoe Papers, WLCL; Bodle, *Valley Forge Winter*, 6.

11. Bodle, *Valley Forge Winter*, 9.

12. Thayer, *Nathanael Greene*, 222; Biddle, "Selections from the Correspondence of Colonel Clement Biddle," 312–13; Ephraim Blaine to William Evans, 12 February 1778, Blaine to Thomas Wharton, 12 February 1778, Blaine, *Letterbook*, 123.

13. Bodle, "Vortex of Small Fortunes," 288; After Orders, 12 February 1778, RG 93, M853, NARA; 6 February 1778, Angell, "Diary," 129. Angell noted that thirty-two subalterns (captain-lieutenants, lieutenants, and ensigns) were called for, but this was not given in the After Orders. Poor Orderly Book, HSP; First New Jersey Continental Regiment Orderly Book, NJHS; Thomas Jones, 13 February 1778, Return of Provisions

&c. Delivered for the Use of the Army at the Commissary Generals Magazine, RG 360, M247, NARA; Philippe-Charles-Jean-Baptiste Tronson du Coudray to Washington, 4 July 1777, *PGW*, 10:184; McKenney, *Organizational History of Field Artillery*, 9, 11; Muller, *Treatise of Artillery*, 178–79; Stevens, *System for the Discipline of the Artillery*, 141.

14. Jones, Return of Provisions &c. Delivered for the Use of the Army at the Commissary Generals Magazine, 13 February 1778, RG 360, M247, NARA; Poor Orderly Book, HSP; After Orders, 12 February 1778, RG 93, M853, NARA.

15. Blaine, An Estimate of Provisions in the Middle District, Ephraim Blaine, 14 February 1778, Blaine, *Letterbook*, 125–26; Washington to Greene, 12 February 1778, *PNG*, 2:281; 12 February 1778, Angell, "Diary," 129; Washington to Wayne, 9 [–12] February 1778, *PGW*, 13:492–93; Risch, *Supplying Washington's Army*, 219–20; "General Anthony Wayne," VFNHP, http://www.nps.gov/vafo/historyculture/wayne.htm (7 May 2021); Stewart, *Foraging at Valley Forge*, 16.

16. Richard Butler to Thomas Wharton, 12 February 1778, De Coppet Collection, Princeton.

17. After Orders, 12 February 1778, RG 93, M853, NARA. Time and budgetary constraints prevented the recovery of more soldiers' names from the pension records in the National Archives.

18. 6 February 1778, Angell, "Diary," 129; George Fleming to Sebastian Bauman, 13 February 1778, Boyle, *Writings from the Valley Forge Encampment*, 1:52; 13 February 1778, Krafft, *Journal*, 18.

19. 11–13 February 1778, Muhlenberg, *Journals*, 130–31.

20. Wayne to Washington, February 1778, Wayne Papers, HSP; 12 February 1778, Angell, "Diary," 129; 12 February 1778, Poor Orderly Book, HSP; 12 February 1778, First New Jersey Continental Regiment Orderly Book, NJHS; 13 February 1778, Wild, "Journal," 106.

21. 12 February 1778, Muenchausen, *At General Howe's Side*, 47; 13 February 1778, Krafft, "Journal," 18.

22. Greene to Biddle, 14 February 1778, *PNG*, 2:283; Index E-G, Tavern Petitions, Chester County Archives and Record Services, West Chester, Pa., https://www .chesco.org/DocumentCenter/View/4009/Tavern-Petitions-1700-1923-Index-E-G ?bidId= (7 May 2021); Futhey and Cope, *History of Chester County*, 527; Ashmead, *History of Delaware County*, 629; Winthrop, "Early Roads in Chester County," 61.

23. Greene to Biddle, 14 February 1778, *PNG*, 2:283

24. Blaine to Evans, 12 February 1778, Blaine, *Letterbook*, 123; 12 February 1778, Muenchausen, *At General Howe's Side*, 47; 22, 28 October 1777, Montresor, *Journals*, 469, 471.

25. 12 February 1778, Muenchausen, *At General Howe's Side*, 47–48; 11, 14 February 1778, Peebles, *John Peebles' American War*, 163, 164; *Philadelphia Evening Post*, 17 February 1778; Katcher, *Encyclopedia of British, Provincial, and German Army Units*, 95, 84; Petition of Jonathan Walton, 24 March 1790, AO13/72/239, 24 February 1790, Attestation of John Graves Simcoe, AO13/72/241, 17 March 1784, Memorial of John Walton, AO13/72/339, Records of the American Loyalist Claims Commission, NA; Thomas B. Allen, *Tories: Fighting for the King in America's First Civil War*, http:// www.toriesfightingfortheking.com/ToryArmy.htm (7 May 2021).

26. Judging by the size of the Seventy-First Foot's icon, both battalions manned this position. By comparison, two smaller icons designate the two-battalion strong Forty-Second Regiment of Foot (the Royal Highlanders or the Black Watch) on Fadden, *A Plan of the City and Environs of Philadelphia*, https://www.loc.gov/item/74692213/, GMD, LC, (7 May 2021); 14 February 1778, Doehlemann, "Diary," 15. Lewis Lochée reckoned the range of "musket shot" as 300 yards, *Elements of Field Fortification*, 37, 135.

27. 15 February 1778, Döhla, *Diary*, xviii, 70; Eelking, *German Allied Troops*, 336, 339; Greene to Washington, 15 February 1778, Robert Ballard to Greene, 15 February 1778, *PNG*, 2:285, 284, 289; 15 February 1778, Prechtel, *Diary*, 16, 131–32; 17 February 1778, Ewald, *Diary*, 120; 15 February 1778, Muenchausen, *At General Howe's Side*, 48.

28. Ballard to Greene, 15 February 1778, *PNG*, 2:284; Duffy, *Military Experience in the Age of Reason*, 207–9; *Moonpage*, https://www.moonpage.com/index.html?go =T&auto_dst=T&m=2&d=15&y=1778&hour=3&min=0&sec=, (7 May 2021).

29. Ballard to Greene, 15 February 1778, *PNG*, 2:284.

30. 17 February 1778, Ewald, *Diary*, 120; Ballard to Greene, 15 February 1778, *PNG*, 2:284; 15 February 1778, Prechtel, *Diary*, 132.

31. 15 February 1778, Döhla, *Diary*, 70; 14 February 1778, Doehlemann, "Diary," 15, 17; 15 February 1778, Prechtel, *Diary*, 131–32.

32. Ballard to Greene, 15 February 1778, *PNG*, 2:284; Greene to Washington, 17 February 1778, *PGW*, 13:570.

33. Greene to Washington, 15 February 1778, *PGW*, 13:546–547; Thayer, *Nathanael Green*, 222–23.

34. Greene to Washington, 15 February 1778, *PGW*, 13:546.

35. Greene to Washington, 15 February 1778, *PGW*, 13:548; Tench Tilghman to Clement Biddle, 15 February 1778, Biddle Papers, HSP. Feeding the cattle that were to feed the army, the horses that drew the wagons and guns, and served the cavalry was a herculean task. Earl of Pembroke [Henry Herbert], *A Method of Breaking Horses, and Teaching Soldiers to Ride*, 114, 115, suggested "Cut straw and a little hay," along with a "quartern [four ounces] of corn" for horses. He thought that ten to twelve pounds daily of hay was "sufficient for most horses." Hinde, *Discipline of the Light-Horse*, 203, recommended "three quarterns of oats a day" and 20 pounds of hay per cavalry mount. Perjés, "Army Provisioning, Logistics and Strategy," 14–17, calculates the seasonal feeding practices of early-modern, Continental European armies. In the winter, horses were fed mostly dry fodder. A typical daily ration included around fifteen to eighteen pounds of hay, and four to seven pounds of straw; or four to seven pounds of oats, nine to eleven pounds of hay, and four to seven pounds of straw; or twenty to twenty-two pounds of hay alone. Peters, *The Rational Farmer*, 59, 60, noted that two- or three-year-old cattle ate 120 pounds in the field per day, while "Stall fed bullocks for fattening, have an allowance of half their weight every 24 hours given them of the above food; for instance, if a bullock weighs 600 weight, he will eat near 300 weight of such food." Peters recommended a mixture of "turnip rooted cabbage" and straw for fattening them prior to slaughter. Sheep, on the other hand, ate from fifteen to twenty pounds of feed daily. The figures did not include whatever grazing the livestock might eat when set out to pasture.

36. Greene to Washington, 15 February 1778, *PGW*, 13:548.

37. Washington to Greene, 16 February 1778, *PGW*, 13:556–557.

38. Greene to Washington, 16 February 1778, *PGW*, 13:557; William J. Heller, "The Gunmakers of Old Northampton," *The Pennsylvania-German Society: Proceedings and Addresses at Allentown, November 2, 1906*, vol. 17 (Lancaster, Pa.: Pennsylvania-German Society, 1908), 7, 9; Jasper Yeates to James Burd, 15 February 1778, Shippen Family Papers, HSP.

39. Greene to Washington, 16 February 1778, *PGW*, 13:557–558; Receipt, 16 February 1778, Blaine Papers, Force Collection, LC.

40. Greene to Washington, 16 February 1778, Washington to Henry Lee, Jr., 17 February 1778, *PGW*, 13:558, 569, 561–62; Blaine to Charles Stewart, 16 February 1778, Boyle, *Writings from the Valley Forge Encampment*, 1:54.

41. 16, 17 February 1778, Greene to Washington, *PGW*, 13:558, 569; John Laurens to Henry Laurens, 17 February 1778, Laurens, *Army Correspondence*, 127; 17 February 1778, Stoudt, *Ordeal at Valley Forge*, 136.

42. 17 February 1778, Greene to Washington, *PGW*, 13:569.

43. 17 February 1778, Greene to Washington, *PGW*, 13:569.

44. 17 February 1778, Greene to Washington, *PGW*, 13:570.

45. 17 February 1778, Greene to Washington, *PGW*, 13:570.

46. 18 February 1778, Greene to Washington, *PGW*, 13:580; *OCA*, 458.

47. 18 February 1778, Greene to Washington, Washington to Greene, *PGW*, 13:580, 581; 18 February 1778, 18 February 1778, Ephraim Blaine to Stewart, Boyle, *Writings from the Valley Forge Encampment*, 1:61.

48. Greene to Washington, 20 February 1778, *PGW*, 13:607; Greene to Henry Knox, 26 February 1778, *PNG*, 2:292, 293. Diarist Christopher Marshall recorded that Greene had seized "four hundred horses" on the forage, *Diary*, 169–70; Regimental Orders issued by Lt. Col. Josiah Harmar to the Sixth Pennsylvania, Harmar Papers, WLCL; Chaloner to Blaine, n.d. [March 1778?], Boyle, *Blaine Letterbook*, 154; 23 February 1778, Weedon, *Orderly Book*, 240.

49. Ephraim Blaine earlier prompted Washington to write just such a proclamation, Blaine to Washington, 4 February 1778, Washington, "Proclamation on Cattle," 18 February 1778, *PGW*, 13:577–578.

50. Greene to Knox, 26 February 1778, *PNG*, 2:293. Well after Greene had returned, orders pointed out the profusion of "carcases of dead horses . . . , Offil of the Commissarys Stalls . . . , [and] Much filth . . . among the Huts," 14 March 1778, "Revolutionary Army Orders," 403.

51. Robert Forsyth to Timothy Pickering, 28 February 1778, Boyle, *Writings from the Valley Forge Encampment*, 2:58; Henry Lee Jr. to Washington, 22 August 1779, *PGW*, 22:221, n. 6; Chaloner to Blaine, n.d. [March 1778?], Boyle, *Blaine Letterbook*, 154.

Chapter Three

1. Nathanael Greene to George Washington, 16 February 1778, *PGW*, 13:557–58.

2. Anderson, *Command of the Howe Brothers*, 299, 300; Gruber, *Howe Brothers*, 254, 287, 288–89, 290; Howe, *Narrative*, 30, 32.

3. See McGready, "Contested Grounds," 35.

4. "Disposition of His Majesty's Ships and Vessels employed in North America under the Command of the Vice Admiral the Viscount Howe," 5 January 1778, "Disposition of Captain Andrew Snape Hamond's Squadron," 23 January 1778, Andrew Snape Hamond to Richard Viscount Howe, 5 February 1778, *NDAR*, 11:39, 196, 292.

5. "Evidence of Major General Grey," "Evidence of Sir Andrew Snape Hamond," *Detail and Conduct of the American War*, 71–72, 73; Des Barres, Knight, and Hunter *A chart of Delawar River*, GMD, LC, https://www.loc.gov/item/75696335/ (7 May 2021); Henry Lee to Washington, 3 November 1777, *NDAR*, 10:388–89; Gardiner, *Navies and the American Revolution*, 20, 54–55, 74.

6. "Disposition of Captain Andrew Snape Hamond's Squadron," 23 January 1778, *NDAR*, 11:196. Faden, *Plan of the City and Environs of Philadelphia*, GMD, LC, https://www.loc.gov/item/74692213/ (7 May 2021), shows Hamond's flagship, *Roebuck*, tied between Pine and Spruce streets. Faden labeled Spruce Street as "Shrub." Earlier maps showed the correct name. Above *Roebuck*, *Camilla* lay at the foot of "Chesnut" Street, while *Delaware* tied up between Arch and Race streets, and *Vigilant* was at the end of Vine Street. Penn/King Street, the north-south road that paralleled the Delaware River, is now beneath Interstate Highway 95.

7. Continental Marine Committee to the Continental Navy Board of the Middle Department, 29 January 1778, Continental Marine Committee to John Barry, 29 January 1778, 11, 26 March 1778, Anthony Wayne to Simeon Jennings, 23 February 1778, *NDAR*, 11:231, 232, 799, 605, 412–13; Jackson, *Pennsylvania Navy*, 285. Tim McGrath's accounts of Barry's actions on the Delaware in the winter of 1778 repeat an incorrect assertion made first in Clark, *Gallant John Barry*, 143, that Barry carried orders from Washington to draft soldiers from Brig. Gen. James Mitchell Varnum's brigade of Connecticut and Rhode Island Continentals to make up for any shortfalls in manning the boats. See McGrath, "I Passed by Philadelphia with Two Boats," 46; and McGrath, *John Barry*, 147–49. No such orders were issued. More than a fortnight passed before Wayne, not Washington, ordered Lieutenant Jennings of the Second Rhode Island to take charge of nineteen soldiers from Varnum's brigade to join Barry in destroying hay along the New Jersey shore of the Delaware River. Nowhere in the 1785 Memorial to Congress did Barry state "I Passed by Philadelphia with Two Boats." See Series I: John Barry, Barry-Hayes Papers, Falvey Memorial Library, Digital Library @ Villanova University, https://digital.library.villanova.edu/Item/vudl:154320?type=AllFields (7 May 2021); Miscite, McGrath, e-mail message to author, 8 July 2010.

8. Matthewman, "Narrative," 178; William Bradford to Thomas Wharton, Jr., 24 January 1778, Hamond to Lord Howe, 1 February 1778, *NDAR*, 11:201, 261–62.

9. John Hazelwood to Washington, 4 February 1778, *NDAR*, 11:283.

10. Hazelwood to Washington, 4 February 1778, *PGW* 13:448; Clark, *Gallant John Barry*, 144; Hamond to Lord Howe, 1 February 1778, *NDAR*, 11:261. Barry acquired four additional boats and crews. See "Journal of H.M.S. *Roebuck*, Hamond," 24 February 1778, *NDAR*, 11:421, n.2; Jedidiah Huntington to Jabez Huntington, 20 February 1778, Huntington Papers, CTHS.

11. William Smallwood to Caesar Rodney, 18 February 1778, Dearborn Collection, Houghton; John Laurens to Henry Laurens, 17 February 1778, Laurens, *Army*

Correspondence, 128; Matthewman, "Narrative," 178; Sickler, *History of Salem County*, 143; Memorial of Hugh Cowperthwaite, 1 February 1788, AO 12/16/193, NA; 23 February 1778, Muenchausen, *At General Howe's Side*, 48.

12. Jackson, *With the British Army in Philadelphia*, 162–64; Lundin, *Cockpit of the Revolution*, 374, 376; Collin, *Journal and Biography*, 245.

13. Wayne to Joseph Ellis, 20 February 1778, GWP, LC; 19 February 1778, Angell, "Diary," 129.

14. Ellis to Wayne, 21 February 1778, Wayne Papers, HSP; Ellis to Wayne, 21 February 1778, GWP, LC; 19 February 1778, Angell, "Diary," 129; 20 February 1778, Peebles, *John Peebles' American War*, 165.

15. Wayne to Washington, 25, 26 February 1778, NDAR, 11:427–28, 438–39; Greene to Washington, 20 February 1778, PGW, 13:607; Thomas Sayre to Wayne, 21 February 1778, Wayne Papers, HSP.

16. Banta, *Sayre Family*, 94; Stryker, *Official Register*, 346; Sayre to Wayne, 21 February 1778, Wayne Papers, HSP; Wayne to Theodore Woodbridge, 22 February 1778, Woodbridge Papers, CTHS.

17. Wayne to Isaac Sherman, 22 February 1778, GWP, LC.

18. Wayne to Woodbridge, 23 February 1778, Woodbridge Papers, CTHS; Risch, *Supplying Washington's Army*, 83; 23 February 1778, Angell, "Diary," 131.

19. Wayne to Barry, 23 February 1778, Wayne to Jennings, 23 February 1778, NDAR, 11:412–13.

20. Wayne to Washington, 25 February 1778, PGW, 13:668–69.

21. Barry to Washington, 26 February 1778, NDAR, 11:440.

22. Wayne to Washington, 25 February 1778, PGW, 13:668; Wayne to William Livingston, 26 February 1778, Wayne Papers, HSP.

23. 24, 25 February 1778, Downman, *Services*, 56; 24 February 1778, Robertson, *Diaries and Sketches*, 163; Hamond, "Journal of H.M.S. *Roebuck*," 24 February 1778, Hamond, "Master's Journal of H.M.S. *Roebuck*," 24 February 1778, James Watt, "Journal of H.M.S. *Delaware*," 26 February 1778, Thomas Spry, "Master's Journal of H.M. Galley *Cornwallis*," 25 February 1778, NDAR, 11:421; 439, 428, 430; 24 February 1778, Muenchausen, *At General Howe's Side*, 48; Ewing, *Military Journal*, 30. Abercromby's brigade was one of the elite formations within Howe's army. Composed of the light companies drawn from each of the British battalions, the brigade mustered about eleven hundred of the army's fittest and most intelligent soldiers. In the regular establishment, each British battalion was authorized eight line-companies and two flank-companies, one of light infantry and another of grenadiers. The Light Infantry Brigade's establishment, like that of the similarly organized Grenadier Brigade, followed a practice in the British Army of creating ad hoc battalions and brigades in field armies from these companies.

24. Hamond, "Master's Journal of H.M.S. *Roebuck*," 25 February 1778, Watt, "Journal of H.M.S. *Delaware*," 27 February 1778, NDAR, 11:428, 457; Peebles, *John Peebles' American War*, 165–66; 1, 2 March 1778, Montresor, *Journals*, 481; 25 February 1778, Muenchausen, *At General Howe's Side*, 48; 25 February 1778, Downman, *Services*, 56. Peebles' rank, captain-lieutenant, like that of Montresor, bridged the gap between captains, who commanded companies, and lieutenants, who seconded captains.

Typically, the captain-lieutenant commanded the colonel's company. In the absence of the colonel, who by the mid-eighteenth century was actually a general officer acting as regimental patron or colonel-commandant, the captain-lieutenant commanded in the colonel's stead. When the colonel was still a colonel and present, his responsibility to command the regiment superseded his command of a company; thus it fell to the captain-lieutenant, although some regimental commanders actually commanded their companies. By the American War for Independence, however, a lieutenant colonel typically exercised command of the regiment, seconded by a major. The two other field officers also had their own companies, but were commanded by the senior lieutenants of their companies. Gen. Lord John Murray was colonel of Peebles's regiment. Interestingly, on 26 May 1772, the War Office reported that "for the future, the Captain-Lieutenants of the Cavalry and Marching Regiments [infantry] shall have Rank, as well in the Army as in their respective Regiments, as Captains; that the present Captain-Lieutenants shall take the said Rank from this Day; and all future Captain-Lieutenants from the Date of their respective Commissions." The British Army maintained the rank until the close of the eighteenth century. The Continental Army also adopted the rank, but not due to generals serving as regimental patrons (colonels). *London Gazette*, 23–26 May 1772.

25. Wayne to Washington, 26 February 1778, *PGW*, 13:677; Simcoe, *Military Journal*, 38–40.

26. Watt, "Journal of H.M.S. *Delaware*," 26 February 1778, Spry, "Master's Journal of H.M. Galley *Cornwallis*," 26 February 1778, *NDAR*, 11:439–40.

27. Wayne to Washington, 25, 26 February 1778, *PGW*, 13:668, 678; Collin, *Journal and Biography*, 242–43. A Swedish mile measured 6.64 miles. Högman, "Old Swedish Units of Measurement," *History*, http://www.hhogman.se/old-units-of-measurement-sweden.htm#xl_Linear_Measure (9 May 2021).

28. Collin, *Journal and Biography*, 244–45; Waldron, "'A True Servant of the Lord'," 96; 25 February 1778, Schmidt, "Extracts from the Diary of the Moravian Congregation at Oldmans Creek," 379.

29. Wayne to Washington, 26 February 1778, *PGW*, 13:677; Stryker, *Official Register of the Officers and Men of New Jersey*, 442; Stewart, *Foraging for Valley Forge*, 6. Wayne estimated the combined strength of the Continental Army's and New Jersey Militia's foragers at no more than five hundred and fifty soldiers. See Wayne to William Livingston, 26 February 1778, Wayne Papers, HSP. Following the British victory at Brandywine on 11 September 1777, British Maj. Gen. Charles Grey led a night bayonet attack against Wayne's camp of the Pennsylvania Line at Paoli. Wayne formed his division and started it out of camp after receiving an alarm from one of his outposts. Grey's attack, however, overwhelmed the rearguard. Wayne demanded a court-martial to clear his name of neglect. He was acquitted in November 1777. Nevertheless, memories of the so-called Paoli Massacre and its tactical lessons played a formative role in his maturation as a commander. Washington's selection of Wayne as Greene's deputy indicated his confidence in the Pennsylvanian. See Nelson, *Anthony Wayne*, 62–64; and McGuire, *Battle of Paoli*.

30. Wayne to Washington, *PGW*, 13:668–71; 26 February 1778, Gruber, *John Peebles' American War*, 166; 24 February 1778, Robertson, *Diaries and Sketches*, 163.

31. 28 February, 1 March 1778, Gruber, *John Peebles' American War*, 166–67; 27 February 1778, Downman, *Services*, 56; 28 February 1778, Muenchhausen, *At General Howe's Side*, 48; 24 February 1778, Robertson, *Diaries and Sketches*, 163; Laye, Extracts from various Standing Orders, NAM.

32. 27 February 1778, Downman, *Services*, 56; 28 February 1778, Muenchausen, *At General Howe's Side*, 48.

33. Wayne to Washington, 25, 26 February 1778, *PGW*, 13:668–71, 677–78; Wayne to Livingston, 25, 26 February 1778, Wayne Papers, HSP.

34. Wayne to Washington, 26 February 1778, *PGW*, 13:677–78; Wayne to Casimir Pulaski, 27 February 1778, Pulaski to Wayne, 27 February 1778, Wayne Papers, HSP; Pulaski to Washington, 27 February 1778, Washington to Pulaski, 1 March 1778, *PGW*, 13:689, 14:14–15; Stewart, *Foraging for Valley Forge*, 7–8.

35. Wayne to Washington, 26 February 1778, *PGW*, 13:677–78; Hamond, "Master's Journal, H.M.S. *Roebuck*," NDAR, 28 February 1778, 11:467; Pulaski to Wayne, 28 February 1778, Wayne Papers, HSP; Simcoe, *Military Journal*, 38, 40–41; Stewart, *Foraging for Valley Forge*, 7–8, 9.

36. Watt, "Journal, H.M.S. *Delaware*," 27 February 1778, Hamond, "Master's Journal, H.M.S. *Roebuck*," 28 February 1778, Spry, "Master's Journal, H.M. Galley *Cornwallis*," 28 February 1778, NDAR, 11:457, 458–59, 467, 468; 28 February 1778, Peebles, *John Peebles' American War*, 166; Smallwood to Washington, 28 February 1778, *PGW*, 13:699; Gardiner, *Navies and the American Revolution*, 73; Canney, *Sailing Warships of the US Navy*, 18; Simcoe, *Military Journal*, 38.

37. Pulaski to Wayne, 28 February 1778, Wayne Papers, HSP; Wayne to Washington, 5 March 1778, *PGW*, 14:72–74; Stewart, *Foraging for Valley Forge*, 7.

38. Peebles noted that the "Coll. got some intelligence of a great Body of the Enemy coming towards us & some shots being fired at the Rangers Picket across the Creek at Keys Mill the Compys. order'd under arms, & soon after desir'd to go into the Barns & be ready to turn out at a moments warng." 1 March 1778, Peebles, *John Peebles' American War*, 167; Simcoe, *Military Journal*, 42–43; Wayne to Washington, 5 March 1778, *PGW*, 14:72–73.

39. Wayne to Washington, 5 March 1778, *PGW*, 14:72–73; Simcoe, *Military Journal*, 43; 2 March 1778, Gruber, *John Peebles' American War*, 167. The Light Infantry Brigade landed at the north end of Philadelphia about 2:00 P.M. on 1 March. Spry, "Master's Journal, H.M. Galley *Cornwallis*," 1 March 1778, NDAR, 11:483.

40. Simcoe, *Military Journal*, 43; Gara, *Queen's American Rangers*, 105; OAC, 203; 2 March 1778, Peebles, *John Peebles' American War*, 167.

41. Wayne to Washington, 5 March 1778, *PGW*, 14:72–73.

42. Simcoe, *Military Journal*, 44–45; Wayne to Washington, 5 March 1778, *PGW*, 14:72–73; Mickle, *Reminiscences of Old Gloucester*, 50; Clement, *Revolutionary Reminiscences*, 7–8. The engagement took place in the vicinity near Market Street between 6th and 7th streets.

43. Simcoe, *Military Journal*, 44–46; Wayne to Washington, 5 March 1778, Pulaski to Washington, 3 March 1778, *PGW*, 14:72–73, 50–51; Gara, *Queen's American Rangers*, 107.

44. Wayne to Washington, 5 March 1778, Pulaski to Washington, 3 March 1778, *PGW*, 14:72–73, 50–51; Simcoe, *Military Journal*, 44–46. Distinctive in their short

green jackets, white breeches, and tall, black, cylindrical, lambskin caps emblazoned with small, white metal gorgets, the Rangers' grenadiers looked nothing like Hessian grenadiers in blue with tall, metal-fronted, conical caps. Wayne, who had faced both rangers and Hessians, was clearly mistaken in his identification.

45. Wayne to Washington, 5 March 1778, Pulaski to Washington, 3 March 1778, *PGW*, 14:72–73, 50–51; Simcoe, *Military Journal*, 45–46; 2 March 1778, Peebles, *John Peebles' American War*, 167; 1 March 1778, Downman, *Services*, 56.

46. *The* (Trenton) *New Jersey Gazette*, 11 March 1778.

47. Wayne to Washington, 5 March 1778, Washington to Wayne, 12 March 1778, Wayne to Washington, 14 March 1778, Washington to Wayne, 15 March 1778, *PGW*, 14:72–73, 166, 180–82, 190; Wayne to Morton, 13 March 1778, Wayne Papers, HSP; John Chaloner to Blaine, n.d. [March 1778?], Boyle, *Blaine Letterbook*, 154.

48. Wayne to Washington, 14 March 1778, Washington to Wayne, 15 March 1778, *PGW*, 14:180–81, 190; Wayne to John Lacey, Jr., 15 May 1778, in Hazard, *Register of Pennsylvania*, 308; 23 March 1778, Weedon, *Orderly Book*, 267; "Revolutionary Army Orders," 50.

49. Bodle, *Valley Forge Winter*, 216–17; Stewart, *Foraging for Valley Forge*, 19–22; Hamond to Linzee, 10 March 1778, *NDAR*, 11:590; Simcoe, *Military Journal*, 46–54; 12 March 1778, Downman, *Services*, 57; 12, 29 March 1778, 5 April 1778, Montresor, *Journals*, 482–84; 6 March 1778, Baurmeister, *Revolution in America*, 155–56, 160; Livingston to Shreve, 23 March 1778, Israel Shreve Revolutionary War Letters, UHL; Shreve, "Personal Narrative," 568; Thompson, *Israel Shreve*, 38.

50. "Articles of Surrender of the British Army Schooner *Alert*," 7 March 1778, "Journal of H.M.S. *Experiment*, Capt. Sir James Wallace," 9 March 1778, "Journal of H.M. Sloop *Dispatch*, Cdr. Christopher Mason," 9 March 1778, *NDAR*, 11:539–40, 559–61; Barry to Washington, 9 March 1778, Smallwood to Washington, 9–10 March 1778, Washington to Barry, 12 March 1778, Smallwood to Washington, 16 March 1778, *PGW*, 14:106–07, 116–18, 154–55, 203–5.

Chapter Four

1. George Washington to Henry Hollingsworth, 16 February 1778, *PGW*, 13:558–59.

2. Washington to Henry Lee Jr., 16 February 1778, Washington to William Smallwood, 16 February 1778, *PGW*, 13:561–62, 563–64.

3. Washington to Lee, 16 February 1778, Washington to Smallwood, 16 February 1778, *PGW*, 13:561–62, 563–64.

4. Washington to Hollingsworth, 16 February 1778, Washington to Smallwood, 16 February 1778, *PGW*, 13:558–59, 563–64; Thomas Jones to Charles Stewart, 16 February 1778, Stewart Papers, FAM; James Mitchell Varnum to Nathanael Greene, 12 February 1778, *PNG*, 2:280.

5. Shy, "The Military Conflict Considered as a Revolutionary War," 219. Bodle, *Valley Forge Winter*, examines the Continental Army's role as a buttress to Pennsylvania's state government and extension of the Continental Congress's authority. For a study of British officers' attitudes regarding popular affection and the prosecution of the war, see Conway, "To Subdue America," 381–407.

6. Ewald, *Treatise on Partisan Warfare*, 68; Gruber, *Howe Brothers*, 92, 113, 145–46, 194–95, 242–44, 346, 350. See Fischer, *Washington's Crossing*, 62–65, 375–79, 172–81, for the most recent discussion of Revolutionary Americans' ways of war and the often-crossed fine line between foraging, plundering, and pillaging. Royster, *Light-Horse Harry Lee*, 9–54, examines Lee's temperament and conduct.

7. Washington to Smallwood, 16 February 1778, *PGW*, 13:563–64; Piecuch and Beakes, *"Light Horse Harry" Lee*, ix–x, 5–18; *OCA*, 345; McGuire, *Philadelphia Campaign*, 8, 20; Chernow, *Washington*, 182; Loescher, *Washington's Eyes*, 5–8. Lesser, *Sinews of Independence*, 56, records that Lee commanded fifty men in December 1777, but makes no mention thereafter. Largely because of the lack of forage for its horses, Washington ordered most of the cavalry to separate encampments. The strength reports do not note any of the cavalry until July 1778. Timothy Pickering to Rebecca White Pickering, 22 January 1778, Pickering Papers, MAHS.

8. 23 December 1777, Smith Diaries, AAS; 21, 22 December 1777, Howe Orderly Book, WLCL; 22, 23, 24, 25 December 1777, Robertson, *Diaries and Sketches*, 162; Richard Butler, [December 1777], Butler Papers, Draper Manuscripts, WHS; Morgan to Washington, 5 January 1778, *PGW*, 13:150.

9. de Jeney, *The Partisan*, 2, 6–7; Clausewitz, *On War*, 102–03. On Lee's life, see Royster, *Light-Horse Harry Lee*.

10. Dallett, *War of the Revolution in Radnor*, 4–7, 16–19.

11. 19 January 1778, Muenchausen, *At General Howe's Side*, 47; Lee to Washington, 4 January 1778, 18 January 1778, *PGW*, 13:141–42, 273–74. For more on Lee, *petite guerre*, and partisan warfare see Herrera, "'[T]he zealous activity of Capt. Lee'," 9–11, 17–19; and Hall, "An Irregular Reconsideration of George Washington and the American Military Tradition," 961–993.

12. Ewald, *Diary of the American War*, 121; Ford, *British Officers Serving in the American Revolution*, 54; Muenchausen, *At General Howe's Side*, 47; Royster, *Light-Horse Harry Lee*, 26; Lee to Washington, 4 January 1778, 20 January 1778, 20 January 1778, *PGW*, 13:141–42, 292–94; Piecuch and Beakes, *Light Horse Harry Lee*," 16–17, refer to Lee's position as being at the Spread Eagle Tavern, although Lee noted his location as "Scotts farm" in his 4 January 1778 letter to Washington; Burns, "New Light on the Encampment of the Continental Army at Valley Forge," 67–70, shows Lee's position west of the tavern. Pickering to Rebecca Pickering, 22 January 1778, Pickering Papers, MAHS, gave Lee's number as "eight in whole." Pickering estimated that "about 150 or 200 of the enemy's dragoons beset the house." Francis Barber to Elias Dayton, 22 January 1778, Sparks Collection, Houghton, reported that Lee had "only his Lieutenant and seven or eight privates," and estimated that there were 150 British soldiers.

13. Muenchausen, *At General Howe's Side*, 47; Lee to Washington, 20 January 1778, 20 January 1778, Washington to Lee, 20 January 1778, *PGW*, 13: 292–94; 23 February 1778, Ewald, *Diary of the American War*, 121; [20 January 1778?], Valley Forge Orderly Book, 20 January 1778–22 February 1778, Orderly Book Collection, WLCL; *OCA*, 352, 519.

14. John Jameson to Washington, 2 February 1778, Jameson to Washington, 31 December 1777, *PGW*, 13:440–41, 81–82. Jameson's command consisted of thirty-five soldiers, eighteen under Capt. Charles Craig (First Troop, Fourth Continental

Light Dragoons), twelve under Maj. Benjamin Tallmadge (Second Continental Light Dragoons), and five under Lt. Addison Lewis (Sixth Troop, First Continental Light Dragoons). Congress had authorized each troop of light dragoons three officers, six noncommissioned officers, one trumpeter, one farrier, one armorer, and thirty-two privates. Maurer, *Dragoon Diary*, 18–19; 13 June 1776, *Proceedings of the Convention of the Delegates for the Counties and Corporations in the Colony of Virginia*, 45–46; Wright, *Continental Army*, 107.

15. Pickering to Rebecca Pickering, 22 January 1778, Pickering Papers, MAHS; W[illiam]. [Bernard] Gifford to Benjamin Holme, 24 January 1778, Piatt Papers, Burton Collection, DPL; George Weedon to John Page, 25 January 1778, Weedon Papers, CHS; William Livingstone to Lord Sterling, 26 January 1778, Alexander (Lord Sterling) Selected Papers, NYHS. Fabulists later inflated the action to mythic proportions, to include the participation of Banastre Tarleton. Others have repeated the claim based on hearsay that the action took place at the Spread Eagle Tavern. No primary evidence has been detected for either of these suggestions, which some modern biographers have uncritically repeated. See Garden, *Anecdotes of the Revolutionary War*, 127–28; Garden, *Anecdotes of the American Revolution*, 134; Woodruff, "Capt. Ferdinand O'Neal," 328–30; Piecuch and Beakes, *"Light Horse Harry" Lee in the War for Independence*, 16–19; and Cole, *Light-Horse Harry Lee*, 55.

16. Hartmann, *American Partisan*, 61; Lee to Washington, 19 February 1778, Smallwood to Washington, 21 February 1778, *PGW*, 13:598–99, 634–35; Smallwood to Caesar Rodney, 18 February 1778, Dearborn Collection, Houghton. Read had been elected vice-president of Delaware but following President John McKinly's capture by the British at the battle of Brandywine, 11 September 1777, Read assumed the office; Read, *Life and Correspondence of George Read*, 92. OCA, 373.

17. Jones to Stewart, 16 February 1778, Stewart Papers, FAM.

18. Smallwood to Washington, 21 February 1778, George Read to Washington, 5 February 1778, Smallwood to Washington, 26 January 1778, *PGW*, 13:634–35, 461–62, 358; Smallwood to McLane, 11 February 1778, McLane Papers, NYHS.

19. Washington to Smallwood, 25 February 1778, *PGW*, 13:667.

20. Bodle, "Ghost of Clow," 27; Turner, "Cheney Clow's Rebellion," 4.

21. Anderson, "Personal Recollections," 53–54; Bodle. "Ghost of Clow," 27.

22. Hancock, *Delaware Loyalists*, 4, 56–57, 24–25; Neville, "For God, King, and Country," 135; Nelson, *American Tory*, 108; Council to Talbot [County] Judges, 16 March 1778, Browne, *Archives of Maryland*, 537. See also Mason, "Association Localism, Evangelicalism, and Loyalism," 23–54. As of 2 September 1777, Caesar Rodney was a brigadier general. By October, however, he had been promoted to major general. *Delaware Archives*, 3:1050, 1250. On African Americans in the American Revolution and War for Independence, see Quarles, *The Negro in the American Revolution*; Frey, *Water from the Rock*; Piecuch, *Loyalists, Indians, and Slaves*; Urwin, "When Freedom Wore a Red Coat," 6–23; Egerton, *Death or Liberty*; Jasanoff, *Liberty's Exiles*; and Van Buskirk, *Standing in Their Own Light*.

23. de Saxe, "Reveries," 256–57.

24. Nelson, *American Tory*, 107–8; Washington to Greene, 12 February 1778, *PGW*, 13:514.

25. Smallwood to Washington, 21 February 1778, *PGW*, 13:634; Smallwood to Rodney, 18 February 1778, Dearborn Collection, Houghton.

26. Hartmann, *American Partisan*, 61; Hollingsworth to Washington, 18 February 1778, Lee to Washington, 19 February 1778, *PGW*, 13:582, 598–99. Hollingsworth's report that there was no supply of meat speaks to the state of communications. Ephraim Blaine had reported on 14 February 1778, that he estimated Elk held 500 barrels of beef and pork, along with 5,000 of flour, 2,000 of bread, 10 of rum, 10 hogsheads of whiskey, 60 of rum, and 6,000 bushels of wheat. Blaine, "An Estimate of Provisions in the Middle District," 14 February 1778, Blaine, *Letterbook*, 125–26.

27. Lee to Washington, 19 February 1778, *PGW*, 13:598–99.

28. Lee to Washington, 19 February 1778, *PGW*, 13:598–99; The hundred roughly corresponds to a township. It is a geographic subdivision within a county with origins in Anglo-Saxon politico-geographic organization in medieval England. Used initially in seventeenth-century Pennsylvania and Delaware, in the United States, the hundred now exists solely in Delaware. Conrad, *History of the State of Delaware*, 449.

29. Lee to Howell, 19 February 1778, Reed Collection, VFNHP; Lee to Howell, 20 February 1778, Howell, *Book of John Howell*, 198–99; Cook, *What Manner of Men*, 35–36.

30. Greene to Washington, 20 February 1778, Lee to Washington, 19 February 1778, *PGW*, 13:607, 599.

31. Washington to Lee, 21 February 1778, *PGW*, 13:631.

32. Lee to Howell, 22 February 1778, Howell, *Book of John Howell*, 199; "Account of Cattle, & Provisions," Howell Papers, GCHS.

33. Smallwood to Allen McLane, [date smudged; 20?] January 1778, William D. Kelley to McLane, 15 February 1778, Smallwood to McLane, 11 February 1778, McLane Papers, 1775–1821, NYHS; Berg, *Encyclopedia of Continental Army Units*, 93, 60–61.

34. Hartmann, *American Partisan*, 61; Lee to Washington, 21 February 1778, *PGW*, 13:632; Read to General Assembly, 21 February 1778, *Delaware Archives*, 2:828.

35. Lee to Washington, 21 February 1778, *PGW*, 13:632, 675–76.

36. Washington to Read, 26 February 1778, *PGW*, 13:675–76; Read to Washington, 2 March 1778, *PGW*, 14:36–38.

37. Lee to Washington, *PGW*, 13:642–43; Hartmann, *American Partisan*, 62.

38. Lee to Washington, 22 February 1778, *PGW*, 13:642–43.

39. Lee to Washington, 22 February 1778, *PGW*, 13:642–43.

40. Washington to Lee, 25 February 1778, *PGW*, 13:661–62.

41. Lee to Howell, 23 February 1778, Howell to Lee, 25 February 1778, Howell, *Book of John Howell*, 200–201.

42. Receipt, John Trump to McLane, 24 February 1778, Robert Porter and George Reynolds to McLane, 25 February 1778, McLane Papers, NYHS.

43. "Account of Cattle, & Provisions," Howell Papers, GCHS; Hinde, *Discipline of the Light-Horse*, 12.

44. "Account of Cattle, & Provisions," Howell Papers, GCHS; Howell to Blaine, 22 February 1778, Smith Collection, MNHP; Blaine to Washington, 28 February 1778, *PGW*, 13:691; John Chaloner to Blaine, n.d. [March 1778?], Blaine, *Letterbook*, 154.

45. "Account of Cattle, & Provisions," Howell Papers, GCHS.

46. "Account of Cattle, & Provisions," Howell Papers, GCHS; Riordan, "1776 Tax information for the Town of New Castle," *New Castle, Delaware Community History and Archaeology Program*, http://nc-chap.org/census/riordan/tax1776.php (7 May 2021).

47. Blaine to Washington, 28 February 1778, *PGW*, 13:691–92.

48. William Shannon to Hollingsworth, 15 March 1778, Feinstone Collection, APS; Broad, "Cattle Plague in Eighteenth-Century England," 104–15; Burgos Cáceres, "The long journey of cattle plague," 1140; Shannon to William Henry, 24 June 1779, Jordan, *Life of William Henry*, 104–5.

49. Bodle, "The Ghost of Clow," 27; Chaloner to Blaine, n.d. [March 1778?], Boyle, *Ephraim Blaine Letterbook*, 154; Mason, "Association Localism, Evangelicalism, and Loyalism," 23–24, 49–53; Council to Colonel Simpson at Accomack, 10 February 1778, Council to Talbot [County] Judges, 16 March 1778, Council to George Dashiell, 16 March 1778, Browne, *Archives of Maryland*, 485–86, 537, 538; Charles Pope to Smallwood, 14 April 1778, Samuel Patterson to Smallwood, 15 April 1778, Smallwood to Henry Laurens, 17 April 1778, *Calendar of Maryland State Papers*, 94–95; Read, *Life and Correspondence of George Read*, 323–24.

50. Bodle, "The Ghost of Clow," 28–29; Patterson to Smallwood, 15 April 1778, *Calendar of Maryland State Papers*, 94–95; John McKinly to Patterson, 17 June 1777, *Delaware Archives*, 2:740; Hancock, *Delaware Loyalists*, 34–35; *OCA*, 446.

Chapter Five

1. Johnson, in "Administration of the American Commissariat," 78–79, contends that Elk was the army's most important magazine in the 1777–1778 campaigns. Risch, *Supplying Washington's Army*; George Washington to Nathanael Greene, 31 March 1778, *PGW*, 14:367; Galloway, "Evidence of Mr. Galloway," *Detail and Conduct of the American War*, 122.

2. Johnson, "Administration of the American Commissariat," 84; Risch, *Supplying Washington's Army*, 173–74; Resolution, 18 June 1777, Resolution, 6 August 1777, JCC, 8: 477, 617; Ephraim Blaine to William Buchanan, 3 November 1777, Blaine, *Letterbook*, 25–26.

3. Resolution, 18 June 1777, Resolution, 9 August 1777, "Report Respecting the Commissary's Department," 10 June 1777, JCC, 8: 477, 627, 433–48; Peter Colt to John Hancock, 4 October 1777, RG 93, M247, NARA; Risch, *Supplying Washington's Army*, 174–75; Thibaut, "This Fatal Crisis," 72–78. Champion eventually resumed his duties purchasing cattle for the army. Colt noted that Champion had been "appointed superintendant of the purchasing live Stock—& is made intirly independent of me." See Colt to Washington, 20 February 1778, *PGW*, 13:603–5; Colt to Samuel Gray, 26 January 1778, Charles Stewart to Gray, 17 February 1778, Colt to Samuel Gray 19 February 1778, Gray Commissary Records, CTHS; Asa Waterman to Henry Champion, 19 February 1778, Champion to Blaine, 28 February 1778, John Chaloner to Champion, 17 March 1778, Revolutionary War Commissary Papers, CTHS.

4. Colt to Champion, 8 November 1777, RG 83, M859, NARA; Gray to Stewart, 16 November 1777, Stewart Papers, FAM; 10 October 1777, *JCC*, 9:790; Buchanan to Washington, *PGW*, 12:222; Colt to Buchanan, 2 September 1777, PCC, M 247, LC; Colt to Hancock, 4 October 1777, RG 93, M247, NARA; Thibaut, "This Fatal Crisis," 74, 157. See Colt to Washington, 20 February 1778, *PGW*, 13:603–5 for a detailed explanation of Colt's difficulties.

5. Hunter, *A sketch of the navigation from Swan Pt. to the River Elk at the head of Chesapeak Bay*, GMD, LC, https://www.loc.gov/item/gm71002217/ (7 May 2021); *Progress of the army from their landing till taking possession of Philadelphia*, GMD, LC, https://www.loc.gov/item/gm71000678/ (7 May 2021); American Philosophical Society, *Map of proposed roads*, GMD, LC, https://www.loc.gov/item/79695387/ (7 May 2021); Gardiner, *Navies and the American Revolution*, 54.

6. Hunter, *A sketch of the navigation from Swan Pt. to the River Elk*, GMD, LC; Varle and Shallus, *Map of the State of Delaware and the Eastern Shore of Maryland*, GMD, LC, https://www.loc.gov/item/2018590123/ (7 May 2021); Selig, *The Washington-Rochambeau Revolutionary Route*, 3–4, 3–6, 3–12; "Elk Landing," *The National Washington-Rochambeau Revolutionary Route Association*, https://w3r-us.org/historic-sites/elk-landing/ (7 May 2021).

7. "Return of Stores by Col. Trumbull to Colo. Buchanan," 8 August 1777, Blaine Papers, Force Collection, LC; Washington to Hancock, 25 August 1777, *PGW*, 11:69.

8. Washington to Hancock, 27 August 1777, *PGW*, 11:78; Blaine to Zebulon Hollingsworth, 30 August 1777, Blaine, *Letterbook*, 5; Jamar, *Hollingsworth Family and Collateral Lines*, 18–20, 32.

9. Deposition of James Johnston, 1832, quoted in Dann, *Revolution Remembered*, 404; Petition of William Welsh of Christiana Bridge, 9 September 1780, RG 360, PCC, M247, NARA.

10. 28 August 1778, Downman, *Services*, 31; 28 August 1777, Montresor, *Journals*, 444; *Progress of the army*, GMD, LC, https://www.loc.gov/item/gm71000678/ (7 May 2021); William John Hale to Admiral & Mrs. J[ohn]. Hale, 30 August 1777, Wilkin, *Some British Soldiers in America*, 227. Bonner-Smith and Royal Naval College, *Commissioned Sea Officers*, 393, list the elder Hale as a superannuated rear admiral as of 1779.

11. Hale to Admiral & Mrs. J. Hale, 30 August 1777, *Some British Soldiers in America*, 227; Daniel Wier to Unidentified, 1 September 1777, Wier Letterbook, HSP; 28 August 1777, Heister, Journal of General von Heister, Lidgerwood Collection, MNHP. Heister's father, Lt. Gen. Leopold Philip de Heister, had been recalled earlier in 1777 following the disaster at Trenton in December 1776. In the eighteenth century, some German officers adopted the French article "de" in place of the German article "von" to indicate their noble status or were referred to as such. French language and culture predominated among educated Europeans during the age of the Enlightenment, and signified learning and sophistication. Frederick the Great (r. 1740–1786) spoke French almost exclusively and popularized the language's usage in the German states' officer corps. It was common for British and German officers to speak and write French, which was the language of translation for both. The title *Freiherr* (free lord), which loosely translated to the French title baron, did not translate as well as the French title, hence the usage of "Baron de" rather than "*Freiherr* von" with officers like Heister.

Other prominent examples of German officers adopting French renditions of their names include the Saxon-born Marshal Maurice de Saxe (Hermann Moritz von Sachsen) and the Franconian-born Maj. Gen. Johann de Kalb (Johann Kalb). Paul D. Lockhart to author, 24 August 2021. See Lockhart, *Drillmaster of Valley Forge*, 29–30; Arzberger, "The choice between the German or French Language," 333–42; 28 August 1777, Montresor, *Montresor Journals*, 443; Philemon Dickinson to Washington, 11 August 1777, John Clark to Washington, 6 October 1777, *PGW*, 11:585–86, 406–7. William Paca to Thomas Johnson, 30 August 1777, Browne, *Archives of Maryland*, 353.

12. Seybolt, "Contemporary British Account of General Sir William Howe's Military Operations in 1777," 77; Carl Leopold Baurmeister to Friedrich Christian Arnold von Jungkenn, 20 July–17 October 1777, Baurmeister, *Revolution in America*, 100–101; Charles Carroll to Charles Carroll, 11 September 1777, Hoffman, Mason, and Darcy, eds., *Dear Papa, Dear Charley*, 1054; Washington to William Aylett, *PGW*, 11:349. Deputy Commissary David Redick wrote that the destruction was "Chiefly Indian Corn; [but] the Salt and Flour was got off." David Redick to Joseph Trumbull, 1 October 1777, Trumbull Papers, CTHS; Charles Stuart to Earl of Bute [John Stuart], 31 August 1777, Stuart-Wortley [Violet Hunter Guthrie Montagu-Stuart-Wortley], *A Prime Minister and His Son*, 116; *Army List* (1777), 97.

13. Joseph Galloway, "Evidence of Mr. Galloway," *Detail and Conduct of the American War*, 125.

14. Washington to Henry Hollingsworth, 6 October 1777, *PGW*, 11:408; Risch, *Supplying Washington's Army*, 65, 220.

15. Maryland Council of Safety to Hollingsworth, 22 October 1777, Council to Charles Rumsey, 22 October 1777, Browne, *Archives of Maryland*, 401, 402; [Ephraim Blaine?], "State of Supplies," 25 December 1777, RG 93, M859, NARA. The Imperial long hundredweight, used in colonial British North America, equaled 112 pounds. Twenty-six hundredweight per location worked out to just over twenty-nine hundred pounds at Lancaster, Wright's Ferry, and York, over four tons total. Imperial Measures of Weight, https://theedkins.co.uk/jo/units/weight.htm (21 August 2021).

16. Washington to Buchanan, 28 December 1777, *PGW*, 13:29.

17. Duncan "Journals," *Naval Miscellany*, 150; Richard Howe to Philip Stephens, 25 October 1777, *NDAR*, 10:288. For the Royal Navy's activities during this period, see Syrett, *Royal Navy in American Waters* and *NDAR*, vols. 9 & 10. Philadelphia's defenders emplaced over sixty *chevaux-de-frise* (literally Frisian horses) in the Delaware River's navigation channel to impede British warships by tearing out the bottoms of ships' hulls. Each individual *cheval-de-frise* was a log topped with an iron spear tip angled downriver and below the water's surface. They measured around thirty feet in length, and were anchored in large, rock-filled cribs. "Preservation of a Cheval-de-frise from the Delaware River," http://twipa.blogspot.com/2013/06/preservation-of -cheval-de-frise-from.html (21 August 2021).

18. Patrick Henry in Council, to Virginia Delegates in Congress, 20 January 1778, *Papers of James Madison*, 219; Henry to Thomas Johnson, 26 January 1778, McIlwaine, *Official Letters of the Governors of Virginia*, 235; 19 January 1778, JCC, 10:62.

19. Maryland Council to Henry, 14 February 1778, *NDAR*, 11:348. The Governor's Council consisted of five men elected yearly by both houses of the Maryland legislature

to advise the governor. *Archives of Maryland, Historical List: Governors' Councils*, https://msa.maryland.gov/msa/speccol/sc2600/sc2685/html/council.html (7 May 2021).

20. Washington to the Board of War, 2–3 January 1778, *PGW*, 13:111, 113; Blaine to John Ladd Howell, 10 February 1778, deCoppet Collection, PUL; Blaine to Robert McGarmont, 10 February 1778, Blaine, *Letterbook*, 122.

21. Blaine to Henry E. Lutterloh, 7 February 1778, Blaine, *Letterbook*, 114.

22. Blaine, "An Estimate of Provisions in the Middle District," 14 February 1778, Blaine to Henry Hollingsworth, 15 February 1778, Blaine, *Letterbook*, 125–26, 127; Return of Stores by Col. Trumbull to Colo. Buchanan, 8 August 1777, Blaine Papers, LC.

23. Buchanan to Blaine, 15 January 1778, RG 360, M 247, NARA; Blaine to Washington, 28 February 1778, *PGW*, 13:691–92.

24. Blaine to Washington, 28 February 1778, *PGW*, 13:691–92.

25. Blaine to Washington, 28 February 1778, *PGW*, 13:691–92; Steiner, *Archives of Maryland*, 616–24; "The Wharf 1742," *Historical Sites*, 14; Smith, *A new and accurate chart of the Bay of Chesapeake*, GMD, LC, https://www.loc.gov/item/74691941/ (7 May 2021).

26. Morris, "Site 44Y088," 50; Middleton, *Tobacco Coast*, 237, 273; Salvatore Mercogliano to author, 22 July 2020.

27. Blaine to Washington, 28 February 1778, *PGW*, 13:691–92.

28. Blaine to Washington, 28 February 1778, *PGW*, 13:692.

29. Blaine to Washington, 28 February 1778, *PGW*, 13:692.

30. Blaine to Washington, 28 February 1778, Smallwood to Washington, 21 February 1778, Washington to Smallwood, 25 February 1778, *PGW*, 13:692, 635, 667. John Ladd Howell reported that "Colo. Blaine directed me to send the Flour on to Charles town on North East by water from George Town by the Assistance of Colo. Wm. Henry—a Magistrate." Howell estimated that Smallwood's soldiers seized 450 barrels of flour and another 1,000 bushels of wheat. Howell to Chaloner, 5 March 1778, Smith Collection, MNHP.

31. Blaine to Howell, 1 March 1778, Howell, *Book of John Howell*, 202.

32. Blaine to Washington, 28 February 1778, *PGW*, 13:692; George Read to Washington, *PGW*, 13:462.

33. On examples and patterns of disaffection, see Bodle, *Valley Forge Winter*, 50, 140, 163–65, 185–88; and Sullivan, *The Disaffected*.

34. For Robert Lettis Hooper, see Hart, "Colonel Robert Lettis Hooper," 60–91; and Kortenhof, "Republican Ideology and Wartime Reality," 193, 201, 208.

35. Kilpatrick, "Thomas Huggins (1748–1788), of Head of Elk, Maryland," *Arborealis*, https://arborealis.ca/2015/12/23/thomas-huggins/ (23 December 2015); Kilpatrick, "A Huggins Thorn in George Washington's Revolutionary Side," *Arborealis*, https://arborealis.ca/2015/12/23/huggins-thorn-in-washingtons-side/ (7 May 2021); *Proceedings of the Conventions of the Province of Maryland*, 80; Blaine to Thomas Huggins, 15 October 1777, Blaine, *Letterbook*, 15; Thomas Jones to Stewart, 22 October 1777, Stewart Collection, FAM.

36. Blaine to Huggins, 18 November 1777, Chaloner to Huggins, 29 December 1777, Blaine, *Letterbook*, 71–72.

37. Chaloner to Buchanan, n.d. [January 1778], Chaloner to Huggins, 4 January 1778, Blaine, *Letterbook*, 79, 76.

38. Maryland Council to Buchanan, 8 January 1778, Browne, *Archives of Maryland*, 461–462; 10 December 1777, JCC, 9:1013–015.

39. Charles Rumsey to Maryland Council of Safety, 19 December 1777, Maryland Council to William Buchanan, 8 January 1778, Browne, *Archives of Maryland*, 438, 461–62; Englehard Yeiser to Thomas Johnson, 9 January 1778, *Calendar of Maryland State Papers*, 85.

40. Smallwood to Washington, 26 January 1778, George Read, Jr. to Washington, 5 February 1778, Washington to Smallwood, 16 February 1778, PGW, 13: 355–56, 460–61, 563.

41. Read to Washington, 5 February 1778, Proclamation on Market at Valley Forge, 30 January 1778, PGW, 13: 460–61, 415–17. In the Proclamation on Market at Valley Forge, Washington announced the prices offered for various kinds, measurements, and qualities of provisions in Pennsylvania, Maryland, and Delaware.

42. Smallwood to Washington, 21 February 1778, PGW, 13:634–35; Jedidiah Huntington to Andrew Huntington, 25 December 1777, Boyle, *Writings from the Valley Forge Encampment*, 3:7; Chaloner to Huggins and Howell, 29 May 1778, Boyle, *Writings from the Valley Forge Encampment of the Continental Army*, 4:159–60.

43. Washington to Read, 22 February 1778, Washington to Smallwood, 25 February 1778, PGW, 13:644–45, 667.

44. Blaine to Huggins, 10 February 1778, Blaine, *Letterbook*, 121; Smallwood to McLane, 11 February 1778, McLane Papers, NYHS.

45. Smallwood to Washington, 26 May 1778, PGW, 15:229; Howell to Chaloner, 5 March 1778, Howell to Chaloner, 26 March 1778, Smith Collection, MNHP.

Conclusion

1. The Continental Army's senior leaders were well-acquainted with mutiny. Over the army's short lifetime, it had experienced over fifty such events. See Nagy, *Rebellion in the Ranks*. Way, "Rebellion of the Regulars," 761–92, recounts the continent-wide mutiny of British regulars in North America following the Seven Years' War. See also Kopperman, "The Stoppages Mutiny of 1763," 241–54; Hendrix, "Spirit of the Corps,"128–40.

2. Personal probity did not hinder Washington from ordering severe measures, as in John Sullivan's 1779 campaign against the Iroquois. Select studies include Graymont, *Iroquois in the American Revolution*, 192–222; Mintz, *Seeds of Empire*; Fischer, *Well-Executed Failure*; Williams, *Year of the Hangman*; and Lee, *Barbarians and Brothers*, 209–31.

3. Fischer, *Washington's Crossing*, 111–14.

4. Nathanael Greene to George Washington, 15 February 1778, PGW, 13:546.

5. Greene to Henry Knox, 26 February 1778, PNG, 2:293; Orderly Book, Ninth Pennsylvania Regiment, SCL.

6. Greene to Washington, 24 April 1779, PNG, 3:427.

7. See Buchanan, *The Road to Charleston* for an authoritative account of Greene in the Southern Department, but also his foraging comrades, Anthony Wayne and Henry Lee, who served under Greene's command.

8. Greene to Anne-Cesar de la Luzerne, 28 April 1781, *PNG*, 8:167–68; Thayer, *Nathanael Greene*, 404, 445–46.

9. Anthony Wayne to Washington, 26 December 1777, Washington to Wayne, 27 December 1777, *PGW*, 13:13–15, 26–27; Draft, [c. 26 December 1777], Wayne Papers, HSP.

10. Greene to Washington, 15 February 1778, Washington to Greene, 16 February 1778, Greene to Washington, 17 February 1778, *PGW*, 13:548, 556, 558.

11. Wayne to Washington, 15 July 1779, 16 July 1779, *PGW*, 21: 508–9, 523; Nelson, *Anthony Wayne*, 62–64, 94–100; *OCA*, 577, 527.

12. Nelson, *Anthony Wayne*, 116–19; Nagy, *Rebellion in the Ranks*, 72, 77.

13. *OCA*, 521; Nelson, *Anthony Wayne*, 120–24; Wayne to Washington, 2 January 1781, 11 January 1781, *Founders Online*, NARA, https://founders.archives.gov/documents/Washington/99-01-02-04417, https://founders.archives.gov/documents/Washington/99-01-02-04507 (7 May 2021); Petition to Wayne, 25 December 1780, Petition to Wayne, 4 January 1781, Wayne to Serjeants and Privates of the Pennsylvania Line, 7 January 1781, Wayne Papers, HSP; Washington to the President of Congress, [Samuel Huntington], 6 January 1781, Washington to Wayne, 16 January 1781, *WGW*, 21:64–66, 112; See Nagy, *Rebellion the Ranks*, 77–166, for the most recent and comprehensive examination of the Pennsylvania Line's mutiny.

14. Lee, *Memoirs*, 438–40; Buchanan, *The Road to Charleston*, 311–14; Nelson, *Anthony Wayne*, 175–76, 225, 228–83, 300.

15. Lee to Washington, 31 March 1778, Washington to Lee, 1 April 1778, *PGW*, 14: 368–69, 379–80; *OCA*, 345, 373; Berg, *Encyclopedia of Continental Army Units*, 60–61.

16. Washington to Lee, 9 June 1779, 6 June 1779, 9 July 1779, *PGW*, 21:116, 91, 401; Royster, *Light-Horse Harry Lee*, 17–24; Piecuch and Beakes, *"Light Horse Harry" Lee*, 29–30.

17. Washington to Lee, 10 July 1779, Lee to Washington, 11 July 1779, *PGW*, 21: 422, 441; Washington to Lee, 10 August 1779, General Orders, 22 August 1779, Lee to Washington, 22 August 1779, *PGW*, 22:83, 209, 210–24.

18. Royster, *Light-Horse Harry Lee*, 148–49, 3–7; *OCA*, 345.

19. McGrath, *John Barry*, 4, 143–70, 424, 499, 350; Barry and Capt. Thomas Read, commanding the frigate *Washington*, scuttled their ships below Bordentown, New Jersey, at White Hill Landing, where the river bottom was soft, and from which the frigates could be easily raised at a later date. The ships lay at the foot of White Hill, located today around 217 Fourth St., Fieldsboro, New Jersey. The eighteenth-century house, altered over the years, remains. On the morning of 7 May 1778, British forces raised *Effingham* and *Washington* and burned them, along with a brig, a sloop, and some fifty other vessels. Jonathan Mifflin to Washington, 3 October 1777, Continental Navy Board of the Middle Department to John Barry, 2 November 1777, Continental Navy Board of the Middle Department to Washington, 10 November 1777, *NDAR*, 10:25, 377, 453–54; V. Adm. Viscount Howe to Secretary of the Admiralty Philip Stephens, 10 May 1778, *NDAR*, 12:321–22; Wayne to Barry, 23 February 1778, *NDAR* 11: 412; McVarish, "White Hill Mansion," sec. 8:10.

20. Stryker, *Official Register*, 341, 349; Morrison, "Colonel Joseph Ellis House," sec. 8:2.

21. Weinstein, "Casimir Pulaski," *Digital Encyclopedia of George Washington*, https://www.mountvernon.org/library/digitalhistory/digital-encyclopedia/article /casimir-pulaski/ (7 May 2021); Lawrence, *Storm Over Savanah*, 100–101.

22. Taaffe, *Philadelphia Campaign*, 72, 96, 103. For a dramatic telling of the First Maryland Continentals' story, see O'Donnell, *Washington's Immortals*.

23. Schmitt, "William Smallwood," *Archives of Maryland*, https://msa.maryland .gov/megafile/msa/speccol/sc3500/sc3520/001100/001134/html/1134bio.html (7 May 2021); Kimmel, *William Smallwood*, 3–4, 7, 10–11; *OCA*, 500–501, 596. Greene to Alexander Hamilton, 10 January 1781, *Papers of Alexander Hamilton*, 531–32; Washington to Lee, 16 February 1778, Washington to William Smallwood, 16 February 1778, *PGW*, 13:561–62, 563–64.

24. Buchanan, *Road to Guilford Courthouse*, 162, 168; Schmitt, "William Smallwood;" Kimmel, *William Smallwood*, 12, 14–17; Greene to Hamilton, 10 January 1781, *Papers of Alexander Hamilton*, 531–32; *OCA*, 501; Greene to Washington, 7 December 1780, *Founders Online*, NARA, https://founders.archives.gov/documents/Washington/99-01 -02-04138 (7 May 2021), https://founders.archives.gov/documents/Washington/99-01 -02-04356 (7 May 2021); "Understanding Maryland Records: Money," http://guide .msa.maryland.gov/pages/viewer.aspx?page=money (22 August 2021).

25. Howe, *Narrative*, 30, 32, 33. Smith, *William Howe* is a thorough examination of Howe's tenure of command and Parliamentary defense.

26. Howe, *Narrative*, 30, 32, 33; Mackesy, *War for America*, 149–52; Anderson, *Command of the Howe Brothers*, 301–7; O'Shaughnessy, *Men Who Lost America*, 105–6.

27. Howe, *Narrative*, 30, 32, 33; Gruber, *Howe Brothers*, 287, 290, 295.

28. Howe to George Germain, 22 October 1777, 30 November 1777, Germain to Howe, 11 December 1777, ser. 1, vol. 6, Germain Papers, WLCL. A week following his letter to Germain, Howe had informed Lt. Gen. Sir Henry Clinton of his request to "retire from this Command, conceiving I have not met with the Support I had a Right to expect from those under whom I am employed." Howe to Henry Clinton, [18] December 1777, Ser. 1, vol. 28, Clinton Papers, WLCL.

29. Howe to Germain, 17 January 1778, Germain to Howe, 4 February 1778, ser. 1, vol. 7, Germain Papers, WLCL; Howe to Germain, 19 April 1778, Howe to Germain, 22 October 1777, Germain to Howe, 27 February 1778, Howe to Germain, 17 January 1778, Germain to Howe, 4 February 1778, Historical Manuscripts Commission, *Stopford-Sackville Manuscripts*, 106, 80, 84, 91, 92; Germain to Clinton, 4 February 1778, ser. 1, vol. 31, Clinton Papers, WLCL; Howe, *Narrative*, 49.

30. Thomas Stirling to William Stirling, 13 April 1778, Letters to Sir William Stirling, Papers, NAS; O'Shaughnessy, *Men Who Lost America*, 121, 122; Biddulph, *Nineteenth and Their Times*, 64; Gruber, "Howe, William," *ODNB*, https://doi.org/10.1093 /ref:odnb/13966 (7 May 2021). From 1 January 1776, Howe, a lieutenant general, had held the "Local Rank" (brevet) of general in America. *Army List* (1778), xviii.

31. Callahan, "Abercromby, Sir Robert" *ODNB*, https://doi.org/10.1093/ref:odnb /47 (7 May 2021); *Army List* (1775), 117; *Army List* (1776), 91; Taaffe, *Philadelphia Campaign*, 98–99, 105–6.

32. Stirling to William Stirling, 29 November 1777, Letters to Sir William Stirling, Papers, NAS.

33. Lloyd, "Stirling, Sir Thomas," *ODNB*, https://doi.org/10.1093/ref:odnb/26535 (7 May 2021); Forbes, *"Black Watch,"* 100, 101–2; Stirling to Anne Graham, 9 August 1776, Stirling to William Graham, 18 April 1782, Stirling to William Graham, 7 June 1783, Additional Papers, Stirling, NLS. Stirling spent some part of 1782 taking the waters at Bath, recuperating from his wound. Finding no relief, he journeyed to Barèges, France, where the thermal waters were reputed to possess curative effects for gunshot wounds. In addition to "injecting, bathing, douching & drinking" to salve his wound, Stirling also sought medical assistance, and reflected on the pleasures of the flesh. He reported to his brother-in-law, William Graham, that "I was an hour today lying on my face while a Surgeon was probing & tugging at a splinter wt his forceps but it is D—obstinate it would not move I might have been making better use of that position in a hundreth part of the time wt the Widow you recommend if she had been here but not being here with one of the Pyranean Nymphs who are as like our Highd Lasses as can be only that they would not throw a pail of Milk in your face was you to put half a crown in their bosom." See Meighan, *Treatise*.

34. Captain Andrew Snape Hamond, RN, to Secretary of the Admiralty Philip Stephens, 26 March 1778, *NDAR*, 11:798.

35. Knight, "Hamond, Sir Andrew Snape," *ODNB*, https://doi.org/10.1093/ref:odnb/12164 (7 May 2021); Mariot Arbuthnot to Earl of Sandwich, 12 September 1780, quoted in Montagu, *Private Papers of Sandwich*, 237.

36. Wright, *Continental Army*, 24, 46.

Bibliography

Manuscript and Archival Sources

American Antiquarian Society, Worcester, Mass.
  Greene, Nathanael. Papers, 1770–1798.
  Smith, John. Diaries, 1776–1778.
American Philosophical Society, Philadelphia, Pa.
  Boyle, Joseph Lee. "'Up to our Knees in Mud for Four Days Past': The Weather and
    the Continental Army, August 1777–June 1778." Unpublished manuscript.
    David Library of the American Revolution, at the American Philosophical
    Society.
  Feinstone, Sol. Collection of the American Revolution, ca. 1760s–1850s.
Chicago History Museum
  Weedon, George. Papers, 1776–1789.
William L. Clements Library, University of Michigan, Ann Arbor
  Clinton, Henry. Papers, 1736–1850.
  Germain, George Sackville. Papers, 1683–1785.
  Harmar, Josiah. Papers 1681–1937.
  Howe, William. Orderly Book, 1776–1778.
  Orderly Book, Valley Forge, 20 January 1778–22 February 1778. Orderly Book
    Collection.
  Simcoe, John Graves. Papers, 1774–1824.
  Turner, Peter. Papers 1774–1789.
Connecticut Historical Society, New Haven, Conn.
  Commissary, Revolutionary War. Papers, 1758–1819.
  Gray, Samuel. Commissary Records, 1777–1782.
  Huntington, Jedidiah. Papers, 1758–1814.
  Trumbull, Joseph. Papers, 1753–1791.
  Wadsworth, Jeremiah. Business and Commissary Records, 1759–1847.
  Woodbridge, Theodore. Papers, 1777–1798.
Detroit Public Library
  Piatt, Jacob. Papers, 1777–1778. Burton Historical Collection.
Fenimore Art Museum, Cooperstown, N.Y.
  Stewart, Colonel Charles. Papers, 1777–1783. Special Collections.
Gloucester County Historical Society, N.J.
  "Account of Cattle, & Provisions Collected by the Party under the Command
    of Capt. Henry Lee." Howell Family. Collection, 1738–1897.
Historical Society of Pennsylvania, Philadelphia, Pa.
  Barnard, Richard. Diary.

Biddle, Clement. Papers.

Shippen Family. Papers.

Society. Collection.

Poor, Enoch. Orderly Book.

Wayne, Anthony. Papers.

Wier, Daniel. Letterbook.

Houghton Library, Harvard University, Cambridge, Ma.

Dearborn, Frederick M. Collection of Military and Political Americana. Part I: The Revolution and the Administration, 1669–1953.

Sparks, Jared. Collection of Documents Concerning the American Revolution.

University of Houston Libraries, Houston, Tex.

Shreve, Israel. Revolutionary War Letters.

Library of Congress, Washington, D.C.

Force, Peter. Collection.

Blaine, Ephraim. Papers, 1765–1805.

Davis, John. Papers, 1775–1783.

Washington, George. Papers, 1592–1943.

Massachusetts Historical Society, Boston

Pickering, Timothy. Papers, 1731–1927.

Morristown National Historic Park, N.J.

Lidgerwood Collection.

Smith, Lloyd W. Collection.

National Archives, Kew, Surrey

Military Despatches, 1777–1778, Board of Trade and Secretaries of State: America and West Indies, Original Correspondence, CO 5/95.

Records of the American Loyalist Claims Commission, AO 13.

National Archives and Records Administration, Washington, D.C.

Continental Congress. Papers. RG 360. M247.

War Department. Collection of Revolutionary War Records. RG 93. M853. M859.

National Archives of Scotland, Edinburgh

Stirling of Ardoch, Letters to Sir William, from his Brother, 1760–1797. Papers of the Family of Stirling Home Drummond Moray, 1236–1920 of Abercairny.

National Army Museum, London

Extracts from Various Standing Orders 1750 (c), and letters of Maj. Gen. Francis Laye, Royal Artillery, to his father while serving in America, 1775–1781; associated with the American War of Independence (1775–1783).

National Library of Scotland, Edinburgh

Graham of Airth and Other Related Families. Additional Papers of the Family, Notably (Graham) Stirling of Ardoch and Strowan, and Stirling of Kippendavie.

New Jersey Historical Society, Newark, N.J.

First New Jersey Continental Regiment. Orderly Book, 1777–1778.

New-York Historical Society, New York

Alexander, William, Lord Stirling. Selected Papers.

McLane, Allen. Papers.

New York Public Library, New York

Buchanan, William. Letters to Thomas Wharton, 1777.

Princeton University Library

De Coppet, Andre. Collection.

Rhode Island Historical Society, Providence

Smith, Sandford B. Papers.

Society of the Cincinnati Library, Washington, D.C.

Barton, Lt. William. Letters, 1777–1779.

Orderly Book. 9th Pennsylvania Regiment, Valley Forge and Elsewhere, 5 January–9 July 1778.

Wayne, Anthony. Letter to Richard Peters, 30 December 1777.

Williams Family. Collection.

Valley Forge National Historic Park

Hurd, Lewis. Diary.

Reed, John. Collection.

Wisconsin Historical Society, Madison

Frontier Wars Papers, Lyman Copeland Draper Manuscripts.

Published Primary Sources

Books

Baurmeister, Carl Leopold. *Revolution in America: Confidential Letters and Journals, 1776-1784, of Adjutant General Major Baurmeister of the Hessian Forces*. Translated by Bernhard A. Uhlendorf. New Brunswick, N.J.: Rutgers University Press, 1957.

Boyle, Joseph Lee, ed. *Writings from the Valley Forge Encampment of the Continental Army, December 19, 1777–June 19, 1778*. 4 vols. Bowie, Md.: Heritage Books, 2000–2002.

Browne, William Hand, ed. *Archives of Maryland*. Vol. 16, *Journal and Correspondence of the Maryland Council of Safety, January 1-March 20, 1777, Journal and Correspondence of the State Council, March 20, 1777–March 28, 1778*. Baltimore: Maryland Historical Society, 1897.

Burnett, Edmund C. *Letters of the Members of the Continental Congress*. Vol. 2, *July 5, 1776–December 31, 1777*. Washington, D.C.: Carnegie Institution, 1923.

———. *Letters of the Members of the Continental Congress*. Vol. 3, *January 1, 1777–December 31, 1778*. Washington, D.C.: Carnegie Institution, 1926.

Bute, Third Earl [John Stuart]. *A Prime Minister and His Son: From the Correspondence of the 3rd Earl of Bute and of Lt.-General the Hon. Sir Charles Stuart, K.B.* Edited by Mrs. E[dward]. [Violet Hunter Guthrie Montagu-Stuart-Wortley] Stuart-Wortley. New York: E.P. Dutton, 1925.

Calendar of Maryland State Papers. No. 4, pt. 1. Red Books. Annapolis, Md.: Hall of Records Commission, 1950.

Chaloner, John. *"My Last Shift Betwixt Us and Death:" The Ephraim Blaine Letterbook, 1777-1778*. Edited by Joseph Lee Boyle. Bowie, Md.: Heritage Books, 2001.

Collin, Nicholas. *Journal and Biography of Nicholas Collin, 1746-1831*. Translated by Amandus Johnson. Philadelphia: New Jersey Society of Pennsylvania, 1936.

Crawford, Michael J., ed. *Naval Documents of the American Revolution*. Vol. 11, *American Theater: October 1, 1777-December 31, 1777, European Theater: October 1, 1777-December 31, 1777*. Washington, D.C.: Naval Historical Center, 1996.

———. *Naval Documents of the American Revolution*. Vol. 11, *American Theater: January 1, 1778—March 31, 1778, European Theater: January 1, 1778-March 31, 1778*. Washington, D.C.: Naval Historical Center, 2005.

———. *Naval Documents of the American Revolution*. Vol. 12, *American Theater: April 1, 1778-May 31, 1778, European Theater: April 1, 1778-May 31, 1778*. Washington, D.C.: Naval Historical Center, 2013.

Dann, John C., ed. *The Revolution Remembered: Eyewitness Accounts of the War for Independence*. Chicago: University of Chicago Press, 1980.

Dearborn, Henry. *Revolutionary War Journals of Henry Dearborn, 1775-1783*. Edited by Lloyd A. Brown and Howard H. Peckham. Chicago: Caxton Club, 1939.

de Jeney, M[ichel]. *The Partisan: Or, the Art of Making War in Detachments with Plans Proper to Facilitate the Understanding of the Several Dispositions, and Movements Necessary to Light Troops, in Order to Accomplish Their Marches, Ambuscades, Attacks and Retreats with Success*. Translated by an officer of the army [Thomas Ellis?]. London: R. Griffiths, 1760.

The Detail and Conduct of the American War under Generals Gage, Howe, Burgoyne, and Vice Admiral Howe. 3rd ed. London: Richardson and Urquhart, 1780.

Döhla, Johann Conrad. *A Hessian Diary of the American Revolution*. Translated and edited by Bruce E. Burgoyne. Norman: University of Oklahoma Press, 1990.

Downman, Francis. *The Services of Lieut.-Colonel Francis Downman, R.A., in France, North America, and the West Indies, Between the Years 1758 and 1784*. Edited by Francis Arthur Whinyates. Woolwich, U.K.: Royal Artillery Institution, 1898.

Ewald, Johann. *Diary of the American War: A Hessian Journal*. Translated and edited by Joseph P. Tustin. New Haven, Conn.: Yale University Press, 1979.

———. *Treatise on Partisan Warfare*. Translated and edited by Robert A. Selig and David Curtis Skaggs. Westport, Conn.: Greenwood, 1991.

Ewing, George. *The Military Journal of George Ewing (1754-1824): A Soldier of Valley Forge*. Yonkers, N.Y.: Thomas Ewing, 1928.

Ford, Worthington Chauncey, ed. *Journals of the Continental Congress, 1774-1789*. Vol. 5, *June 5, 1776 to October 8, 1776*. Washington, D.C.: Government Printing Office, 1906.

———. *Journals of the Continental Congress, 1774-1789*. Vol. 6, *October 9, 1776 to December 31, 1776*. Washington, D.C.: Government Printing Office, 1906.

———. *Journals of the Continental Congress, 1774-1789*. Vol. 9, *October 31-December 31, 1777*. Washington, D.C.: Government Printing Office, 1907.

Garden, Alexander. *Anecdotes of the American Revolution: Illustrative of the Talents and Virtues of the Heroes and Patriots, Who Acted the Most Conspicuous Parts Therein*. 2nd ser. Charleston, S.C.: A.E. Miller, 1828.

—————. *Anecdotes of the Revolutionary War in America: With Sketches of Character of Persons the Most Distinguished, in the Southern States, for Civil and Military Services*. Charleston, S.C.: A.E. Miller, 1822.

Graydon, Alexander. *Memoirs of His Own Time: With Reminiscences of the Men and Events of the Revolution*. Edited by John Stockton Littell. Philadelphia: Lindsay & Blakiston, 1846.

Greene, Nathanael. *The Papers of General Nathanael Greene*. Vol. 2, *1 January 1777–16 October 1778*. Edited by Richard K. Showman. Chapel Hill: University of North Carolina Press for the Rhode Island Historical Society, 1980.

—————. *The Papers of General Nathanael Greene*. Vol. 3, *18 October 1778–10 May 1779*. Edited by Richard K. Showman. Chapel Hill: University of North Carolina Press for the Rhode Island Historical Society, 1983.

—————. *The Papers of General Nathanael Greene*. Vol. 8, *30 March–10 July 1781*. Edited by Dennis M. Conrad. Chapel Hill: University of North Carolina Press for the Rhode Island Historical Society, 1995.

Hazard, Samuel, ed. *Pennsylvania Archives*. Ser. 1. Vol. 5. Philadelphia: Joseph Severns, 1853.

—————. *Pennsylvania Archives*. Ser. 1. Vol. 6. Philadelphia: Joseph Severns, 1853.

—————. *The Register of Pennsylvania*. Vol. 3. Philadelphia: W. F. Geddes, 1829.

Hinde, Robert. *The Discipline of the Light-Horse*. London: W. Owen, 1778.

Historical Manuscripts Commission. *Report on the Manuscripts of Mrs. Stopford-Sackville of Drayton House, Northamptonshire*. Vol. 2. Hereford, U.K.: HM Stationery Office, 1910.

Hoffman, Ronald, Sally D. Mason, and Eleanor S. Darcy, eds. *Dear Papa, Dear Charley: The Peregrinations of a Revolutionary Aristocrat, as Told by Charles Carroll of Carrollton and his Father, Charles Carroll of Annapolis, with Sundry Observations on Bastardy, Child-Rearing, Romance, Matrimony, Commerce, Tobacco, Slavery, and the Politics of Revolutionary America*. Vol. 2. Chapel Hill: University of North Carolina Press for the Omohundro Institute of Early American History and Culture, 2001.

Howe, William. *The Narrative of Lieut. Gen. Sir William Howe in a Committee of the House of Commons, on the 29th of April, 1779*. 3rd ed. London: H. Baldwin, 1781.

Howell, Frances. *The Book of John Howell and His Descendants. . . .* vol. 1. New York: Frances Howell, 1897.

Kelly, Patrick. *The Universal Cambrist and Commercial Instructor. . . .* Vol. 1. London: for the author, 1811.

Krafft, John Charles Philip von. *Journal of John Charles Philip von Krafft, Lieutenant in the Regiment von Bose, 1776–1784*. Edited by Thomas H. Edsall. New York: n.p., 1888.

Laurens, Henry. *The Papers of Henry Laurens*. Vol. 12, *November 1, 1777–March 15, 1778*. Edited by David R. Chesnutt. Columbia: University of South Carolina Press for the South Carolina Historical Society, 1990.

Laurens, John. *The Army Correspondence of Colonel John Laurens in the Years 1777-8*. New York: Publications of the Bradford Club, 1867.

Hamilton, Alexander. *Papers of Alexander Hamilton*. Vol. 2, *1779–1781*. Edited by Harold C. Syrett. New York: Columbia University Press, 1961.

Lee, Henry. *Memoirs of the War in the Southern Department of the United States*. Vol. 2, Philadelphia: Bradford & Inskeep, 1812.

Livingston, William. *The Papers of William Livingston*. Vol. 2, *July 1777–December 1778*. Edited by Carl E. Prince and Dennis P. Ryan. Trenton: New Jersey Historical Society, 1980.

Lochée, Lewis. *Elements of Field Fortification*. London: for the author, 1783.

Madison, James. *The Papers of James Madison*. Vol. 1, *16 March 1775–16 December 1779*, ed. William T. Hutchinson and William M. E. Rachal. Chicago: University of Chicago Press, 1962.

Marshall, Christopher. *Extracts from the Diary of Christopher Marshall Kept in Philadelphia and Lancaster during the American Revolution, 1774–1781*. Edited by William Duane. Albany, N.Y.: Joel Munsell, 1877.

McIlwaine, H. R., ed. *Official Letters of the Governors of Virginia*. Vol. 1, *The Letters of Patrick Henry*. Richmond: Virginia State Library, 1926.

Meighan, Christopher. *A Treatise of the Nature and Powers of Bareges's Baths and Waters.* . . . London: T. Meighan, 1742.

Montagu, John. *The Private Papers of John, Earl of Sandwich: First Lord of the Admiralty, 1771–1782*. Vol. 3, *May 1779–December 1780*. Edited by G.R. Barnes and J.H. Owen. [London]: Navy Records Society, 1932.

Montresor, John. *The Montresor Journals*. Edited by G.D. Scull. New York: New-York Historical Society, 1882.

Muenchausen, Friedrich von. *At General Howe's Side, 1776–1778: The Diary of General William Howe's Aide-de-Camp, Captain Friedrich von Muenchausen*. Translated by Ernst Kipping. Annotated by Samuel Stelle Smith. Monmouth Beach, N.J.: Philip Freneau Press, 1974.

Muhlenberg, Henry Melchior. *The Journals of Henry Melchior Muhlenberg*. Vol. 3, *1777–1787*. Translated by Theodore G. Tappert and John W. Doberstein. Philadelphia: Evangelical Lutheran Ministerium of Pennsylvania and Adjacent States and Muhlenberg Press, 1958.

Muller, John. *A Treatise of Artillery* . . . *: To which is Prefixed, an Introduction, with a Theory of Powder Applied to Fire-arms*. 2nd ed. London: John Millan, 1768.

Peebles, John. *John Peebles' American War: The Diary of a Scottish Grenadier, 1776–1782*. Edited by Ira D. Gruber. Mechanicsburg, Pa.: Stackpole, 1998.

Pembroke, Earl of [Henry Herbert]. *A Method of Breaking Horses, and Teaching Soldiers to Ride*. 2nd ed., rev. London: J. Hughes, 1762.

Peters, Matthew. *The Rational Farmer: Or a Treatise on Agriculture and Tillage* . . . , 2nd ed. London: W. Flexney, 1771.

Prechtel, Johann Ernst. *A Hessian Officer's Diary of the American Revolution*. Translated and edited by Bruce E. Burgoyne. Bowie, Md.: Heritage, 1994.

The Proceedings of the Convention of the Delegates for the Counties and Corporations in the Colony of Virginia. Richmond: Ritchie, Trueheart, & Du-Val, 1816.

Proceedings of the Conventions of the Province of Maryland, Held at the City of Annapolis, in 1774, 1775 & 1776. Baltimore: James Lucas & E. K. Deaver, 1836.

Public Archives Commission. *Delaware Archives*. 3 vols. Wilmington, Del.:
Mercantile, 1911–1919.

Robertson, Archibald. *His Diaries and Sketches in America, 1762–1780*. New York:
New York Public Library, 1930.

Simcoe, John Graves. *Simcoe's Military Journal*. . . . 1784. Reprint. New York:
Bartlett & Welford, 1844.

Smith, Paul H., ed. *Letters of Delegates to Congress, 1774–1789*. Vol. 8, *September 18,
1777–January 31, 1778*. Washington, D.C.: Library of Congress, 1981.

———. *Letters of Delegates to Congress, 1774–1789*, vol. 9, *February 1–May 31, 1778*.
Washington, D.C.: Library of Congress, 1982.

Steiner, Bernard Christian, ed. *Archives of Maryland*. Vol. 42, *Proceedings and Acts of
the General Assembly, 1740–1744*. Baltimore: Maryland Historical Society, 1923.

Stevens, William. *A System for the Discipline of the Artillery of the United States of
America, or, the Young Artillerist's Pocket Companion*. New York: William A. Davis,
1797.

Stoudt, John Joseph, ed. *Ordeal at Valley Forge: A Day-by-Day Chronicle from
December 17, 1777 to June 18, 1778, Compiled from the Sources*. Philadelphia:
University of Pennsylvania Press, 1963.

Trumbull, Jonathan. *Collections of the Massachusetts Historical Society: The Trumbull
Papers*. 7th ser., vol. 2, pt. 3. Boston: Massachusetts Historical Society, 1902.

Washington, George. *The Papers of George Washington: Revolutionary War Series*.
Vol. 10, *11 June 1777–18 August 1777*. Edited by Frank E. Grizzard, Jr. Charlottesville:
University Press of Virginia, 2000.

———. *The Papers of George Washington: Revolutionary War Series*. Vol. 11,
19 August 1777–25 October 1777. Edited by Philander D. Chase. Charlottesville:
University of Virginia Press, 2002.

———. *The Papers of George Washington: Revolutionary War Series*. Vol. 12,
October–December 1777. Edited by Frank E. Grizzard, Jr., and David R. Hoth.
Charlottesville: University of Virginia Press, 2002.

———. *The Papers of George Washington: Revolutionary War Series*. Vol. 13,
December 1777–February 1778. Edited by Edward G. Lengel. Charlottesville:
University of Virginia Press, 2003.

———. *The Papers of George Washington: Revolutionary War Series*. Vol. 14,
March 1778–April 1778. Edited by David R. Hoth. Charlottesville: University of
Virginia Press, 2004.

———. *The Papers of George Washington: Revolutionary War Series*. Vol. 21, *1 June–
31 July 1779*. Edited by William M. Ferraro. Charlottesville: University of Virginia
Press, 2012.

———. *The Papers of George Washington, Revolutionary War Series*. Vol. 22,
1 August–21 October 1779. Edited by Benjamin L. Huggins. Charlottesville:
University of Virginia Press, 2013.

———. *The Writings of George Washington from the Original Manuscript Resources,
1745–1799*. Vol. 21, *December 22, 1780–April 26, 1781*. Edited by John C.
Fitzpatrick. Washington, D.C.: Government Printing Office, 1937.

Weedon, George. *Valley Forge Orderly Book of General George Weedon*. . . . New York: Dodd, Mead, 1902.

Wilkin, W.H., ed. *Some British Soldiers in America*. London: Hugh Rees, 1914.

Articles and Chapters

Anderson, Enoch. "Personal Recollections of Captain Enoch Anderson, an Officer of the Delaware Regiments in the Revolutionary War." Edited by Henry Hobart Bellas. *Papers of the Historical Society of Delaware* 16 (1896): 3–61.

Angell, Israel. "The Israel Angell Diary, 1 October 1777–28 February 1778." Edited by Joseph Lee Boyle. *Rhode Island History* 58, no. 4 (November 2000): 107–38.

Armstrong, Samuel. "From Saratoga to Valley Forge: The Diary of Lt. Samuel Armstrong." Edited by Joseph Lee Boyle. *Pennsylvania Magazine of History and Biography* 121, no. 3 (July 1997): 237–70.

Biddle, Clement. "Selections from the Correspondence of Colonel Clement Biddle." *Pennsylvania Magazine of History and Biography*, 42, no. 4 (January 1918): 310–43.

Brigham, Paul. "A Revolutionary Diary of Captain Paul Brigham, November 19, 1777–September 4, 1778." Edited by Edward A. Hoyt. *Vermont History* 34, no. 1 (January 1966): 3–30.

de Saxe, Maurice. "My Reveries upon the Art of War." In *Roots of Strategy: The Five Greatest Military Classics of All Time*. Translated and edited by Thomas R. Phillips, 177–300. 1940. Reprint, Harrisburg, Pa.: Stackpole, 1985.

Doehlemann, Johann Christoph. "Diary of Johann Christoph Doehlemann, Grenadier Company, Ansbach Regiment, March 1777–September 1778." Translated by Karl Walther and Henry J. Retzer. *Journal of the Johannes Schwalm Historical Association* 11 (2008): 11–17.

Duncan, Henry. "Journals of Henry Duncan, Captain, Royal Navy 1776–1782." In *The Naval Miscellany*. Vol.1, *Publications of the Navy Records Society*. Edited by John Knox Laughton, 105–219. [London]: Naval Records Society, 1902.

Matthewman, Luke. "Narrative of Lieut. Luke Matthewman of the Revolutionary Navy, from the *New York Packet*, 1778." *The Magazine of American History with Notes and Queries* 2, no. 3 (March 1878): 175–85.

McMichael, James. "Diary of Lieutenant James McMichael, 1776–1778." Edited by William P. McMichael. *Pennsylvania Magazine of History and Biography* 16, no. 2 (July 1892): 129–59.

Morton, Robert. "Diary of Robert Morton," *Pennsylvania Magazine of History and Biography* 1, no. 1 (1877): 1–39.

"Revolutionary Army Orders: For the Main Army under Washington. 1778–1779." *Virginia Magazine of History and Biography* 14, no. 4 (April 1907): 97–407.

"Revolutionary Army Orders: For the Main Army under Washington, 1778–1779." *Virginia Magazine of History and Biography* 15, no. 1 (July 1907): 44–56.

Schmidt, Frederick. "Extracts from the Diary of the Moravian Congregation at Oldmans Creek, N.J., 1777–78. Rev. Frederick Schmidt, pastor" *Pennsylvania Magazine of History and Biography* 35, no. 139 (July 1911): 378–79.

Seybolt, Robert Francis, ed. "A Contemporary British Account of General Sir William Howe's Military Operations in 1777." *Proceedings of the American Antiquarian Society*, n.s., 40 (1930): 69–92.

Shreve, John. "Personal Narrative of the Services of Lieut. John Shreve of the New Jersey Line of the Continental Army." *Magazine of American History* 3, pt. 2, no. 7 (July 1879): 564–79.

Waldo, Albigence. "Valley Forge, 1777–1778: Diary of Surgeon Albigence Waldo, of the Connecticut Line." *Pennsylvania Magazine of History and Biography* 21, no. 3 (October 1897): 299–323.

Wild, Ebenezer. "The Journal of Ebenezer Wild (1776–1781) Who Served as Corporal, Sergeant, Ensign, and Lieutenant in the American Army of the Revolution." *Proceedings of the Massachusetts Historical Society*. Ser. 2, vol. 6 (October 1890): 78–160.

Periodicals

London Gazette
Philadelphia Evening Post
The (Trenton) *New Jersey Gazette*

Constitutions

Delaware Constitution. 1776.
Pennsylvania Constitution. 1776.

Maps and Charts

American Philosophical Society, *Map of proposed roads through the southeastern part of Pennsylvania, the northeastern part of Maryland, and the northern part of Delaware*. [Philadelphia: American Philosophical Society, 1771]. Map. Geography and Map Division, Library of Congress. https://www.loc.gov/item/79695387/. 7 May 2021.

Churchman, John. *To the American Philosophical Society, this map of the peninsula between Delaware & Chesopeak bays, with the said bays and shores adjacent drawn from the most accurate surveys is humbly inscribed by John Churchman.* [Philadelphia?: 1778?]. Map. Geography and Map Division, Library of Congress. https://www.loc.gov/item/73691622/. 7 May 2021.

Des Barres, Joseph F. W, John Knight, and John Hunter. *A chart of Delawar River from Bombay Hook to Ridley Creek, with soundings &c taken by Lt. Knight of the Navy.* [London, 1779]. Map. Geography and Map Division, Library of Congress. https://www.loc.gov/item/75696335/. 7 May 2021.

Faden, William. *A Plan of the City and Environs of Philadelphia: With the Works and Encampments of His Majesty's Forces under the Command of Lieutenant General Sir William Howe, K.B.* London: William Fadden, 1779. Map. Geography and Map Division, Library of Congress. https://www.loc.gov/item/74692213/. 7 May 2021.

Hunter, John. *A sketch of the navigation from Swan Pt. to the River Elk at the head of Chesapeak Bay. Sketch of the River Elk, at the head of Chesapeak Bay.* [1777] Map. Geography and Map Division, Library of Congress. https://www.loc.gov/item /gm71002217/. 7 May 2021.

Kitchin, Thomas. *Seat of War in the Environs of Philadelphia.* [London Printed for R. Baldwin, 1777]. Map. Geography and Map Division, Library of Congress. https://www.loc.gov/item/gm71002457/. 7 May 2021.

Progress of the army from their landing till taking possession of Philadelphia. [1777?]. Map. Geography and Map Division, Library of Congress. https://www.loc.gov /item/gm71000678/. 7 May 2021.

Smith, Anthony. *A new and accurate chart of the Bay of Chesapeake, with all the shoals, channels, islands, entrances, soundings, and sailing-marks, as far as the navigable part of the rivers Patowmack, Patapsco and north-east.* London: Robert Sayer & John Bennett, 1776. Map. Geography and Map Division, Library of Congress. Library of Congress. https://www.loc.gov/item/74691941/. 7 May 2021.

Varle, Charles, and Francis Shallus. *A map of the state of Delaware and the Eastern Shore of Maryland: with the soundings of the Bay of Delaware.* [Philadelphia?: n.p., 1801]. Map. Geography and Map Division, Library of Congress. https://www.loc .gov/item/2018590123/. 7 May 2021.

Published Secondary Sources

Books

Anderson, Troyer Steele. *The Command of the Howe Brothers during the American Revolution.* New York: Oxford University Press, 1936.

Ashmead, Henry Graham. *History of Delaware County, Pennsylvania.* Philadelphia: L.H. Everts, 1884.

Atwood, Rodney. *The Hessians: Mercenaries from Hessen-Kassel in the American Revolution.* Cambridge: Cambridge University Press, 1980.

Banta, Theodore M. *Sayre Family: Lineage of Thomas Sayre, a Founder of Southampton.* New York: De Vinne, 1901.

Biddulph, John. *The Nineteenth and Their Times: Being an Account of the Four Cavalry Regiments in the British Army That Have Borne the Number Nineteen and of the Campaigns in Which They Served.* London: John Murray, 1899.

Bodle, Wayne K. *The Valley Forge Winter: Civilians and Soldiers in War.* University Park: Pennsylvania State University Press, 2002.

Bowler, R. Arthur. *Logistics and the Failure of the British Army in America, 1775–1783.* Princeton, N.J.: Princeton University Press, 1975.

Buchanan, John. *The Road to Charleston: Nathanael Greene and the American Revolution.* Charlottesville: University of Virginia Press, 2019.

———. *The Road to Guilford Courthouse: The American Revolution in the South.* New York: John Wiley & Sons, 1997.

Buel, Richard, Jr. *In Irons: Britain's Naval Supremacy and the American Revolutionary Economy.* New Haven, Conn.: Yale University Press, 1998.

Canney, Donald L. *Sailing Warships of the US Navy*. Annapolis, Md.: Naval Institute Press, 2001.

Carp, E. Wayne. *To Starve the Army at Pleasure: Continental Army Administration and American Political Culture, 1775-1783*. Chapel Hill: University of North Carolina Press, 1984.

Chernow, Ron. *Washington: A Life*. New York: Penguin, 2010.

Clark, William Bell. *Gallant John Barry, 1745-1803: The Story of a Naval Hero of Two Wars*. New York: Macmillan, 1938.

Clausewitz, Carl von. *On War*. Indexed ed. Edited and translated by Michael Howard and Peter Paret, Princeton, N.J.: Princeton University Press, 1984.

Clement, John. *Revolutionary Reminiscences of Camden County (Originally Part of "Old Gloucester"), State of New Jersey*. Camden, N.J.: S. Chew, 1876.

Cole, Ryan. *Light-Horse Harry Lee: The Rise and Fall of a Revolutionary Hero*. Washington, D.C.: Regnery, 2019.

Conrad, Henry C. *History of the State of Delaware: From the Earliest Settlement to the Year 1907*. Vol. 2. Wilmington, Del.: Henry C. Conrad, 1908.

Cook, Fred J. *What Manner of Men: Forgotten Heroes of the American Revolution*. New York: William Morrow, 1959.

Dallett, Francis James. *The War of the Revolution in Radnor (1776-1778)*. Revised by Phil Graham. [Radnor, Pa.]: Radnor Historical Society, 1976.

Doerflinger, Thomas M. *A Vigorous Spirit of Enterprise: Merchants and Economic Development in Revolutionary Philadelphia*. Chapel Hill: University of North Carolina Press for the Institute of Early American History and Culture, 1986.

Duffy, Christopher. *The Military Experience in the Age of Reason, 1715-1789*. London: Routledge & Kegan Paul, 1987.

Eelking, Max von. *The German Allied Troops in the North American War of Independence, 1776-1783*. Translated by J.G. Rosengarten. Albany, N.Y.: Joel Munsell's Sons, 1893.

Egerton, Douglas R. *Death or Liberty: African Americans and Revolutionary America*. New York: Oxford University Press, 2009.

Fagan, Brian. *The Little Ice Age: How Climate Made History, 1300-1850*. New York: Basic Books, 2000.

Futhey, J. Smith and Gilbert Cope. *History of Chester County, Pennsylvania, with Genealogical and Biographical Sketches*. Philadelphia: Louis H. Everts, 1881.

Gara, Donald J. *The Queen's American Rangers*. Yardley, Pa.: Westholme, 2015.

Gardiner, Robert ed. *Navies and the American Revolution, 1775-1783*. Annapolis, Md.: Naval Institute Press in association with the National Maritime Museum, 1996.

Gaylord, Willis, and Luther Tucker, eds. *American Husbandry: Being A Series of Essays on Agriculture*. Vol. 1. New York: Harper, 1840.

Fischer, David Hackett. *Washington's Crossing*. New York: Oxford University Press, 2004.

Fischer, Joseph R. *A Well-Executed Failure: The Sullivan Campaign Against the Iroquois, July-September 1779*. Columbia: University of South Carolina Press, 1997.

Forbes, Archibald. *The "Black Watch": The Record of an Historic Regiment*. London: Cassell, 1896.

Frey, Silvia R. *Water from the Rock: Black Resistance in a Revolutionary Age*. Princeton, N.J.: Princeton University Press, 1991.

Graymont, Barbara. *The Iroquois in the American Revolution*. Syracuse, N.Y.: Syracuse University Press, 1972.

Gruber, Ira D. *The Howe Brothers and the American Revolution*. Chapel Hill: University of North Carolina Press, for the Omohundro Institute of Early American History and Culture, 1972.

Hancock, Harold Bell. *The Delaware Loyalists*. 1940. Reprint, Boston: Gregg Society, 1972.

Hartmann, John W. *The American Partisan: Henry Lee and the Struggle for Independence, 1776-1780*. Shippensburg, Pa.: Burd Street, 2000.

Historical Sites: Charlestown, Cecil County, Maryland: Incorporated in 1742. [Charlestown, Md.?]: Historical Charlestown, n.d.

Jackson, John W. *The Pennsylvania Navy: The Defense of the Delaware*. New Brunswick, N.J.: Rutgers University Press, 1974.

———. *With the British Army in Philadelphia, 1777-1778*. San Rafael, Calif.: Presidio, 1979.

Jamar, Mary Hollingsworth. *Hollingsworth Family and Collateral Lines of Cooch-Gilpin-Jamar-Mackall-Morris-Stewart*. Philadelphia: Historical Publication Society, 1944.

Jasanoff, Maya. *Liberty's Exiles: American Loyalists in the Revolutionary World*. New York: Alfred A. Knopf, 2011.

Joint Chiefs of Staff. Joint Publication (JP) 3-0, *Joint Operations*. Washington, D.C.: Joint Chiefs of Staff, 2008.

Jordan, Francis, Jr. *The Life of William Henry of Lancaster, Pennsylvania, 1729-1786: Patriot, Military Officer, Inventor of the Steamboat*. Lancaster, Pa.: New Era, 1910.

Kimmel, Ross M. *In Perspective: William Smallwood*. [Mt. Victoria], Md.: Smallwood Foundation, 2000.

Lawrence, Alexander A. *Storm Over Savanah: The Story of Count d'Estaing and the Siege of the Town in 1779*. Athens: University of Georgia Press, 1951.

Lee, Wayne E. *Barbarians and Brothers: Anglo-American Warfare, 1500-1865*. New York: Oxford University Press, 2011.

Lender, Mark Edward. *Cabal!: The Plot against George Washington*. Yardley, Pa.: Westholme, 2019.

Lockhart, Paul. *The Drillmaster of Valley Forge: The Baron de Steuben and the Making of the American Army*. New York: Harper Collins, 2008.

Loescher, Burt Garfield. *Washington's Eyes: The Continental Light Dragoons*. Fort Collins, Colo.: Old Army, 1977.

Ludlum, David M. *Early American Winters, 1604-1820*. Boston: American Meteorological Society, 1966.

Lundin, Charles Leonard. *Cockpit of the Revolution*. Princeton, N.J.: Princeton University Press, 1940.

Mackesy, Piers. *The War for America, 1775-1783*. Cambridge, Mass.: Harvard University Press, 1964.

Maurer, C.F. William. *Dragoon Diary: The History of the Third Continental Light Dragoons*. Bloomington, Ind.: Author House, 2005.

McGrath, Tim. *John Barry: An American Hero in the Age of Sail*. Yardley, Pa.: Westholme, 2010.

McGuire, Thomas J. *Battle of Paoli*. Mechanicsburg, Pa.: Stackpole, 2000.

———. *The Philadelphia Campaign*. Vol. 1, *Brandywine and the Fall of Philadelphia*. Mechanicsburg, Pa.: Stackpole, 2006.

McKenney, Janice E. *The Organizational History of Field Artillery, 1775–2003*. Washington, D.C.: Center of Military History, 2007.

Metcalf, Henry Harrison, ed. *Laws of New Hampshire, Including Public and Private Acts and Resolves with an Appendix Embracing the Journal of the Committee of Safety*. Vol. 4, *Revolutionary Period, 1776–1784*. Bristol, N.H.: Musgrove, 1916.

Mickle, Isaac. *Reminiscences of Old Gloucester: or Incidents in the History of the Counties of Gloucester, Atlantic and Camden, New Jersey*. Philadelphia: Townsend Ward, 1845.

Middleton, Arthur Pierce. *Tobacco Coast: A Maritime History of the Chesapeake Bay in the Colonial Era*. Newport News, Va.: Mariner's Museum, 1953.

Mintz, Max M. *Seeds of Empire: The American Revolutionary Conquest of the Iroquois*. New York: New York University Press, 1999.

Montgomery, Morton L. *History of Berks County, Pennsylvania, in the Revolution, from 1774 to 1783*. Reading, Pa.: Charles F. Haage, 1894.

Murray, Williamson, and Peter R. Mansoor, eds. *Hybrid Warfare: Fighting Complex Opponents from the Ancient World to the Present*. New York: Cambridge University Press, 2012.

Nagy, John. *Rebellion in the Ranks: Mutinies of the American Revolution*. Yardley, Pa.: Westholme, 2007.

Nelson, Paul David. *Anthony Wayne: Soldier of the Early Republic*. Bloomington: Indiana University Press, 1985.

Nelson, William H. *The American Tory*. 1961. Reprint. Boston: Northeastern University Press, 1992.

O'Donnell, Patrick K. *Washington's Immortals: The Untold Story of an Elite Regiment Who Changed the Course of the Revolution*. New York: Atlantic Monthly, 2016.

O'Shaughnessy, Andrew Jackson. *The Men Who Lost America: British Leadership, the American Revolution and the Fate of the Empire*. New Haven, Conn.: Yale University Press, 2013.

Piecuch, Jim. *Loyalists, Indians, and Slaves in the Revolutionary South, 1775–1782*. Columbia: University of South Carolina Press, 2008.

———and John Beakes. *"Light Horse Harry" Lee in the War for Independence: A Military Biography of Robert E. Lee's Father*. Charleston, S.C.: Nautical & Aviation, 2013.

Quarles, Benjamin A. *The Negro in the American Revolution*. 1961. Reprint, Chapel Hill: University of North Carolina Press for the Omohundro Institute for Early American History and Culture, 1996.

Read, William Thompson. *Life and Correspondence of George Read: A Signer of the Declaration of Independence, with Notices of Some of His Contemporaries*. Philadelphia: J.B. Lippincott, 1870.

Risch, Erna. *Supplying Washington's Army*. Washington, D.C.: U.S. Army Center of Military History, 1981.

Royster, Charles. *Light-Horse Harry Lee and the Legacy of the American Revolution*. New York: Alfred A. Knopf, 1981.

Ruddiman, William F. *Plows, Plagues, and Petroleum: How Humans Took Control of Climate*. Princeton, N.J.: Princeton University Press, 2005.

Selig, Robert A. *The Washington-Rochambeau Revolutionary Route: Statement of National Significance*. Rev. ed. Washington, D.C.: National Park Service, 2003.

Sickler, Joseph S. *The History of Salem County, New Jersey: Being the Story of John Fenwick's Colony, the Oldest English Speaking Settlement on the Delaware River*. Salem, N.J.: Sunbeam, 1937.

Smith, David. *William Howe and the American War of Independence*. London: Bloomsbury, 2015.

Stewart, Frank H. *Foraging at Valley Forge by General Anthony Wayne in Salem and Gloucester Counties, New Jersey, with Associated Happenings and Foraging in Salem County for the British Army in Philadelphia by Colonel Mawhood and Major Simcoe, 1778*. Woodbury, N.J.: Gloucester County Historical Society, 1929

Sullivan, Aaron. *The Disaffected: Britain's Occupation of Philadelphia During the American Revolution*. Philadelphia: University of Pennsylvania Press, 2019.

Syrett, David. *The Royal Navy in American Waters, 1775–1783*. Aldershot, UK: Scolar, 1989.

———. *Shipping and the American War, 1775–1783: A Study of British Transport Organization*. London: Athlone, 1970.

Taaffe, Stephen R. *The Philadelphia Campaign, 1777–1778*. Lawrence: University Press of Kansas, 2003.

Thayer, Theodore. *Nathanael Greene: Strategist of the American Revolution*. New York: Twayne, 1960.

Thompson, William Y. *Israel Shreve: Revolutionary War Officer*. Ruston, La.: McGinty Trust Fund, 1979.

Trussell, John B.B., Jr., *Birthplace of an Army: A Study of the Valley Forge Encampment*. Harrisburg: Pennsylvania Historical and Museum Commission, 1976.

———. *The Pennsylvania Line: Regimental Organization and Operations, 1775–1783*. Harrisburg: Pennsylvania Historical and Museum Commission, 1993.

Tylden, G[eoffrey]. *Horses and Saddlery: An Account of the Animals Used by the British and Commonwealth Armies from the Seventeenth Century to the Present Day with a Description of the Equipment*. London: J.A. Allen, 1965.

United States Army. *FM 3-0: Operations*. Washington, D.C.: Department of the Army, 2008.

US Bureau of the Census. *Historical Statistics of the United States: Colonial Times to 1957*. Washington, D.C.: Government Printing Office, 1960.

Van Buskirk, Judith L. *Standing in Their Own Light: African American Patriots in the American Revolution*. Norman: University of Oklahoma Press, 2017.

Williams, Glenn F. *Year of the Hangman: George Washington's Campaign Against the Iroquois*. Yardley, Pa.: Westholme, 2005.

Wright, Robert K., Jr. *The Continental Army*. Washington, D.C.: Center of Military History, 1983.

Articles and Chapters

Arzberger, Steffen. "The choice between the German or French Language for the German nobility of the late 18th Century." In *Germanic Language Histories "from Below," 1700-2000*. Edited by Stephan Elpass, Nils Langer, Joachim Scharloth, and Wim Vendenbussche, 333-42. Berlin: Walter de Gruyter, 2007.

Bailey, James S. "Two Winters of Discontent: A Comparative Look at the Continental Army's Encampments at Valley Forge and Jockey Hollow." In *Pennsylvania's Revolution*. Edited by William Pencak, 306-334. University Park: Pennsylvania State University Press, 2010.

Bodle, Wayne. "Generals and 'Gentlemen': Pennsylvania Politics and the Decision for Valley Forge." *Pennsylvania History* 62, no. 1 (Winter 1995): 59-89.

———. "The Ghost of Clow: Loyalist Insurgency in the Delmarva Peninsula." In *The Other Loyalists: Ordinary People, Royalism, and the Revolution in the Middle Colonies, 1763-1787*. Edited by Joseph Tiedemann, Eugene R. Fingerhut, and Robert W. Venables, 19-44. Albany: State University of New York Press, 2009.

Broad, John. "Cattle Plague in Eighteenth-Century England." *Agricultural History Review* 31, no. 2 (1983): 104-15.

Burgos Cáceres, Sigfrido. "The long journey of cattle plague." *Canadian Veterinary Journal* 52 (October 2011): 1140.

Burns, Franklin L. "New Light on the Encampment of the Continental Army at Valley Forge." *Tredyffrin Easttown Historical Club Quarterly* 2, no. 3 (July 1939): 51-81.

Conway, Stephen. "To Subdue America: British Officers and the Conduct of the Revolutionary War." *William and Mary Quarterly* 43, no. 3 (July 1986): 381-407.

Dorland, W.A. Newman. "The Second Troop Philadelphia City Cavalry." *Pennsylvania Magazine of History and Biography* 45, no. 3 (July 1921): 257-91.

Friedemann, Theodore E., Herman F. Kraybill, and C. Frank Consolazio. "The Uses of Recommended Dietary Allowances in Military Nutrition." *American Journal of Public Health* 49, no. 8 (August 1959): 1006-12.

Hall, John W. "An Irregular Reconsideration of George Washington and the American Military Tradition." *Journal of Military History* 73, no. 3 (July 2014): 961-93.

Heller, William J. "The Gunmakers of Old Northampton." In *The Pennsylvania-German Society: Proceedings and Addresses at Allentown, November 2, 1906*. Vol. 17, 3-14. Lancaster, Pa.: Pennsylvania-German Society, 1908.

Herrera, Ricardo A. "Foraging and Combat Operations at Valley Forge, February–March 1778." *Army History* 79 (Spring 2011): 6-29.

———. "'[O]ur Army will hut this Winter at Valley forge': George Washington, Decision-Making, and the Council War." *Army History* (Fall 2020): 6-26.

———. "'[T]he zealous activity of Capt. Lee': Light-Horse Harry Lee and *Petite Guerre*." *Journal of Military History* 79, no. 1 (January 2015): 9-36.

Hart, Charles Henry. "Colonel Robert Lettis Hooper: Deputy Quarter Master General in the Continental Army and Vice President of New Jersey." *Pennsylvania Magazine of History and Biography* 36, no. 1 (January 1912): 60-91.

Huber, Thomas M. "Compound Warfare: A Conceptual Framework." In *Compound Warfare: That Fatal Knot*, edited by Thomas M. Huber, 1–9. Fort Leavenworth, Kans.: U.S. Army Command and General Staff College Press, 2002.

Kopperman, Paul. "The Stoppages Mutiny of 1763." *Western Pennsylvania Historical Magazine* 69, no. 3 (July 1986): 241–54.

Kortenhoff, Kurt Daniel. "Republican Ideology and Wartime Reality: Thomas Mifflin's Struggle as the First Quartermaster General of the Continental Army, 1775–1778." *Pennsylvania Magazine of History and Biography* 122, no. 3 (July 1998): 179–210.

Maar, Charles. "The High Dutch and Low Dutch in New York, 1624–1924." *The Quarterly Journal of the New York State Historical Association* 5, no. 4 (October 1924): 317–29.

Marshall, Thomas, and Philip Reade, "Massachusetts at Valley Forge." Pt. 3. *The Magazine of History, with Notes and Queries* 20, no. 6 (June 1915): 265–69.

Mason, Keith. "Association Localism, Evangelicalism, and Loyalism: The Sources of Discontent in the Revolutionary Chesapeake." *Journal of Southern History* 56, no. 1 (February 1990): 23–54.

McGrath, Tim. "I Passed by Philadelphia with Two Boats." *Naval History* 23, no. 3 (June 2009): 44–49.

McGready, Blake. "Contested Grounds: An Environmental History of the 1777 Philadelphia Campaign." *Pennsylvania History: A Journal of Mid-Atlantic Studies* 85, no. 1 (Winter 2018): 32–57.

Neville, Barry Paige. "For God, King, and Country: Loyalism on the Eastern Shore during the American Revolution." *International Social Science Review* 84, nos. 3–4 (2009): 135–56.

Newcomb, Benjamin. "Washington's Generals and the Decision to Quarter at Valley Forge." *Pennsylvania Magazine of History and Biography* 117, no. 4 (October 1993): 309–29.

Olsen, Stanley J. "Food Animals of the Continental Army at Valley Forge and Morristown." *American Antiquity* 29, no. 4 (April 1964): 506–9.

Perjés, G[eza]. "Army Provisioning, Logistics and Strategy in the Second Half of the 17th Century." *Acta Historica Academiae Scientiarum Hungaricae* 16, no.1/2 (1970): 1–52.

Purvis, Thomas. Patterns of Ethnic Settlement in Late Eighteenth-Century Pennsylvania." *The Western Pennsylvania Historical Magazine* 70, no. 2 (April 1987): 107–22.

Shy, John. "The Military Conflict Considered as a Revolutionary War." In *A People Numerous and Armed: Reflections on the Military Struggle for Independence*, rev. ed., edited by John Shy, 213–244. Ann Arbor: University of Michigan Press, 1990.

Turner, Joseph Brown. "Cheney Clow's Rebellion." *Papers of the Historical Society of Delaware* 57 (1912): 3–16.

Urwin, Gregory J. W. "When Freedom Wore a Red Coat: How Cornwallis' 1781 Campaign Threatened the Revolution in Virginia." *Army History* 20 (Summer 2008): 6–23.

Waldron, Richard. "'A True Servant of the Lord': Nils Collin, the Church of Sweden, and the American Revolution in Gloucester County." *New Jersey History* 126, no. 1 (2011): 96–103.

Way, Peter. "Rebellion of the Regulars: Working Soldiers and the Mutiny of 1763–1764." *William and Mary Quarterly* 57, no. 4 (October 2000): 761–92.

Winthrop, Grace. "Early Roads in Chester County." *Tredyffrin Easttown Historical Club Quarterly* 24, no. 2 (April 1986): 59–66.

Woodruff, Caldwell. "Capt. Ferdinand O'Neal of Lee's Legion." *William and Mary Quarterly* 23, no. 3 (July 1943): 328–330.

Yagi, George, Jr., "Surviving the Wilderness: The Diet of the British Army and the Struggle for Canada, 1754–1760." *Journal of the Society for Army Historical Research* 89, no. 357 (Spring 2011): 66–86.

Unpublished Secondary Sources

Hendrix, Scott N. "The Spirit of the Corps: The British Army and the Pre-National Pan-European Military World and the Origins of American Martial Culture, 1754–1783." PhD diss., University of Pittsburgh, 2005.

Johnson, Victor Leroy. "The Administration of the American Commissariat during the Revolutionary War." PhD diss., University of Pennsylvania, 1941.

McVarish, Douglas C. "National Register of Historic Places Registration: White Hill Mansion, Fieldsboro, New Jersey." Collingswood, N.J.: Friends of White Hill, 2020.

Morris, John William, III, "Site 44Y088: The Archaeological Assessment of the Hull Remains at Yorktown, Virginia." MA thesis, East Carolina University, 1991.

Morrison, Craig. "National Register of Historic Places Registration: Colonel Joseph Ellis House, Haddon Heights, New Jersey." Haddon Heights Historic Preservation Commission, 1988.

Thibaut, Jacqueline. "This Fatal Crisis: Logistics, Supply, and the Continental Army at Valley Forge, 1777–1778." Vol. 2, "The Valley Forge Historical Report." Valley Forge National Historical Park, Pa.: U.S. Department of the Interior, National Park Service, 1980.

Reference Works

A List of the General and Field Officers, as They Rank in the Army. . . . London: J. Millan, 1775.

A List of the General and Field Officers, as They Rank in the Army. . . . London: J. Millan, 1776.

A List of the General and Field Officers, as They Rank in the Army. . . . London: J. Millan, 1778.

Berg, Fred Anderson. *Encyclopedia of Continental Army Units: Battalions, Regiments, and Independent Corps*. Harrisburg, Pa.: Stackpole, 1972.

Bonner-Smith, David, and Royal Naval College. *The Commissioned Sea Officers of the Royal Navy, 1660-1815*. Vol 1, *A–F*. Greenwich, U.K.: National Maritime Museum, 1954.

Ford, Worthington C., comp. *British Officers Serving in the American Revolution, 1774-1783*. Brooklyn: Historical Printing Club, 1897.

Heitman, Francis B., ed. *Historical Register of the Continental Army during the War of the Revolution, April, 1775, to December, 1783*. New, rev. & enl. ed. Washington, D.C.: Rare Book Shop, 1914.

Johnson, Henry P., ed. *The Record of Connecticut Men in the Military and Naval Service during the War of the Revolution, 1775-1783*. Hartford, Conn.: 1889.

Lesser, Charles H., ed. *The Sinews of Independence: Monthly Strength Reports of the Continental Army*. Chicago: University of Chicago Press, 1976.

Linn, John Blair, and William H. Egle, eds. *Pennsylvania in the War of the Revolution, Battalions and Line: 1775-1783*. Vol. 1. Harrisburg, Pa.: Lane S. Hart, 1880.

Katcher, Philip R.N. *Encyclopedia of British, Provincial, and German Army Units, 1775-1783*. Harrisburg, Pa.: Stackpole, 1973.

Matthew, H. C. G., and Brian Harrison, eds. *Oxford Dictionary of National Biography Oxford Dictionary of National Biography*. Oxford: Oxford University Press, 2004. Online ed., edited by Lawrence Goldman, January 2008.

Purvis, Thomas L. *Colonial America to 1763*. New York: Facts on File, 1999.

Resavy, Frank, and Thomas McNichol. *Continental Army: Valley Forge Encampment, 1777-1778*. N.p.: 2008?

Stryker, William S., comp., *Official Register of the Officers and Men of New Jersey in the Revolutionary War*. Trenton, N.J.: William. T. Nicholson, 1872.

Zupko, Ronald E. *A Dictionary of Weights and Measures for the British Isles: The Middle Ages to the Twentieth Century*. Philadelphia: American Philosophical Society, 1985.

Digital Sources

Allen, Thomas B. *Tories: Fighting for the King in America's First Civil War*. http://www.toriesfightingfortheking.com/ToryArmy.htm. 7 May 2021.

Archives of Maryland, Historical List: Governors' Councils, 1777-1838. https://msa.maryland.gov/msa/speccol/sc2600/sc2685/html/council.html. 7 May 2021.

Barry-Hayes Papers. Series I: John Barry. Falvey Memorial Library. Digital Library Villanova University. https://digital.library.villanova.edu/Item/vudl:154320?type=AllFields. 7 May 2021.

Callahan, Raymond. "Abercromby, Sir Robert (1740?-1827)." *Oxford Dictionary of National Biography Oxford Dictionary of National Biography*. Edited by H. C. G. Matthew and Brian Harrison. Oxford: Oxford University Press, 2004. Online ed. Edited by Lawrence Goldman, January 2008. https://doi.org/10.1093/ref:odnb/47. 7 May 2021.

"Elk Landing." *The National Washington-Rochambeau Revolutionary Route Association*. https://w3r-us.org/historic-sites/elk-landing/. 7 May 2021.

"General Anthony Wayne." Valley Forge National Historical Park. http://www.nps.gov/vafo/historyculture/wayne.htm. 7 May 2021.

"George Washington: Revolutionary War." *Founders Online*. National Archives and Records Administration. https://founders.archives.gov/?q=%20Author%3A%22 Washington%2C%20George%22%20Period%3A%22Revolutionary%20War%22&s =1111211111&r=1. 7 May 2021.

Gruber, Ira D. "Howe, William, fifth Viscount Howe (1729–1814)." *Oxford Dictionary of National Biography Oxford Dictionary of National Biography*. Edited by H. C. G. Matthew and Brian Harrison. Oxford: Oxford University Press, 2004. Online ed. Edited by Lawrence Goldman, January 2008. https://doi.org/10.1093 /ref:odnb/13966. 7 May 2021.

Herrera, Ricardo A. "From Small Things: How a Staff Ride Became Two Articles and a Book Project." *Reflections on War and Society: Dale Center for the Study of War and Society Blog*. University of Southern Mississippi, 11 September 2015, https://dalecentersouthernmiss.wordpress.com/2015/09/11/from-small -things-how-a-staff-ride-became-two-articles-and-a-book-project/. 8 May 2021.

Högman, Hans. "Old Swedish Units of Measurement," *History*, http://www .hhogman.se/old-units-of-measurement sweden.htm#xl_Linear_Measure. 9 May 2021.

Imperial Measures of Weight. *Imperial Weights and Measures*, https://theedkins.co .uk/jo/units/weight.htm. 21 August 2021.

Index E-G, Tavern Petitions, 1700–1923. Chester County Archives and Record Services, West Chester, PA. https://www.chesco.org/DocumentCenter/View /4009/Tavern-Petitions-1700-1923-Index-E-G?bidId=; J. 7 May 2021.

Kilpatrick, Alison. "A Huggins Thorn in George Washington's Revolutionary Side." *Arborealis*. https://arborealis.ca/2015/12/23/huggins-thorn-in-washingtons-side/. 7 May 2021.

———. "Thomas Huggins (1748–1788), of Head of Elk, Maryland." *Arborealis*, https://arborealis.ca/2015/12/23/thomas-huggins/. 23 December 2015.

Knight, Roger. "Hamond, Sir Andrew Snape, first baronet (1738–1828)." *Oxford Dictionary of National Biography Oxford Dictionary of National Biography*. Edited by H. C. G. Matthew and Brian Harrison. Oxford: Oxford University Press, 2004. Online ed. Edited by Lawrence Goldman, January 2008. https://doi.org/10.1093 /ref:odnb/12164. 7 May 2021.

Kulikoff, Allan. "The Economic Crisis of the Revolutionary Era." Paper presented at 5th Annual Conference, Program in Early American Economy & Society, Library Company of Philadelphia, 7 May 2021. http://www.librarycompany.org /Economics/PDF%20Files/kulikoff.pdf. 7 May 2021.

Lloyd, E.M. "Stirling, Sir Thomas, of Strowan, fifth baronet (1733–1808)." Revised by Roger T. Stearn. *Oxford Dictionary of National Biography Oxford Dictionary of National Biography*. Edited by H. C. G. Matthew and Brian Harrison. Oxford: Oxford University Press, 2004. Online ed. Edited by Lawrence Goldman, January 2008. https://doi.org/10.1093/ref:odnb/26535. 7 May 2021.

"Preservation of a Cheval-de-frise from the Delaware River," *This Week in Pennsylvania Archaeology*, http://twipa.blogspot.com/2013/06/preservation-of-cheval-de-frise -from.html. 21 August 2021.

Riordan, Liam. "1776 Tax information for the Town of New Castle." *New Castle, Delaware Community History and Archaeology Program.* http://nc-chap.org/census /riordan/tax1776.php. 7 May 2021.

Schmitt, James. "William Smallwood (1732–1792)." MSA SC 3520-1134. *Archives of Maryland (Biographical Series).* https://msa.maryland.gov/megafile/msa/speccol /sc3500/sc3520/001100/001134/html/1134bio.html. 7 May 2021.

"Understanding Maryland Records: Money." *Maryland State Archives: Guide to Government Records.* http://guide.msa.maryland.gov/pages/viewer.aspx?page =money. 22 August 2021.

Valley Forge Legacy: The Muster Roll Project. http://valleyforgemusterroll.org. 7 May 2021.

"Waning Gibbous Moon, 3:00 a.m., 15 February 1778." *Moonpage.* https://www .moonpage.com/index.html?go=T&auto_dst=T&totphase =WAXING+CRESCENT+%2812.54%25+full%29&m=2&d=15&y=1778&hour =3&min=0&sec=0. 7 May 2021.

Weinstein, Quinton. "Casimir Pulaski." In *The Digital Encyclopedia of George Washington.* Edited by James P. Ambuske. Mount Vernon Ladies' Association, 2012–2020. https://www.mountvernon.org/library/digitalhistory/digital -encyclopedia/article/casimir-pulaski/. 7 May 2021.

"Whiskey Barrels," *The Barrel Mill.* https://www.thebarrelmill.com/barrels. 7 May 2021.

Index

Continental Navy, 2, 85, 123, 167–71, 203n7; *Effingham*, 85, 171, 216n19; *Lexington*, 85; *Washington*, 85, 216n19
Continentals. *See* Continental Army
Conway, Maj. Gen. Thomas, 60
Cooch's Bridge (Delaware) Battle of, 1, 141
Coone, Pvt. Israel, 122
Cooper's Creek (New Jersey), 85, 100, 104–05
Cooper's Bridge (New Jersey), 106–07
Cooper's Ferry (New Jersey), 85–97, 101–07, 173, 179–81
corn, 31–33, 39, 46, 53–57, 139, 145, 198n51, 201n35, 213n12
Cornwallis, Lt. Gen. Charles, Earl, 47, 165, 179
Couch, Thomas, 133
Cowperthwaite, Hugh, 87
Craig, Capt. Charles, 209n14
Creek Indians, 168
Crewe, Maj. Richard, 115–16
Cuff, "Negro," 133
Cumberland County (Pennsylvania), 15
Cumberland Island (Georgia), 171
cwt. *See* hundredweight

Darby (Pennsylvania). *See* Derby
David, "Negro," 133
Dearborn, Lt. Col. Henry, 30
Dehaven, Pvt. James, 122
Delaware, 73, 76, 87, 92, 120, 128–38, 157, 163; central, 2, 128, 134, 159; Continentals, 117–20, 124–27, 169; currency, 132; deserters in, 129; disaffection in, 130; enslaved, 133; farmers, 124; government of, 119, 128–29, 197n46; governor of, 26. *See also* president; and Grand Forage of 1778, 2, 77, 110, 121, 126, 131, 136, 174; horses in, 131; hundreds, 128, 210n28; Loyalists in, 120; Militia, 2, 117, 120, 124–27, 134–35, 156; northern, 2, 148; people of, 4, 112–13; president of, 155, 197n46, 209n16. *See*

also governor; provisions in, 13, 57, 129, 215n41; Regiment, *see* Continentals; shore, 108, 130, 155; southern, 134; winter in, 119
Delaware Bay, 82, 143
Delaware River, 13–15, 28, 53–57, 78, 87, 120–21, 136, 149–51, 182, 203nn6, 7; British shipping on, 108; crossing, 28, 77, 88, 92, 99–104, 160, 172, 178–81; current, 18, 48, 82, 95; defenses along, 64, 130, 143; ice, 28, 48, 84, 160; islands, 74, 84; mudflats, 84; navigating, 28, 84; obstacles in, 213n17; ports along, 54; Royal Navy command of, 80; sandbars, 84; shipping channel, 82, 84, 181; tidal movements of, 82–84; tributaries of, 85, 139. *See also* Continental Navy, Royal Navy; weather
deputy commissary general for hides (Continental Army), 134
Derby (Pennsylvania), 47–48, 59–69, 113–15, 163–66
Derby Road (Pennsylvania), 64
deserters, 11, 121, 127–29, 170, 193n13
desertion, 19, 75. *See also* deserters.
Deshane, Valentine, 133
disaffected, 13–16, 54–56, 112, 121, 128–30, 151–53, 159, 170
disaffection, 54, 69, 96, 120, 130, 214n33
disease, 19
Döhla, Pvt. Johann Conrad, 68
Doehlemann, Cpl. Johann Christoph, 68
Donop, Col. Carl Emil Kurt von, 140
Dover (Delaware), 110, 117–19, 126–28, 131–32, 145
Downman, Lt. Col. Francis, 92, 99, 106
Doyle, Capt. John, 60, 103–04, 106
Drew, Capt. Seth, 31
drivers (wagon), 9, 25, 35–38, 57, 132–33, 143, 145. *See also* teamsters; wagoneers
Duane, James, 23
Duck Creek (Delaware), 117, 134
Duer, William, 27
Dunk's Ferry (New Jersey), 92

Dungeness Plantation (Georgia), 171
Dunham, Azariah, 32–33
Dutch population, 55, 199n9

Eastern Department, 136–37
Easton (Pennsylvania), 32
Edgemont Road (Pennsylvania), 63
Ewald, Capt. Johann, 54, 68, 112, 115
economics, 19, 54, 72, 80, 133, 157
Edwards's Tavern (Pennsylvania), 63
Elk (Maryland), 110, 118, 123, 132–52,
    156–57, 210n26, 211n1
Elk Ferry (Maryland), 138
Elk River, 138–41. 147
Ellis, Brig. Gen. Ellis, 88, 94–106,
    167–68, 172
Ellrodt, Capt. Christian Philipp von,
    67–68
England, 13, 175–78, 182, 210n28
English population, 54–55
enslaved, 112, 120, 133, 141, 159, 175.
    See also African Americans; slaves
Eutaw Springs (South Carolina), Battle
    of, 164
Evesham Meeting House (New Jersey),
    100–02
Ewald, Capt. Johann, 54, 68, 112, 115

Fallen Timbers (Indiana), Battle of, 168
Farley, Capt. Michael, 196n23
farmers, 7–14, 33, 37–45, 52–54, 78, 90,
    115, 133, 149–51, 166; avarice, 7, 39;
    concealment by, 71–73, 89–90, 130,
    150–51; Delaware, 123–24; labor, 37;
    local, 4, 72; New Jersey, 55, 89;
    Pennsylvania, 11, 55, 63, 89; selling
    to, 130; theft from, 41
farms, 53, 128, 151; plundered, 47
Ferguson, Pvt. Robert, 122
field army, 5, 161–64, 182. See also
    Forward Operating Base; Valley Forge
Fieldsboro (New Jersey), 217n19
Fillinbuilt, Pvt. William, 122
fish, 10, 43–44, 57, 73, 139, 145, 157,
    198n51

Fleming, Capt.-Lt. George, 59
Flemington (New Jersey), 17
Flesh. See meat
flour, 147; baking of, 34; barrel weight,
    197n51; distribution of, 31; gathering
    of, 2, 77, 153, 159; impressment of, 7,
    39; rations, 33–34, 43–44; shortages
    of, 32, 34, 39, 50, 157; seizure of, 149;
    supplies of, 6, 57, 142–49, 210n26;
    sold to British, 11; transportation of,
    35, 57, 70, 77, 132, 139–45, 150–53,
    163, 213n12, 214n30
fodder, 10–13, 18, 46, 50, 70, 201n35.
    See also forage (livestock feed);
    foraging; Grand Forage of 1778
forage (livestock feed); British Army's
    need for, 10, 13, 18, 46–48, 54;
    Continental Army's need for, 2, 6,
    17–18, 45, 50, 63, 208n7; destruction
    of, 91–92, 108; militia denial of forage,
    16; preparation of, 10. See also fodder;
    foraging; impressment; Grand Forage
    of 1778; teamsters; wagon brigades;
    wagon masters; wagoneers; wagons
foraging, 215n7; British, 11–14, 18,
    46–50, 54–57, 64–66, 88, 99–103, 108,
    113, 175–80; Continental, xi, 5, 11,
    18, 34–45, 100, 136, 151, 155–57.
    See also fodder; forage (livestock feed);
    Grand Forage of 1778; impressment;
    teamsters; wagon brigades; wagon
    masters; wagoneers; wagons
Forsyth, Capt. Robert, 60, 77
Fort Billingsport (New Jersey), 143
Fort Mercer (New Jersey), 143
Fort Mifflin (Pennsylvania), 17, 143
Fort Washington (New York), 162
Forward Operating Base, xi. See also
    Valley Forge
Frankford (Pennsylvania), 66
French navy, 144
frumenty, 69

Galloway, Joseph, 136, 141
Gates, Maj. Gen. Horatio, 25, 164, 174

Pennsylvania, 1, 6, 18, 37, 52–57, 91, 97–99, 107, 131–32, 143–48, 152; adjutant general, 37; Assembly, 167; backcountry, 159; British invasion of, 119; constitutional convention, 42; Continental Line, 29, 61, 107, 167–68, 205n29, 216n13; council, 26–28, 34–42, 71; Council of Safety, 7; currency, 132; disaffection in, 13; east, 2; farmers, 54–55, 78; forage and fodder in, 18; foraging in, 37–38, 54; *Franklin* (Pennsylvania Navy galley), 85; government of, 1, 2, 7, 14–18, 73, 160–61, 167, 173, 197n46, 207n5; and Grand Forage of 1778, 2–4, 51–52, 57; hundred, 210n28; impressment in, 27; Loyalists in, 54–55; Militia, 2, 14–18, 24, 28, 42, 124–27, 139, 194n27, 199n4; *Montgomery* (Pennsylvania Navy ship), 85; Navy, 2, 17, 84–87; Pennsylvanians, 4, 29, 69, 76, 87, 107, 121; president of, 14, 197n46; provisions in, 9, 32, 138, 215n41; quartering in, 17; southeast, 1–2, 11, 18, 50, 54, 87–89, 119, 159–60, 164; struggle for, 13, 50, 160, 183; supplies in, 34; winter in, 4

Peters, Matthew, 201n35
Peters, Richard, 25, 27
Pettengill, Capt. Joseph, 31
Peterson, Widow, 131
petite guerre, 47, 114, 128, 135, 208n11. *See also* partisan warfare
Peyton, Lt. Henry, 108, 122
Phipps, Capt. Hon. Charles, 82
Philadelphia Campaign of 1777–78, xi, 1–4, 37, 46, 78, 152, 162–63, 177–78
Philadelphia (city), 51–55, 82–87, 100, 104–07, 121, 139–41, 172, 181, 203n6; bridges and ferries of, 48, 52, 64–66, 74; British capture of, 24, 141–42; British defenses of, 66–67; British evacuation of, 176–78; British occupation of, xi, 2–5, 79, 87, 99, 119, 136, 165; British operations from, 18, 46, 67, 93, 115, 179–80, 206n39; British strength in, 2, 193n1; British Army wintering in, 11; civilian provisioning of, 11, 55, 72, 149, 155, 163; communications with, 177; Continental Army's defenses of, 24, 213n17; Continental Army prisoners in, 73–75; Continental Army's proximity to, 1, 51, 63, 108, 114–16, 128, 163; economic and political importance of, 46, 54, 80; foraging for, 46–48, 66; islands near, 14, 52, 70; merchants, 20, 128, 137; military discipline in, 47–49; population of, 54; reducing Continental defenses, 143, 181; struggle to control lands nearby, 13, 17–18, 112, 151, 160–81; sustaining, 46; winter in, 29, 64

Philadelphia (County), 9–11, 15–16, 32, 53–57, 108, 119
Pickering, Col. Timothy, 6, 13, 25, 47, 113–16, 208n12
Pine Street (Philadelphia), 203n6
Pointer, Pvt. George, 122
political, 121, 133, 157, 171–72, 210n28; conflict, 13; decentralization, 35; exercise of power, 1, 73; environment, 1, 54, 119–20, 133, 159; importance of Philadelphia, 46, 80; leadership, 112, 152, 167–68, 183–84; loyalties, 11, 72, 157; necessity, 1, 17; power, 11; survival, 119; and war, 19, 119–20, 161, 165, 183–84
politicians. *See* politics
Pope, Lt. Col. Charles, 135
pork, 6, 32–33, 39, 53, 57, 73, 117–19, 123, 125–26, 139–40, 142, 145, 150, 153, 198n51, 210n26
Port Penn (Delaware), 92, 95
Porter, Robert, 131
potatoes, 47
Power, Pvt. Robert, 122
Prechtel, Lt. Johann Ernst, 68
Presbyterians, 54, 55
prices, 6, 37–39, 45, 76, 130, 137, 153, 215n41

Princeton (New Jersey), xii, 28, 142
Proclamation on Market, 215n41
property, 41–42, 76; accountability for, 36, 52, 132; compensation for, 91, 121, 126; concealment of, 73, 90; damage or destruction, 42, 47, 53, 87; enslaved, 133; impressment of, 7, 38, 133; owners, 20; respect for, 7, 71, 121; rights, 38; seizure of, 7, 28, 41, 53, 73, 150, 154, 163; valuation of, 125. *See also* property rights.
property rights, 7, 38, 113, 121–23, 128. *See also* property
provender, 14, 52, 71, 91, 182,
Providence Meeting House (Pennsylvania), 70–72
provincials, *see* Loyalists
Pulaski, Brig. Gen. Casimir, 17, 100–07, 116, 167–69, 173, 180
Putnam, Maj. Gen. Israel, 195n15

Quakers, 39, 52, 54–55, 87, 97, 163
quartermaster (British), 113
Quartermaster General (Continental Army), 20–25, 37, 50–53, 90, 125, 134–44, 148, 152, 159, 164; collapse of, 6; deputy, 32–35, 69–71, 110–12, 125, 145, 152; expenditures of, 8; forage department, 23; functioning of, 20, 35; impressment by, 38; limited authority of, 5, 19; lack of wagons, 9, 34–35; lack of impressment authority, 9, 36, 56; reform of, 23; wagon department, 23. *See also* Thomas Mifflin
Quenouault, Lt. Paul, 124–27
quintals, 198 (n. 15)

Race Street (Philadelphia), 203n6
Raccoon Creek (New Jersey), 91–95
Radnor Meeting House (Pennsylvania), 114
rain. *See* weather
Rangle Town. *See* Wrangle Town
Ransdell, Lt. Thomas, 60, 74–75

rations, 31–34, 43–44, 56–57, 69, 73–75, 142, 197n51, 201n35
Read, President George, Jr., 117, 128–29, 155–56, 209n16
Reading (Pennsylvania), 24, 32–35, 70
Redick, David, 213n12
Reitzenstein, Lt. Wilhelm Friedrich Ernst von, 67
republican virtue, 19–20, 24, 76
Reynolds, George, 131
Rhode Island, 13, 46, 57, 61, 87, 112, 137, 143; Continentals, 203n7
rice, 31
Richardson, Col. William, 120
riflemen. *See* rifles
rifles, 13, 113, 199n7
rinderpest, 134
Rollins, John, 133
Rodney, Maj. Gen. Caesar, 117–21, 125–26, 209n22
Rosamond, Pvt. Robert, 123
Ross, Col. George, 35–36
Royal Navy, 2, 11, 18, 93, 126, 130, 138, 143–49, 171–72, 181–82; and Delaware River conditions, 18, 88; Delaware River operations, 80, 93, 100–04, 108–09, 143; 213n17; Delaware River Squadron, 80–82, 109, 181; strength, 84
—vessels: *Adventure*, H.M. Store Ship, 82; *Augusta*, H.M.S., 84; *Camilla*, H.M.S., 92, 203n6 *Cornwallis*, H.M. Galley, 82–84, 95; *Delaware*, H.M. Armed Ship, 82, 95, 101, 203n6; *Eagle*, H.M.S. 138; *Experiment*, H.M.S., 82; *Merlin*, H.M. Sloop, 84; *Pearl*, H.M.S., 82, 93; *Pembroke*, H.M. Tender, 92–95; *Philadelphia*, H.M. Galley, 82–84; *Roebuck*, H.M.S. 82, 92, 203n6; *Vigilant*, H.M. Armed Ship, 82, 203n6; *Viper*, H.M. Armed Vessel, 82; *Zebra*, H.M. Sloop, 82, 93–95
rum, 48, 56, 97, 140, 145, 157, 198n51, 210n26
Rumford, Capt. Jonathan, Jr., 124, 156

43–44, 120, 132, 136–39, 145, 151; strategic location of, 1–2, 10–13, 19, 50, 55–56, 63, 74, 148, 160–61, 165, 182–84; strength of Continental Army at, 2, 9, 14, 123, 193n13; need for uniforms, 27, 193n13; vulnerability of, 5, 18, 61, 164, 175–78, 183; wagons at, 146; as winter quarters, 1, 11, 20, 29, 159–61, 166–67, 183, 196nn17–18; winter, 28–29, 59–60. *See also* Forward Operating Base

Van Dyke, Maj. John, 108

Varnum, Brig. Gen. James Mitchell, 9, 60–61, 91, 112, 203n7

vessels, 2, 48, 80–87, 108–09, 138–48, 177, 181, 216n19. *See also* British Army; Continental Navy; Royal Navy; transports; victualers

victualers, 46. *See also* British Army; transports; vessels

Vine Street (Philadelphia), 203n6

Virginia, 45, 57, 60, 76, 113–14, 120–23, 139, 165, 198n51; Bland's, Maj. Theodorick, Regiment of Virginia Horse, 113; governor, 26, 143; Capes, 141–43; Continental Line, 26, 62, 67–68, 75, 107; legislature, 26; Navy, 143; service, 169; supplies from, 136

Wallace, Capt. Sir James, 82

Wagons. *See* wagons

wagon brigades, 9, 33, 56, 126, 132, 145–48, 196n27. *See also* wagons

wagon masters, 38, 90

wagoneers, 9–10, 36, 133–36, 159. *See also* drivers (wagon); teamsters

wagons, 29–33, 39–42, 74, 78, 132, 140–50,. 157, 201n35; and British foragers, 11, 47–48, 93–96, 103; and British provisions, 11, 46; carrying capacity, 43, 57, 142, 197n51; collecting, 63, 132; compensation for, 36–37; concealment of, 44, 73; and footbridge, 29; impressment of, 7–9, 34–38, 56, 71–72, 77, 110, 127, 150;

maintenance of, 36–37, 43; and road conditions, 9, 30, 97; scarcity of, 9, 34–38, 43–44, 55–57, 69–71, 75–77, 128, 142–46, 153, 157, 163; travel, rate of, 90, 97; for Valley Forge, 31, 75, 109, 125–26, 136, 146, 157

War Office (British), 205n24

Washington, Gen. George, 4–6, 20, 29, 47, 116, 163, 167–75, 193n1, 208n7, 215n2

—as commander-in-chief: accepting risk, 1–4, 14, 18, 50, 57, 184; aptitude as commander, 4, 19, 28, 119, 142, 161, 183–84; Continental Army, 183; decision-making process, 1–4, 29, 50, 160–61; intelligence on provisions, 11, 57, 149–51; intelligence on British Army operations, 14, 50, 102, 114; maturation as commander, xi–xii, 5, 160, 184; Pennsylvania Militia, 14–18; Pennsylvania Navy, 85; Philadelphia Campaign of 1777–78, 1, 24; on seniority and date of rank, 100, 173; as strategist, 1–2, 50, 119–21, 130, 159–61, 182; as tactician, 28, 78, 160–62, 174; talent discernment, 162, 166–70, 205n29; trust in subordinates, xii, 5, 52–55, 70, 112–14, 126–27, 133, 161–63, 168, 184, 193n5; wintering at Valley Forge, 1, 20, 29, 136

—logistics: clothing the Continental Army, 25–28; Commissary General's Department, 20–23, 138, 148, 155–56; compensating farmers, 14; Elk (Maryland) magazine, 139–44, 155–56; foraging, 34, 39, 45; Grand Forage of 1778, 2–5, 14, 18, 49–63, 69–78, 91–94, 107–13, 117–36, 159–62, 166–78, 184, 203n7; impressment, 38–39, 45, 71, 149; logistical system, 136; observations on livestock, 53; Proclamation on Cattle, 76, 202n49; Quartermaster General's Department, 20–23; sustaining Continental Army at Valley Forge, 13–14, 45, 111–19, 150, 183

—civil-military affairs, 17–18, 41, 119–21, 127, 151, 160; Delaware government, 26, 129; Maryland government, 26; New Jersey government, 17; Pennsylvania government, 14, 26–27; Virginia government, 26
—Second Continental Congress: Board of War, 26–27, 198n52; obedience to, 17

water of life, *see* whiskey

Waters, Cpl. John, 122

Watt, Cdr. James, 82, 95, 108

Wayne, Brig. Gen. Anthony, 164–82, 195n10, 203n7, 205n29; aptitude as commander, 52, 168–69; and Grand Forage of 1778, 14–16, 52–53, 59–62, 70–72, 77–80, 84–110, 123, 136, 159, 215n7; maturation of, 166–68; and Pennsylvania Continental Line, 29, 168; statue, xi; Washington's trust in, xii, 52, 161, 168, 184

weather, xi, 6, 20, 36, 88, 196n17; cold, 9, 16, 28–30, 48, 59, 99, 103, 182; flooding, 9, 59, 64; freezing, xi, 4, 10, 29, 40, 48, 84–86; frost, 103; gales, 103; good, 9, 28, 41, 88; ice, 18, 28, 48, 64, 84, 160; inclement, 9–10, 62, 143; mud, 29–30, 59, 63–64; and navigation, 143; protection from, 97–99; rain, 9–10, 29, 59, 64, 84, 88, 99, 142; sleet, 88, 103; snow, 4, 9, 28–30, 59, 84, 88, 97, 103, 142; temperatures, 28–29; thawing, 10, 29, 84; variations, 8–10, 28, 164; warm, 28, 41, 157; wind, 28, 62. *See also* Little Ice Age

Webb, Col. Charles, 31

Weedon, Brig. Gen. George, 6, 60, 116

Welsh, William, 140

West Chester (Pennsylvania), 52

West Indies, 180

Western Confederacy, 168

Wharton, Thomas, 6–7, 14–17, 34–45

wheat, 39, 69, 141, 147–48, 153, 159, 163, 198n51, 210n26; collecting, 130, 148; growing, 53; price of, 39; purchase of, 7; impressment of, 7; seizure of, 39, 43, 214n30; selling, 55; stocks of, 57, 145, 149, 163

Whigs, 72–74, 87–89, 107, 121

Whippin Town, 91

whiskey, 6, 29, 39, 56, 69 145, 198 (n. 51), 210n26

White, Cnt. John, 122

White Hill (New Jersey), 217n19

Whitemarsh (Pennsylvania), Battle of, 1, 29–30, 47–50, 78–79, 160

Wier, Daniel, 46, 140

Wild, Sgt, Ebenezer, 62

Wiley, Capt. John, 31

Wilkinson, Capt., 125

Wilkinson, Lt. Col. James, 25

Willis, Far. Zachariah, 122

Wilmington (Delaware), 72, 78, 87, 93, 110, 118–26, 131–34, 139–40, 148, 155–67, 174–75

Witherspoon, Capt. Thomas, 124–27, 133

Woodbridge, Capt. Theodore, 60, 89–91

woodcutters, 46, 54, 64

Woodford, Brig. Gen. William, 60

Worcester County (Maryland), 154

Wrangle Town (New Jersey), 90–91

Wright, Pvt. John, 123

Wright's Ferry (Pennsylvania), 34, 142, 213n15

Yeiser, Englehard or Englehard, 154

York (Pennsylvania), 34, 35, 142, 213n15

York County (Pennsylvania), 9, 15

Yorke, Andrew, 89

Yorktown (Virginia), 139; Siege of, 161, 165, 179